# EMPOWERMENT-ORIENTED SOCIAL WORK PRACTICE WITH THE ELDERLY

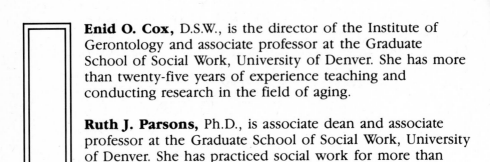

**Enid O. Cox,** D.S.W., is the director of the Institute of Gerontology and associate professor at the Graduate School of Social Work, University of Denver. She has more than twenty-five years of experience teaching and conducting research in the field of aging.

**Ruth J. Parsons,** Ph.D., is associate dean and associate professor at the Graduate School of Social Work, University of Denver. She has practiced social work for more than twenty years with a variety of clients, including families, children, and the elderly.

# EMPOWERMENT-ORIENTED SOCIAL WORK PRACTICE WITH THE ELDERLY

**Enid O. Cox**
*University of Denver*

**Ruth J. Parsons**
*University of Denver*

Brooks/Cole Publishing Company
Pacific Grove, California

ITP™ The trademark ITP is used under license.

A CLAIREMONT BOOK

Brooks/Cole Publishing Company
A Division of Wadsworth, Inc.

Printed in the United States of America

10  9  8  7  6  5  4  3  2  1

**Library of Congress Cataloging-in-Publication Data**
Cox, Enid Opal,
    Empowerment-oriented social work practice with the elderly / Enid
O. Cox and Ruth J. Parsons.
        p.   cm.
    Includes bibliographical references and index.
    ISBN 0-534-20634-4 :
    1. Social work with the aged.   I. Parsons, Ruth J.,
    II. Title.
    HV1451.C684   1993
362.6—dc20                                                    93-17997
                                                              CIP

Sponsoring Editor:  Claire Verduin
Editorial Associate:  Gay C. Bond
Production Coordinator:  Fiorella Ljunggren
Production:  Lifland et al., Bookmakers
Manuscript Editor:  Jane Hoover
Permissions Editor:  Karen Wootten
Interior Design:  Quica Ostrander
Cover Design:  Vernon T. Boes
Interior Illustration:  Gail Magin
Typesetting:  Bookends Typesetting
Printing and Binding:  Malloy Lithographing, Inc.

*In memory of Myra Torgerson Gisb*
*for ber enduring support and faith*
*and*
*to Barbara Joseph, June Dunn, and Virginia Fraser*
*for longstanding support and inspiration*
*in the struggle for social justice*

*Enid O. Cox*

*To George, Marci, and Kassa*
*for their patience and support*

*Ruth J. Parsons*

# CONTENTS

## 3 The Empowerment-Oriented Practice Model 31

## PART TWO EMPOWERMENT-ORIENTED INTERVENTIONS APPLIED TO LEVELS OF PRACTICE 61

## 4 Empowerment and the Arena of Social Policy 63

## 5   Social Service Delivery: An Arena for Empowerment-Oriented Practice   81

## Empowerment-Oriented Interventions with Groups and Individuals   99

## Increasing Knowledge and Skills for Late Life Survival   119

## *Generating Survival Income and Health Care Resources   145*

 ## *Family Caregiving   165*

## Care Receivers   189

## Empowerment-Oriented Social Work in Nursing Homes   207

## Late Life Housing and In-Home Services   233

# PREFACE

The 1990s challenge social work practitioners who serve older Americans to review their approach to practice by intervening in ways that empower both themselves and their clients to fully engage in the tasks of self-care and productive participation in society. *Empowerment-Oriented Social Work Practice with the Elderly* can help these practitioners by providing a model of practice that combines personal strategies (direct service or clinical interventions) with political strategies (indirect service or social action). An empowerment-oriented approach encourages the active participation of clients in dealing with the personal as well as the interpersonal and political aspects of their problems. Empowerment-oriented practitioners foster the fullest possible engagement and contribution of elderly individuals as they face the struggles of late life.

This text provides a philosophical framework that can be easily integrated into many existing practice models, as well as guidelines for empowerment-oriented practice that can be applied across systems and in any service setting. Although many gerontological social workers use empowerment-oriented strategies in their work, few have a fully developed concept of the empowerment-oriented practice model presented in this text. This model not only rationalizes such strategies but also helps social work students and practitioners to review their work critically in terms of its contribution to the empowerment process and to generate new strategies.

Many service programs targeting the elderly and their families will welcome the introduction of an empowerment-oriented approach. Gerontological social workers who are committed to an empowerment-oriented practice model, however, may have to develop a sanction base for its use within their agencies. Although empowerment-oriented strategies can be employed with individuals in most settings, their use with small groups to facilitate social action is often resisted or prohibited. Consequently, empowerment-oriented social workers must collaborate with colleagues who share their values and practice orientation. A network of practitioners working in a variety of agencies can provide vital support for the efforts of all the individual workers.

# Organization of the Book

The text is divided into three parts. Part One, "Theoretical Framework for Empowerment-Oriented Practice," consists of three chapters. These introduce the current issues affecting work with the elders, discuss the aging process and the potential for a sense of powerlessness among the elderly, and describe the empowerment-oriented practice model.

Chapter 1 provides an introduction to the issues and problems faced by gerontological social workers in the 1990s and discusses the diversity, stereotypes, and strengths of the elderly population. Chapter 2 presents an overview of the aging process and describes the political, social, and economic factors that can contribute to feelings of powerlessness in late life. Chapter 3 outlines a model of empowerment-oriented practice, including its underlying philosophy and overall goals as well as key practice components such as assessment and strategies for intervention.

Part Two, "Empowerment-Oriented Interventions Applied to Levels of Practice," consists of three chapters. These elaborate on the application of empowerment orientation at different levels of practice: social policy, service delivery, and work with small groups and individuals.

Chapter 4 suggests strategies that are useful for engaging clients in the policy-making process. Chapter 5 focuses on issues affecting the delivery of social and health care services; it identifies common problems in the provision and receipt of services and offers strategies to help clients develop, change, and control these services. Chapter 6 discusses the implementation of empowerment-oriented practice on a one-to-one basis, as well as within small groups.

Part Three, "Empowerment-Oriented Interventions: Selected Practice Examples," consists of six chapters that describe the implementation of empowerment-oriented strategies in selected problem areas or practice settings that are of special interest and concern in the field of gerontology today.

Chapter 7 discusses empowerment-oriented interventions designed to foster the knowledge and skills necessary for late life survival. The focus is on education, communication, peer counseling, mediation, and advocacy because these skills are vital to the survival of elderly persons and their ability to help others; volunteers with these skills are needed by many community service agencies. Chapter 8 explores a number of effective empowerment-oriented strategies that address the problems of insufficient income and inadequate health care; education, self-help, and collective action are emphasized. Chapters 9 and 10 concentrate on the problems and concerns of caregivers and care receivers. The focus is on the knowledge and strengths necessary to create a caring atmosphere that can reduce feelings of powerlessness in both the caregiver and the care receiver. Chapter 11 describes empowerment-oriented practice in nursing homes, which is especially important because of the disempowering nature of institutional life. Chapter 12 suggests interventions that are useful to elderly people who face decisions or problems in the areas of housing and in-home services. Educational strategies are key in this arena of practice because of the growing variety of housing options and the need for supervision of in-home care.

## *Acknowledgments*

We would like to acknowledge those colleagues, friends, students, practitioners, and clients who have developed the ideas in this book and put them into practice. We are especially indebted to the Colorado Association of Gerontological Social Workers for its examples and commitment to empowerment-oriented practice and to Marta Arnold, Jean Bogar, Bob Brown, Matthew Burroughs, Pat Corwin, Ramona Garcia, Martin Howell, Vicki Jordan, Judy Leonardelli, Kris Mason, Donna Oneisan, Mary-Margaret Schomp, Kathy Tessmer, and Lori Tomlinson for their special help and contributions. We want to thank Barbara Stewart for supplying resources on care receiver interventions and Mile-High United Way for providing resources on mediation. We also thank Neysa Folmer for her supportive assistance in the development of this manuscript.

*Enid O. Cox*
*Ruth J. Parsons*

# EMPOWERMENT-ORIENTED SOCIAL WORK PRACTICE WITH THE ELDERLY

# One

# THEORETICAL FRAMEWORK FOR EMPOWERMENT-ORIENTED PRACTICE

 # OUR AGING SOCIETY: THE CHALLENGE TO SOCIAL WORK PRACTICE

Interest in gerontological social work escalated throughout the 1980s and continues to grow in the 1990s. A major cause of this heightened interest is the increase in the number of elderly people in American society. This chapter will briefly discuss some characteristics of the aging of American society, note some of the major related social policy issues that are emerging, and describe the challenges facing gerontological social workers as a result.

This book does not include a comprehensive overview of the aging process or of the demographic characteristics of the aging population. Introductory gerontology texts, social policy texts, public policy reports, and the popular press clearly articulate demographic trends and provide up-to-date knowledge regarding the aging process (see, for example, Atchley, 1991; Bass, Kutza, & Torres-Gil, 1990; Kart, 1990; Spencer, 1989). For the purpose of understanding the challenges facing gerontological social workers, however, we will begin by briefly discussing some of the demographic factors of most immediate concern to social work practice. Descriptive information related to selected problem areas, such as housing and in-home services, has also been included in later chapters as background for discussions of practice interventions.

## DEMOGRAPHIC FORCES

More than 31,559,000 persons aged 65 and over are currently living in the United States. Of this number, 3,254,000 are over 85 years old. People over 65 now represent more than 12% of the total population, and projections suggest that this segment of the population will increase to 68,500,000 and represent 22.9% of the total population by 2050 (U.S. Census Bureau, 1990).

More important with respect to traditional health and social work concerns are the changes occurring within the elderly population. Increased longevity among the elderly has led some gerontologists to divide the older population into age categories. Atchley (1991) suggests the following categories: the *young-old* (65 to 75), the *middle-old* (75 to 84), and the *old-old* (85 and over). Population projections for 2000 indicate that slightly over half of the older population will be in the young-old group, about 35% will be in the middle-old group, and about 15% will be in the old-old group. Thinking about the elderly in terms of these categories has a number of implications for the future, including the following:

- The growing number of people aged 75 and over strongly suggests an increasing need for health and social services.
- A movement toward redefining "old age" in American society shifts the focus of concern toward old-old and middle-old in considerations of eligibility for health and social services, including social security. The implications of such a shift suggest a need for reintegration of the young-old into productive labor activities.
- Interest in the needs of the young-old related to continued employment and new employment opportunities, preparation for retirement, and caregiving responsibilities is gaining momentum.

These trends signal that the problems and potential contributions of older Americans will become increasingly complex issues. For example, what chronological age will be used to define the status "elderly"?

Lesnoff-Caravaglia's (1988) observation that chronological, physiological, and psychological age rarely coincide adds a dimension that underscores the differences among individuals in terms of aging phenomena. The diversity among the elderly makes standard expectations about aging difficult to establish. Consequently, social workers are challenged to develop services that are more individualized and capable of addressing the needs of increasingly distinguishable groups within the elderly population.

Other demographic trends important for social welfare services include:

- *Increasing numbers of single or widowed elderly women.* The sex ratio among the older population is expected to be only 65 men per 100 women in 2000, and only 38 men per 100 women in the old-old population (Atchley, 1991).
- *Increasing percentages of ethnic minorities among the older population.* While the proportion of elderly blacks in the population is growing, the proportion of elderly whites is declining and the proportion of other races is remaining about the same. An exception to the latter generalization is the growth of a number of Asian groups (Atchley, 1991).

- *Higher levels of formal education among the elderly.* In 2009 nearly one-fifth of the older population will be college graduates (Atchley, 1991).

- *Greater availability of late life income among specific populations of the elderly.* Income statistics for the elderly show increased wealth among people 65 and over. This fact has been widely publicized. However, 1990 census reports show 15.3% of people aged 65 to 74, 24.1% of those aged 75 to 84, and 28.9% of those aged 88 and over are in or near poverty (below 124% of the poverty level) (U.S. Census Bureau, 1990). This trend must be carefully interpreted with respect to the ability of the elderly to take care of their needs. Circumstances important to this consideration include the lack of adequate health care provision in the United States, questionable reliability and stability of pension funds and other sources of income, the impact of inflation on income, and the great diversity of income and health status within the elderly population.

- *Improvement in the health status of the elderly.* This trend is particularly evident among the young-old.

- *An increase in the ratio of elderly people to working-age individuals.* This trend raises concerns about potential limitation of income and support from social security and other employment-related economic bases, as well as the availability of caregivers.

Social workers must not only understand these changing population dynamics and their implications, but must also respond to them by designing services that address the changing needs of both the elderly and society as a whole.

## POLICY IMPLICATIONS AND DIRECTIONS

Demographic changes, coupled with the changing image of the elderly as a group, have stimulated both action and controversy. The shifting image of the elderly during the past three decades has affected the perceptions of both the public and policy makers. In the 1960s and 1970s the elderly were most often characterized by scholars, advocates, and the media as poor, sick, and in need. During the 1980s this image changed to one of a wealthy elderly population using resources needed by younger members of society (Longman, 1987; Moody, 1988). Visible activism by senior advocacy groups such as the American Association of Retired Persons (AARP), the National Council of Senior Citizens (NCSC), the Older Women's League (OWL), and the Gray Panthers has added to a general perception of the elderly as an organized, self-focused population

(Binstock, 1990).* Resentment of such activism has led to characterizations of the elderly as overusers of resources, with labels such as "greedy geezers" (Atchley, 1991). Perceptions of the life-styles and needs of this fast-growing population have influenced the ways in which Americans think about social welfare policy.

## Health Care Issues

Social security and Medicare combined are approaching 30% of the national budget (Binstock, 1990). This fact alone generates great interest in the aging of our society. The growing number of elderly people, especially in the middle-old and old-old ranges, has greatly increased the demand for health care and social services. This greater demand has come at a time when the cost of health care in this country is escalating, the quality of health care is being challenged, and many Americans of all ages are unable to afford appropriate health care (Callahan, 1987). Unfortunately, the elderly are often blamed for the health care crisis, primarily because they are disproportionately represented among the users of the system. Binstock states:

> Perhaps the most serious scapegoating of the aged—in terms of vulnerability of older persons and, possibly, of all persons in our society—has been with respect to health care. A widespread concern about escalating health care costs has somehow been refocused from the health care providers, suppliers, administrators and insurers—the parties responsible for setting the prices of care—to the elderly patients for whom health care is provided. (1990, p. 79)

## Welfare Issues

The elderly have also gained prominence with regard to their alleged "overuse" of social welfare resources in the arena of income. Social security is considered by many to be an entitlement based on lifelong contributions. However, economic factors, such as the national deficit, have forced a new look at all aspects of federal expenditures. Within this context of scarcity and economic decline, some public policy makers have characterized social security as a social welfare transfer program that should be based on need rather than contribution. This view raises the issue of fairness to those of all ages. To some, social security transfers represent a tremendous drain on funds that could be better spent for other age groups or to balance the federal budget. Gallup poll respondents, however, continue to disapprove of "cuts in entitlement programs such as Social Security, Medicare and the like to reduce the deficit" (*Gallup Report,* 1987, p. 25).

*A list of acronyms appears on page 263.

The increasing utilization of social welfare resources by the elderly has led to a number of policy and philosophical reactions. These reactions include:

- The development of the Intergenerational Equity Movement (Hewitt & Howe, 1988; Longman, 1987; Pollack, 1988), which calls for a redistribution of social welfare resources now used by the elderly to younger groups.

- An increase in academic research on and societal attention to "diversity" among the elderly population (Atchley, 1991; Axinn, 1989; Bass, Kutza, & Torres-Gil, 1990; Crystal & Shea, 1990; Pollack, 1988), which leads to a more individualized, or subgroup-specific, exploration of the needs of the elderly and tends to support the recommendation of some policy analysts that means testing should be the basis for provision of resources to this group.

- The development of a political theme that emphasizes "productivity" over redistribution as a guide for thinking about social policy and the elderly in the 1990s and beyond (Karger and Stoesz, 1990; Moody, 1990).

These changes in the perception of social policy that concerns the elderly have important implications for social workers engaged in empowerment-oriented practice. The task of empowerment-oriented practice is to assure that the elderly have a viable role in the formulation and implementation of social policy that affects their lives. Consequently, understanding and thereby finding effective ways to influence the current policy direction are crucial. The dynamically changing characteristics of the elderly population, including its changing size and resources, are variables critical to the future of social policy and social work practice.

## STRENGTHS AND CONTRIBUTIONS OF THE ELDERLY POPULATION

The demographic trends among the elderly, coupled with society's response to the current and potential impact of these trends on social welfare policy, illustrate the vital role an aging populace plays in the economic and social life of the United States. Demographic characteristics such as increasing longevity, good health among the young-old, and better income status among the elderly bode well for the future of the aging population. The political perspective that the elderly constitute a potential drain on societal resources ignores the reality of the present and future strengths of this age group and its contributions to society.

Statistical reviews often do not identify the strengths of the aging population. Also not often described in the literature are the contributions of the elderly to the economy as workers, taxpayers, paying consumers, and providers of monetary support for children and others; to the family unit as caregivers for older relatives, children, grandchildren, and spouses; to the community as volunteers meeting critical needs; and to the society as a whole through political participation (including the strong support of senior advocacy groups for intergenerational issues).

Even though participation in activities outside the home declines with age, adults have been found to have a core of leisure activities that persists across the life course, although the means for carrying out such activities may be altered by aging (Hooyman & Kiyak, 1988). Type of organizational participation and type and level of activities vary by gender and socioeconomic status.

Among people who are 65 and older, 10% are formal volunteers, compared with 23% of Americans in general. When volunteerism is defined more informally, 37% of the elderly population are involved (Hooyman & Kiyak, 1988). Of people 65 to 74 years old, 68% provide informal help to friends and relatives by running errands, doing household chores, or watching children (Herzog & House, 1991). Several volunteer organizations are composed entirely of the elderly. These include the Retired Senior Volunteer Program (RSVP), which has over 700 projects in schools, hospitals, day care centers, and nursing homes and supervises more than 300,000 older volunteers (Hooyman & Kiyak, 1988); the Foster Grandparents Program, which pairs the elderly with disabled children; the Senior Companion Program, which provides senior-to-senior assistance; and the International Executive Service Corps of Retired Executives, made up of retired executives who volunteer their skills. These represent only a few well-known national programs. It is estimated that 40% of the elderly volunteer through local programs, religious organizations, hospitals, and schools (Herzog and House, 1991).

There are many myths about the elderly that promote stereotyping and negative images. The following list (Harrigan & Farmer, 1992) enumerates some of them:

- Old people are physically ill.
- Old people are underactive.
- Old people cannot do physical activities.
- Old people are depressed and sleep all the time.
- Old people are not attractive.
- Old people are not interested in sex.
- Old people are set in their ways and cannot change.
- Old people are senile.
- Old people cannot learn anything new; nor can they remember anything.
- Old people cannot think and solve problems.

***A wealth of knowledge and experience to share***
*(Photo courtesy of Senior Resource Center, Wheatridge, Colorado)*

- Old people withdraw from society, are alienated through the generation gap, and desire to be left alone.
- Old people are unable and don't want to work.*

Although most of us have held some of these beliefs ourselves or have heard them voiced by others, they are, in fact, all myths—that is, information generally accepted but not true.

The truth is that chronic physical conditions vary greatly in the elderly, with some groups having more physical ailments than others. The belief that unattractiveness is associated with being old is a youth-oriented cultural value, not a truth. Many people remain very active throughout their late life years. Depression is found in only 10–20% of the elderly population. Older people actually sleep less than younger age groups. People remain sexually capable and active throughout late life unless medication or chronic illness prevents such activity. Older people

---

* From "Myths and Facts of Aging" by M. P. Harrigan and R. L. Farmer, in *Gerontological Social Work* by R. L. Schneider and N. P. Kropf (Eds.). Copyright © 1992 by Nelson-Hall Publishers. Reprinted by permission.

are quite capable of problem solving and of changing to adapt to their environment. Short-term memory loss is common among the elderly, but senility occurs in only 5% of people over 65 (Harrigan & Farmer, 1992). Older people generally do not withdraw or disengage from society in spite of the loss of many socially valued formal roles. Many studies have provided truths regarding aging, and these facts are important for gerontological social workers (see, for example, Antonucci & Akiyama, 1991; Beaver & Miller, 1992; Hancock, 1990; Harrigan & Farmer, 1992; Henig, 1981; Salthouse, 1991).

Older people's strengths and capacities are especially important to empowerment-oriented social workers, the core of whose practice is the transfer of knowledge and skills for survival and enhancement of late life. Lowy (1988) suggests that education strategies are becoming ever more important to social welfare interventions in general.

## SOCIAL WORK PRACTICE AND THE ELDERLY

Social work as a profession placed little emphasis on the elderly population until the late 1950s (Lowy, 1979). The 1960s brought new and increased resources into the field through departments of public assistance, the Economic Opportunity Act (1964), and the Older Americans Act (1965). As agents of the departments of public welfare, social workers were able to provide protective and casework services to elderly who were receiving public old age pensions. The community action agencies funded through the Economic Opportunity Act offered opportunities for community-based social work activities, including community organizing and economic self-sufficiency programs targeting the elderly. The Older Americans Act allowed for social casework and social group activity, as well as education and organizing activities. In the early 1970s, pressure was brought to bear on the mental health system to place more emphasis on programs to meet the needs of the elderly.

### Retrenchment

The radical cuts in human services in the 1980s dismantled most of the sources of public social services for the elderly. Funding of medical services for this age group, especially through Medicare and Medicaid, was greatly expanded during the same period. The consequence was the medicalization of most services to seniors. Because positions were not available in public social service departments and there was an increasing need among the elderly for social and emotional assistance, social work professionals were forced to seek positions within medically controlled settings, such as senior health clinics, hospitals, and home health care agencies.

Cuts in funding for socially oriented programs were accompanied by a movement to increase the use of volunteers and untrained para-professionals who could be employed for minimal wages to fill the service gap. *Case management* replaced professional casework services, and case management often came down to nothing more than the provision of information and referral services. Although the National Association of Social Workers has attempted to define case management in a manner equivalent to social casework, this definition is far from being universally accepted. Also, health professionals have done much to "medicalize" the concept of case management in many settings.

Social work professionals today find that they must articulate what professional social work can contribute to the needs of an aging society and must develop the resources and settings for making this contribution. A strong beginning has been made toward establishing—or re-establishing—the role of social work in the field of gerontology.

Social workers in nursing homes, hospitals, home health care agencies, and other medical-model settings are providing interventions that focus on the social and emotional needs of the elderly as they cope with sickness and disability. The important role of social work in assisting older people to find and access long-term care services, housing, income, and other needed resources is also apparent in many of these settings (Monk, 1990). Social workers in these settings, however, often find themselves limited by a medical-model focus on illness and by a lack of attention to the social/emotional/political aspects of human life. In addition, inadequate staffing and lack of sanction for work with families to develop support and self-help networks and for the initiation of other key social work interventions are often inhibiting factors.

In the wide range of nonmedical gerontological settings, such as senior centers, legal service centers, employment programs, volunteer projects, and so on, professional social workers must often contend with limited resources and untrained staff in attempting to achieve solutions to the problems such programs are designed to address. Practitioners find themselves trying to attend to clients' needs without adequately paid and trained personnel and without a system of comprehensive services (Monk, 1990).

## The Future

What about the future of social work practice? Peterson (1990) reports that approximately 26% of practicing social workers serve the elderly. The National Institute on Aging (1987) estimates that 60,000 to 70,000 professionally trained social workers will be needed in 2020. Monk (1990) notes that this estimate is based on the increasing number of frail elderly (old-old) and does not consider the emerging demand from the young-old, including early retirees. All estimates of the need for social workers in the future are, of course, subject to the complex and rapidly changing relationship between need and resources.

The dramatic demographic changes, the great diversity within the aging population, the wealth of resources and strengths among the elderly, and the increasing need for health services and health-related social services due to the greater number of old-old pose a great challenge to the social work profession. An ever increasing repertoire of knowledge and skills is necessary for assisting those elderly who suffer from disabilities and the families who suffer with them. Social work services for the elderly must attempt to reinstate preventive and socially based interventions. In addition, they must create programs and intervention strategies that facilitate empowerment of the elderly and their families. Congruent with the empowerment approach, gerontological social workers must be capable of contributing to the development of social policy and services in such a way as to facilitate a partnership between themselves and the elderly. This partnership must support the fullest possible development of strengths and potential in the elderly population, which constitutes a vital, productive, and integrated force in American society.

A key task of social workers involved in this process includes the assessment of the tasks, challenges, and problems encountered by people as they age. Chapter 2 focuses on common challenges. Even though diversity of sex, age, ethnic background, and social class (including income and resource levels) is a reality in all age groups, late life brings some common negative experiences that typically include physical, mental, and economic decline. An improved understanding of these problems and the state of powerlessness they can cause will enable empowerment-oriented social workers to develop increasingly effective interventions that counter or prevent the experience of powerlessness.

## SUMMARY

The growing number of elders in American society has created an increasing interest in and attention to this segment of the population. The diversity and complexity of this age group make generalizations very difficult and challenge social workers to create interventions appropriate to distinguishable subgroups.

Specific trends within the older population include increasing numbers of elderly women, ethnic minorities, and people aged 85 and over, as well as higher education levels, increased availability of income, and improved health status among the young-old.

Ongoing changes in the demographics of the elderly population, coupled with economic problems, have resulted in a shifting image of the elderly—from poor, sick, helpless, and needy to wealthy, greedy "gobblers" of resources. Increased concern about the costs of medical care focuses on the elderly as a group, rather than on the health care system. Furthermore, the rising percentage of federal social welfare spending going to older people is viewed as a consequence of greed among the elderly, rather than as due to the growing numbers of elderly. Such slanted perceptions have caused much research and policy analysis to focus on the elderly as a potential political problem.

A view of the elderly as a resource drain fails to take into account their many tangible and intangible contributions to society. Contributions such as volunteerism (both formal and informal) are not components of the view of the elderly as users or takers. Myths about aging and the elderly increase negative stereotyping and age discrimination. Most of the common myths about elders have been exposed as falsehoods by research.

Social workers' services to the elderly have mirrored society's shifting image of this population—from infantilized caretaking to an emphasis on improving employment opportunities and instituting self-sufficiency programs. Retrenchment of funding sources has both cut services available to the elderly and generated an emphasis on elders' volunteerism. Case management is the theme of the 1990s in social work practice, to the detriment of many social and emotional issues involved in the aging process. Limited resources have forced social workers to be creative in seeking ways to provide services. Empowerment is a necessary component of the provision of services to the elderly.

# REFERENCES

Antonucci, T., & Akiyama, H. (1991). Social relationships and aging well. *Generations, 15*(1), pp. 39–44.

Atchley, R. C. (1991). *Social forces and aging* (7th ed.). Belmont, CA: Wadsworth.

Axinn, J. (1989). Women and aging: Issues of adequacy and equity. In D. Garner & S. Mercer (Eds.), *Women as they age: Challenge, opportunity, and triumph.* New York: Hawthorne.

Bass, S. A., Kutza, E. A., & Torres-Gil, F. M. (Eds.). (1990). *Diversity in aging: Challenge facing planners and policy makers in the 1990s.* Glenview, IL: Scott, Foresman.

Beaver, M. L., & Miller, D. A. (1992). *Clinical social work practice with the elderly* (2nd ed.). Pacific Grove, CA: Brooks/Cole.

Binstock, R. (1990). The politics and economics of aging and diversity. In S. A. Bass, E. A. Kutza, & F. M. Torres-Gil (Eds.), *Diversity in aging.* Glenview, IL: Scott, Foresman.

Callahan, D. (1987). *Setting limits: Medical goals for an aging society.* New York: Simon & Schuster.

Crystal, S., & Shea, D. (1990). Cumulative advantage, cumulative disadvantage, and inequality among elderly people. *The Gerontologist, 30*(4), pp. 437–443.

*Gallup Report.* (1987). August–November, *263,* pp. 25–27.

Hancock, B. L. (1990). *Social work with older people* (2nd ed.). Englewood Cliffs, NJ: Prentice-Hall.

Harrigan, M. P., & Farmer, R. L. (1992). The myths and facts of aging. In R. L. Schneirder & N. P. Kript (Eds.), *Gerontological social work.* Chicago: Nelson-Hall.

Henig, R. M. (1981). *The myth of senility.* New York: Anchor.

Herzog, A. R., & House, J. S. (1991). Productive activities and aging well. *Generations, 1*(3), pp. 10–13.

Hewitt, P. S. & Howe, N. (1988). Future of generational politics. *Generations, 7*(3), pp. 10–13.

Hooyman, N. R., & Kiyak, H. A. (1988). *Social gerontology.* Boston: Allyn and Bacon.

Karger, H. I., & Stoesz, D. (1990). *American social welfare policy: A structural approach.* White Plains, NY: Longman.

Kart, C. S. (1990). *Realities of aging: An introduction to gerontology.* Boston: Allyn and Bacon.

Lesnoff-Caravaglia, G. (1988). Aging in a technological society. In G. Lesnoff-Caravaglia (Ed.), *Aging in a technological society.* New York: Human Sciences Press.

Longman, P. (1987). *Born to pay: The new politics of aging in America.* Boston: Houghton Mifflin.

Lowy, L. (1979). *Social work with the elderly.* New York: Harper & Row.

Lowy, L. (1988). Human service professionals: Their role in education for older people. *Generations, 15*(2), pp. 31–37.

Monk, A. (1990). *Handbook of gerontological services* (2nd ed.). New York: Columbia University Press.

Moody, H. R. (1988). *Abundance of life: Human development policies for an aging society.* New York: Columbia University Press.

Moody, H. R. (1990). The politics of entitlement and the politics of productivity. In S. A. Bass, E. A. Kutza, & F. M. Torres-Gil (Eds.), *Diversity in aging.* Glenview, IL: Scott, Foresman.

National Institute on Aging. (1987). *Personnel for health needs of the elderly: Through 2020.* Washington, DC: U.S. Government Printing Office.

Peterson, D. A. (1990). Personnel to serve the aging in the field of social work: Implications for educating professionals. *Social Work, 35,* pp. 412–418.

Pollack, R. (1988). Serving intergenerational needs. *Generations,* 7(3), pp. 14–18.

Salthouse, T. A. (1991). Cognitive facets of aging well. *Generations,* 15(1), pp. 35–38.

Spencer, G. (1989). Projections of the population of the United States, by age, sex and race: 1988 to 2080. *Current Population Report Series, 1018,* p. 25.

U.S. Census Bureau. (1990). *Current population reports* (No. 1057, March, p. 25). Washington, DC: U.S. Government Printing Office.

# UNDERSTANDING POWERLESSNESS AMONG THE ELDERLY

This chapter discusses powerlessness as a factor in all human existence and, more specifically, considers the nature of and special circumstances that can generate a feeling of powerlessness in elderly people. It also examines the common experiences of the elderly—such as physical, mental, support, and resource decline—that can contribute to feelings of powerlessness.

## INTRODUCTION

Two closely related assumptions are basic to the empowerment-oriented practice model presented in this book:

1. *All* human beings are potentially competent, even in extremely challenging situations.
2. *All* human beings are subject to various degrees of *powerlessness.*

A basic tenet of empowerment-oriented social work practice is that older people who experience radical changes and adverse circumstances are able to counter powerlessness personally and/or politically. The elderly strive for effectiveness in their lives, just as younger people do. They want to be—and are potentially capable of being—participants in the creation and governing of their own environment. They do not naturally and willfully fade out of the political, economic, and social scenes.

Loss of efficacy on the part of elders results less from loss of competence than from the power differential in the interaction between elderly people and the environmental systems with which they are involved. Health problems, loss of significant support systems, and forced disengagement from major social institutions often impose a limitation on elders' choices that results in decreased power to make decisions about their lives—and eventually in loss of control and disenfranchisement. We believe this process can be prevented or greatly modified.

This book introduces a model that emphasizes empowerment in social work practice with elders and suggests intervention strategies that facilitate the process of helping elderly people to assert more control over their own lives. All human beings sometimes feel powerless and experience different levels of political consciousness regarding oppression, but an at-risk population such as the elderly feels powerlessness most acutely. *Powerlessness* is defined as a lack of access to the resources, knowledge, and skills that are necessary to solve one's own problems, including the ability to participate effectively in social change.

In her important book on empowerment, Solomon (1976) conceived powerlessness as deriving from at least three sources: (1) the attitudes of members of the oppressed population themselves, (2) the interaction between victims of oppression and the large environmental systems that impinge on them, and (3) the larger environmental structure—that is, the structural arrangements of social systems that are not responsive to victims of oppression and, indeed, serve to perpetuate the oppression. These factors are connected to and feed on one another. Internal attitudes of powerlessness are reinforced by experiences in which attempts to solve problems are blocked, and external perceptions of a given group as powerless are reinforced as internal attitudes intensify. A sense of powerlessness emerges when "an individual feels or expects his actions not to produce desired outcomes; that although he is not living the life he would like, there is nothing he can do about it" (Maze, 1987, p. 1).

Differences in the power to make desired changes in one's life can result from class structure and from differences in status deriving from sex, race, ethnicity, religion, age, sexual preference, physical and mental ability, or combinations of these characteristics (the latter category includes aged women of color, for example) (Staples, 1990).

## Empowerment

*Empowerment* has been defined by Staples (1990) as "(1) to gain power; (2) to develop power, to take or seize power; (3) to facilitate or enable power; (4) to give, grant, or permit power" (p. 29). In her synthesis of empowerment literature, Torre (1985) concluded that "empowerment is a process through which people become strong enough to participate within, share in the control of, and influence events and institutions which affect their lives" and that, in part, "empowerment necessitates that people gain particular skills, knowledge and sufficient power to influence their lives and the lives of those they care about" (p. 61).

In his study of the empowerment process, Kieffer (1981) identified the following requisites for empowerment:

- A personal attitude, or *sense of self,* that promotes active social involvement
- The capacity for *critical analysis* of the social and political systems that define one's environment
- An ability to develop *action strategies* and cultivate resources for attainment of one's goals
- An ability to act in an efficacious manner *in concert with others* to define and attain collective goals

Empowerment is both a process in which people become engaged and an outcome of such engagement. "In a nutshell, empowerment is helping people assure or reclaim control over their own destiny—it focuses on the capacity of people to function in their own behalf" (Akins, 1985, p. 10).

## *Empowerment-Oriented Practice*

Empowerment-oriented social work practice is a model through which social workers can assist older people to utilize their strengths, abilities, and competencies in order to mobilize their resources toward problem solving and ultimately toward empowerment. Empowerment-oriented practice recognizes that elders frequently experience substantial loss of power for a variety of reasons. The definition and process of empowerment-oriented practice will be elaborated on in Chapter 3 and elsewhere throughout this book. The remainder of this chapter focuses on the life changes experienced by many elders and their families—changes that often bring great challenges in late life. These challenges, while stimulating a variety of individual responses, can lead to feelings of powerlessness.

## *LATE LIFE EXPERIENCES AND POWERLESSNESS*

The powerlessness that elders may feel must be understood in the context of powerlessness among all groups. As suggested in the beginning of this chapter, powerlessness has both internal and external dynamics and is generated by an interactive process.

## *The Interactive Process Underlying Powerlessness*

In general, powerlessness is viewed as a construct of continuous interaction between individuals and their environment. It comprises an

attitude of self-blame, a sense of generalized distrust, a feeling of alienation from resources necessary for social influence, an experience of disenfranchisement and economic vulnerability, and a sense of hopelessness
in the sociopolitical struggle (Kieffer, 1984).

A person's level of political consciousness, concrete personal experiences in meeting late life needs, and participation in the change and
control of the immediate environment are all aspects of his or her degree
of empowerment. Many groups in our society perceive themselves to
be without power in the face of the political-economic system, religious
systems, social welfare institutions, and even their communities, peer networks, and families. This perception of a lack of power may derive from
a variety of factors, including economic insecurity, absence of experience
in the political arena, lack of access to information, absence of financial
support, lack of training in abstract or critical thought, and physical or
emotional stress (Conway, 1979; Sennett & Cobb, 1972).

Weakening of support groups contributes to a sense of powerlessness.
Nisbet (1953) identifies the weakening of primary groups in society (for
example, families and communities) as one source of feelings of alienation, fear, and disconnectedness between people, which eventually result
in a decreased ability to work together toward common goals. Self-
devaluation contributes to the perpetuation of powerlessness among the
elderly. Solomon (1976) argues that powerlessness results in part from
membership in a stigmatized group, whose members often adopt society's negative stereotypes, internalizing them and incorporating them into
their own self-image. Consequently, members of such a group are less
able to view themselves as capable and deserving of the right or the power
to change their lives.

As suggested in Chapter 1, great diversity exists among elderly people
with respect to financial resources, health status, the quality of support
networks, and responses to crises and other events in their lives. However,
many elders experience certain critical changes and challenges that are
strongly related to powerlessness. These common experiences include
risk of economic insecurity, physical and mental stress, and weakening
of social support. Such challenges are often faced by elderly people
without adequate preparation, by either themselves or their families. They
and their families may be isolated from others with similar problems or
lack the knowledge and access to resources that could improve their circumstances. Feelings of powerlessness have often been the result for many
elders and their families.

Although a cushion is afforded those older people who have substantial resources, most people are faced with some significant losses in late
life. Losses experienced by elders include *personal losses,* such as changes
in physical and mental health and the death or decline of significant others.
In addition, *social losses,* which are more easily understood in terms of
the political-economic system, are experienced by most elders to one
degree or another. These social losses include retirement (for many, an

important diminishment of financial adequacy and/or independence and a significant loss of role) and loss of other meaningful life roles. Elders who have experienced a lifetime of poverty or limited financial resources or who have suffered discrimination because of ethnic minority status, female status, or class-related factors are even more threatened by the challenges of late life.

Regardless of the fact that the situation may vary from individual to individual, certain kinds of losses are more common to the elderly than to the population in general. Also, society tends to generalize about elders as a group and to discriminate against them on the basis of negative stereotypes. Figure 2.1 suggests the interrelationship of external losses, the internal sense of loss related to these experiences, the internalized sense of powerlessness, and larger societal images of aging and the elderly.

## Personal Losses

Experiences common to many elders that constitute personal losses include physical and mental decline and loss of support systems.

***Physical Decline***   Some degree of physical decline is inherent in the aging process. Energy is diminished because of the body's decreased capacity to deliver oxygen and nutrients. By age 80, a person's body can take in only half the oxygen it could at age 40 (Atchley, 1991). Muscle strength remains relatively constant through age 70, but maximum work output declines steadily after age 40 (Shock & Norris, 1970). The decline in energy does not interfere with low to moderate levels of work, but it does result in longer recovery time from illness or injury.

Aging may also result in decreases in physical stature, mobility (as a result of the onset of arthritis and the degeneration of connective tissue), and physical coordination. Other physical signs of aging include wrinkled skin, age spots, gray hair, and midriff bulge—all characteristics commonly devalued in American society.

The wide variation in the health status of older people suggests that poor health is not inevitably associated with aging. As a group, however, older people do suffer disproportionately from some chronic conditions. These include heart disease, arthritis, hypertension, diabetes, lower body (back and spine) impairment, asthma, and hearing and vision impairment. Nearly 86% of people over 65 suffer from one or more such conditions, and about half of those experience limitations in activity as a result (AARP, 1991; Atchley, 1985). More than 25% of elders aged 85 and over need assistance with some instrumental activities of daily living (Atchley, 1991). Studies also show a greater incidence of chronic conditions among elders of lower socioeconomic status than in the general population (Cohen & Brody, 1981).

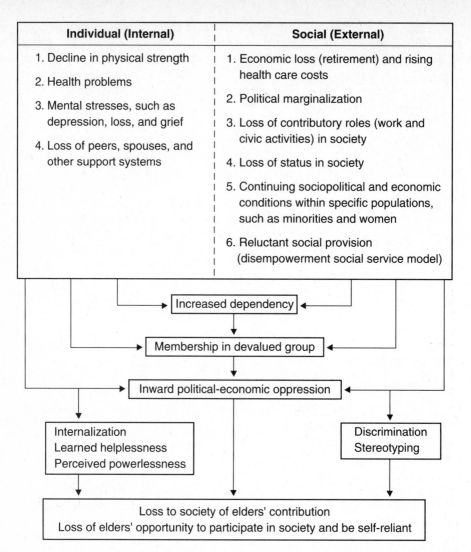

| Individual (Internal) | Social (External) |
|---|---|
| 1. Decline in physical strength | 1. Economic loss (retirement) and rising health care costs |
| 2. Health problems | 2. Political marginalization |
| 3. Mental stresses, such as depression, loss, and grief | 3. Loss of contributory roles (work and civic activities) in society |
| 4. Loss of peers, spouses, and other support systems | 4. Loss of status in society |
| | 5. Continuing sociopolitical and economic conditions within specific populations, such as minorities and women |
| | 6. Reluctant social provision (disempowerment social service model) |

Increased dependency

Membership in devalued group

Inward political-economic oppression

Internalization
Learned helplessness
Perceived powerlessness

Discrimination
Stereotyping

Loss to society of elders' contribution
Loss of elders' opportunity to participate in society and be self-reliant

***Figure 2.1    Factors Contributing to Loss of Power by Elders***

The social consequences of health impairments can reinforce perceptions of powerlessness. Atchley (1991) notes two types of social consequences: "(1) social limits imposed by other people's perceptions of the condition and (2) functional limits imposed by the condition itself" (p. 79). He notes that the perceptions of others can limit employment and social opportunities as well as affect self-perception.

***Mental Decline***    Another personal loss that is a potential source of feelings of powerlessness is mental incapacity. Although verbal abilities and remote memory are relatively unaffected by normal aging, a modest impairment of short-term memory, a decrease in speed of learning, a slowing of reaction time, and some degree of mild forgetfulness are common in old age (Veith & Borson, 1986).

Biological factors are associated with a number of mental disorders. The association between degenerative changes in the central nervous system and Alzheimer's-type dementia is well established (Veith & Borson, 1986). Alzheimer's disease is the most common form of dementing illness, affecting approximately 4 million Americans. Approximately 10% of the population over 65 is afflicted with the disease. The proportion rises to 47.2% of those over 85, which is one of the fastest-growing segments of the U.S. population (Coons, 1991). Other mental dysfunctions that cluster in the older population are non–Alzheimer's-type dementia, depression, and late-onset paranoia. Studies over the last several decades have documented that between 15% and 25% of older people have serious symptoms of some mental disorder (AARP, 1991). Depression is substantially more common among the elderly than in the younger population (Hooyman & Kiyak, 1988). Depression in elders may not be biologically based but may be related to the social aspects of aging, such as role loss.

In terms of general social functioning, age-related decrements in mental acuity affect only a small proportion of the population under 70 (Atchley, 1985). Although some mental changes are clearly associated with the aging process, the incidence, severity, and consequences of these changes vary dramatically among the aging population. Thus, generalizations simply cannot be made. However, even a slight loss of memory can be a source of loss, a challenge to one's self-image, and, consequently, a source of feelings of powerlessness.

**Loss of Support Systems**    The term *support system* refers to a relationship that involves the giving and receiving of assistance, which is viewed by both the giver and the receiver as significant to maintaining the psychological, social, and physical integrity of the receiver (Lopata, 1975). Support systems can be formal or informal: informal support is provided by family and friends; formal support is provided by the social service system or other social institutions.

The death of a loved one is a common source of loss of support for older people. The aging process typically brings with it the deaths of friends and cohorts as well as spouses and other family members. The death of a pet is also a great loss for some elders. Death, however, is not the only form of loss related to support group strength. Income, personal assistance, and emotional support can also be lost when disability affects members of one's support network.

Clearly, the major support system for elders is family. The loss of informal support, whether through death or through relocation away from a familiar place, increases elders' isolation as well as their dependence on more formal systems of support. Dependence on formal support systems is discussed more fully later as an issue that is more directly associated with the political economy of aging.

## Sociopolitical Factors in Loss

Minkler and Estes (1984, 1991) maintain that the major problems of the elderly in American society are socially constructed. According to Maze (1987), the problems are products of the American class society, in which "some individuals and groups have much greater power than others to influence the definition of social problems and to specify the policy interventions that address those problems" (p. 1). Phillipson (1982, p. 38) describes the process by which elderly people become members of a marginal or "less useful and needed population" in society as their skills become less necessary to the work force, making them vulnerable to loss of employment in a capitalistic system. The need of the younger population for jobs, the antiquation of older employees' knowledge and skills, their poor health, and their higher salaries may all contribute to the marginalization of the elderly in the workplace.

***Retirement*** Retirement has become an increasingly accepted social institution, although mandatory retirement was made illegal for most positions. According to Kingston (1990),

> The labor force participation of men 60 and over has dropped from 45.5% in 1950 to 16.3% in 1987, and participation of men aged 55 through 64 has declined from 86.9% to 67.6% during this period. Women's participation in the labor market at age 65 and above has remained fairly stable; however, the participation rate of women aged 55 through 64 has increased from 27.0% in 1950 to 42.7% in 1987. (pp. 271–272)

The availability of pensions, social security, and other forms of late life income is believed to have a significant impact on these trends. Other factors related to the political economy—such as class differences among the elderly, a shrinking labor market, rapidly changing technology, age discrimination, and poor health of some workers—also affect employment trends among the elderly.

Many elders are caught in a dilemma by the mixed messages of social policy on late life employment. Early retirement programs continue to encourage exit from the work force; at the same time, concerns regarding the need to reexamine the institution of retirement are being expressed. Elderly retirees are faced with the prospect of twenty to thirty years of need for income after retirement. Even though income statistics (see Chapter 1) show greatly improved late life income for many groups among the elderly, income needs in late life are indeterminate. Late life income needs are difficult to determine because of uncertainty regarding longevity, inflation, and adequacy and stability of private pension plans, social security, other public pensions, and other income sources. In addition, the medical costs that may accrue to any individual cannot be predicted. At this point, adequate public coverage for most long-term care needs does not exist.

The social meaning of retirement also adds a challenging dimension to late life for many retirees. The extremely strong work ethic in this society has been internalized by most older Americans. Employment is often a source of pride and identity. Clearly, the more a person's life is tied up with work, the more difficult retirement will be. Some people look forward to escape from the workplace, and they experience little social loss; however, retirement nearly always results in loss of meaningful relationships as well as income.

***Role Loss*** The number of roles typically occupied by an individual remains stable between the ages of 50 and 64 but steadily declines after 65 (Atchley, 1991). The most common example of a role frequently lost with age is the work role, but roles in community organizations, neighborhood associations, churches, and even families may also be lost. Families often react to aging members, especially as some degree of disability and/or financial dependence sets in, with a reverse paternalism—as if the elderly person is no longer a viable participant but rather someone in need of care. If roles provide a major source of self-esteem and growth—as role theory suggests they do—then the loss of roles is clearly a major loss for the elderly.

***Age Discrimination*** Another well-documented phenomenon that enters the life of people as they age is age discrimination. Discrimination in employment is one area that strongly affects older women and low-income elders who require employment income to sustain a minimal standard of living. Wineman (1990) states that, despite the passage of the Age Discrimination Act in 1967, "stereotypes of older persons' ability to perform on the job, their perceived health concerns, and the notion of increased costs of their employment persist some fifteen years after enactment" (p. 396). Although much has been done in the area of education of employers, many elderly people find themselves severely hampered by age discrimination in their late life efforts to keep or find work.

There are many other types of discrimination, some strongly linked to other stereotypes of the elderly. Hancock (1990) suggests some stereotypes that may provide support for discriminatory treatment of the elderly: the belief that most elderly persons are disabled and in poor health, the belief that older people inevitably withdraw from the mainstream of society as they grow older (remnants of the disengagement theory), the belief that senility accompanies old age, and the belief that elderly persons are unable to learn new knowledge and skills. Subtle forms of discriminatory behavior—such as asking a younger companion what an elderly person wants when the elder is shopping or waiting to order food at a restaurant—are often as emotionally disturbing as more blatant age discrimination.

***Dependency***   Independence is strongly valued in American society, and dependence is strongly devalued (Clark & Anderson, 1967; Karger & Stoesz, 1990; Morris, 1979; Rokeach, 1973). In a culture where individualism may well be the most highly prized virtue, there is little place for dependency and its implied lack of capacity to choose (Quinn, 1984; Simmel, 1977). Nevertheless, as a result of the kinds of losses described above, many elders find themselves facing a degree of dependency at some point in life.

The negative image of dependence held by this society works to stigmatize elders as a group. Internalized by elders themselves, this negative image may result in a decreased sense of self-esteem, a sense of loss, depression, and, eventually, a state of learned helplessness. Maze (1987) suggests that older people become powerless as "they cease to act upon the environment as agents affecting it, and begin to passively accept an existence within that environment as an object or consequence of it" (p. 1). Elders' lack of information about the aging process itself and the general lack of critical thought about the position of elders in society have also worked to reinforce self-devaluation.

A final potential source of disempowerment that faces those elders who become dependent with respect to income and/or personal care needs is the need for formal support from health and social services. This is explored below.

## Social Policy and Health and Social Services

American social policy and the health and social services that are developed in response to that policy have been described as strong contributors to social control and the creation of helplessness and a sense of powerlessness among those who must rely on them (Abramovitz, 1986; Estes & Lee, 1985; Galper, 1975, 1980; Minkler & Estes, 1991; Phillipson, 1982).

The elderly, often for the first time, find themselves faced with the need for assistance. Social provisions such as Medicaid, state old age pensions, and other means-tested forms of assistance are available in limited supply and with a stigma attached. The difficult act of asking for help is made more difficult by a reluctant, complex, and often adversarial social welfare system. Establishing eligibility often forces one to deal with public workers who are anxious to deny requests because of limitations on fiscal resources and who perhaps hold negative attitudes about dependency. If and when assistance is provided, quality assurance is very limited.

Furthermore, recipient status is often tenuous because of changing eligibility requirements and other funding-related program changes.

Changes in social policy during the 1980s have made the receiving of assistance more difficult for all groups, including the elderly. Privatization of social and health services—the shift from government sponsorship to private sector provision—has led to a number of philosophical and policy changes, including:

- A shift in the perceived status of resources or services from being a social or political right to being a charitable contribution (Estes, 1989)
- A shift of the cost of services out of the feasible price range of many potential clients (Abramovitz, 1986)
- A shift, at least to some degree, toward reducing the monitoring power of the government, which creates more difficulty with quality assurance (Starr, 1989)
- A shift from centralized providers to multiple, competing entities, making services more difficult to locate and causing rapid changes in availability of services as agencies come and go, or, in some cases, a shift to profit-oriented oligopolies that limit access to those most in need (Karger & Stoesz, 1990).

In short, elders who must seek assistance from formal support services often must endure humiliating and frustrating experiences. Later chapters will describe in more detail some of the problems encountered and discuss empowerment-oriented interventions designed to counter some of them.

## SUMMARY

Practitioners must understand both the real and the perceived losses of aging and must recognize how the two reinforce each other. Social workers are challenged to build upon the strengths of the elderly and to provide interventions that assist them to avoid disempowerment or to become empowered to make decisions about their own lives. An overall understanding of the relationship of the circumstances of the elderly to the political economy and the relationship of late life changes to dominant values of American society is crucial in enabling practitioners to identify feelings of powerlessness and actions based on these feelings. Comprehension of the complexity of the phenomenon of powerlessness among the elderly is a necessary context for application of the empowerment-oriented practice model, outlined in Chapter 3.

Because the aging process is both internal and external, loss of efficacy in elders' lives may result in increased powerlessness. Empowerment-oriented practice is geared toward increasing a sense of personal efficacy, improving knowledge and skills for critical analysis of one's situation, formulating action, and taking action to attain collective goals.

Interactions between the personal and social dynamics of aging give impetus to perceived powerlessness among the elderly. Personal losses include physical decline, mental decline, and loss of support systems. Social factors include retirement, role loss, age discrimination, and dependency. Social policies and social services are designed in a way that tends to further stigmatize and infantilize the elderly. An empowerment-oriented approach seeks to counter the resulting internalized powerlessness in the elderly population.

# *REFERENCES*

AARP (American Association of Retired Persons). (1991). *Aging America* (DHHS Publication No. FCOA 91-28001). Washington, DC: U.S. Government Printing Office.

Abramovitz, M. (1986). The privatization of the welfare state: A review. *Social Work, 31*(4), pp. 257–262.

Akins, R. E. (1985). Empowerment: Mastering independence of the older adult. *Aging Network News, 11* (5), p. 10–12.

Atchley, R. C. (1985). *Social forces and aging* (4th ed.). Belmont, CA: Wadsworth.

Atchley, R. C. (1991). *Social forces and aging* (6th ed.). Belmont, CA: Wadsworth.

Clark, M., & Anderson, B. (1967). *Culture and aging.* Springfield, IL: Charles C. Thomas.

Cohen, J. B., & Brody, J. A. (1981). The epidemiologic importance of psychosocial factors in longevity. *American Journal of Epidemiology, 14,* pp. 451–461.

Conway, M. (1979). *Rise gonna rise.* New York: Anchor Books.

Coons, D. H. (1991). *Specialized dementia care units.* Baltimore: Johns Hopkins University Press.

Estes, C. L. (1989). The future of gerontology: Golden purpose or tarnished promise? *The Connection, A* (2), pp. 8–9.

Estes, C. L., & Lee, P. R. (1985). Social, political and economic background of long-term care policy. In C. Harrington, R. Neueiner, & C. Estes (Eds.), *Long-term care of the elderly.* Beverly Hills, CA: Sage.

Galper, J. H. (1975). *The politics of social service.* Englewood Cliffs, NJ: Prentice-Hall.

Galper, J. H. (1980). *Social work practice: A radical perspective.* Englewood Cliffs, NJ: Prentice-Hall.

Hancock, B. L. (1990). *Social work with older people.* Englewood Cliffs, NJ: Prentice-Hall.

Hooyman, N. R., & Kiyak, H. A. (1988). *Social gerontology.* Boston: Allyn and Bacon.

Karger, H. J., & Stoesz, D. (1990). *American social welfare policy: A structural approach.* New York: Longman.

Kieffer, C. H. (1981). *The emergence of empowerment.* Unpublished doctoral dissertation, University of Michigan, Ann Arbor.

Kieffer, C. H. (1984). Citizen empowerment: A developmental perspective. *Prevention in Human Services, 3* (2/3), pp. 9–35.

Kingston, E. R. (1990). Public income security programs for the elderly. In A. Monk (Ed.), *Handbook of gerontological services* (2nd ed.). New York: Columbia University Press.

Lopata, H. (1975). Support systems in elderly urbanites: Chicago of the 1970's. *The Gerontologist, 15*(35), pp. 370–374.

Maze, T. (1987). Empowerment: Reflections on theory and practice. *Aging Network News, 9*(5), p. 1.

Minkler, M., & Estes, C. (Eds.). (1984). *Readings in the political economy of aging.* Farmingdale, NY: Baywood.

Minkler, M., & Estes, C. (Eds.). (1991). *Critical perspectives on aging: The political and moral economy of growing old.* Farmingdale, NY: Baywood.

Morris, R. M. (1979). *Social policy of the American welfare state* (2nd ed.). New York: Longman.

Nisbet, R. (1953). *Community and power.* New York: Oxford University Press.

Phillipson, C. (1982). *Capitalism and the construction of old age.* London: MacMillan.

Quinn, W. H. (1984). Autonomy, interdependence and developmental delay in older generations of the family. In W. H. Quinn & G. Hughston (Eds.), *Independent aging.* Rockville, MD: Aspen.

Rokeach, M. (1973). *The nature of human values.* New York: Free Press.

Sennett, R., & Cobb, J. (1972). *The hidden injuries of class.* Garden City, NY: Vintage.

Shock, N. W., & Norris, A. H. (1970). Neuromuscular coordination as a factor in age changes in muscular exercise. In D. Brunner & E. Jokl (Eds.), *Physical activity and aging.* New York: S. Karger.

Simmel, G. (1977). The metropolis and mental life. In R. L. Warren (Ed.), *Perspectives on the American community* (3rd ed.). Chicago: Rand McNally.

Solomon, B. (1976). *Black empowerment: Social work in oppressed communities.* New York: Columbia University Press.

Staples, L. H. (1990). Powerful ideas about empowerment. *Administration in Social Work, 14*(2), pp. 29–42.

Starr, P. (1989). The meaning of privatization. In S. B. Kamerman & A. I. Kahn (Eds.), *Privatization and the welfare state.* Princeton, NJ: Princeton University Press.

Torre, D. (1985). *Empowerment: Structured conceptualization and instrument development*. Unpublished doctoral dissertation, Cornell University, Ithaca, NY.

Veith, R. C., & Borson, S. (1986). Does age made a difference? *Generations, 10*(3), pp. 9–13.

Wineman, J. (1990). Services to older and retired workers. In A. Monk (Ed.), *Handbook of gerontological services* (2nd ed.). New York: Columbia University Press.

# THE
# EMPOWERMENT-ORIENTED
# PRACTICE MODEL

This chapter describes the essential elements of the empowerment-oriented practice model. The usual components of social work practice are modified by the principles of empowerment. In this practice model, assessment and interventions are conceptualized in terms of four dimensions of problem-solving. Empowerment-oriented practice requires that attention be given to all dimensions of problems presented by clients. Consciousness raising, education, and action are key activities linking the various dimensions.

## *UNDERSTANDING EMPOWERMENT*

### *Examples of Empowerment-Oriented Interventions*

The following case examples describe empowerment-oriented practice and are referred to throughout this chapter. The elderly people described in them lived in a city with a population of approximately 100,000. The empowerment-oriented social worker was employed by a multipurpose agency that operated a number of separate activity sites (senior centers) throughout the city. These sites provided space for meals programs, educational programs, and meetings of both small groups and larger organizations, such as the American Association of Retired Persons (AARP) and the National Association of Retired Federal Employees (NARFE). Many community service agencies, such as the visiting nurse services and the community mental health centers, also used these sites for service activities. The agency also provided support and meeting space for the Citywide Council of Senior Organizations (CCSO). This council became active in local political decision making when the needs of elderly citizens were involved. In addition, it addressed state and federal issues to a limited extent. Overlap of membership between the CCSO and local chapters of national senior organizations (AARP, NCSC, OWL, etc.) allowed the CCSO to make suggestions to those organizations via members who were active in both.

## CASE EXAMPLE: Mrs. B.

Mrs. B. was a 79-year-old widow who had retired as a supervisor of nurses in the visiting nurse program. Mrs. B. had one son, who lived in another state. At the time the worker met her, Mrs. B. had lost most of her sight and was unable to read or drive. She had become depressed and would not go out when friends called to invite her to dinner or other functions. A friend of Mrs. B. called and asked the worker to visit Mrs. B. and see why she had become so withdrawn. Mrs. B. allowed the worker to visit; she explained that she could no longer be "useful" and did not want to be a "burden" to her friends.

*Worker Interventions* Initial visits with Mrs. B. focused on her problems coping with her inability to read and drive. At the worker's suggestion, she explored several services for the blind, and she eventually learned to read Braille. The worker discussed with Mrs. B. many of the issues and problems that other seniors were experiencing with respect to health care and social services. She also solicited Mrs. B.'s advice concerning a number of proposed changes in health care programs and agency activities. She emphasized how Mrs. B.'s expertise was needed by senior action groups and for health education programs being provided at the agency's activity sites. Mrs. B. began to volunteer for specific tasks; she was willing to accept transportation to activities when she went to assist others. Some of her former friends were also volunteers, and consequently she began to go out more often for social events. She eventually became politically active and began to work regularly as a participant on and consultant to the CCSO.

## CASE EXAMPLE: Mr. F.

Mr. F. was a 72-year-old retired salesman who lived in a senior highrise. He had an 88-year-old sister for whom he had provided care for a number of years. He helped her with housework, cooking, shopping, and walking, and he managed her finances. They had had a number of disputes with the building's management arising out of management's concern about the sister's disability. Elderly residents of the high-rise were required by Housing and Urban Development (HUD) regulations to be capable of independent living. The worker became involved when a hospital social worker asked for assistance, explaining that Mr. F. had been hospitalized for a hernia operation and was to be released soon. He was very concerned about the status of his sister now that he was temporarily unable to care for her.

*Worker Interventions*   Initial visits with Mr. F. focused on providing temporary assistance for his sister through volunteer programs and a local homemaker program and obtaining temporary visiting nurse service for Mr. F. Mr. F. had been a good friend to many high-rise residents, so formal support systems were supplemented by his friends. Mr. F. was still concerned about the rule requiring independent status for continued residency and also about the lack of affordable services for older people who had health care needs. The worker invited him to attend a CCSO meeting and a small group meeting of older men who were caregivers. The worker also introduced Mr. F. to Mrs. B., and he began to provide transportation for her and attend numerous meetings related to health care and preventive health education. Mrs. B. initiated discussion in the CCSO about the high-rise's rule regarding independence. The CCSO made this issue one of its priorities, entering into negotiations with high-rise management in the city and corresponding with the HUD authorities responsible for the ruling. Mr. F. was very pleased with these efforts and passed out handbills in high-rises throughout the city to gain support for them. When his sister needed more care than he could provide, Mrs. B. helped them to access all available assistance and to communicate effectively with service providers when problems occurred.

## CASE EXAMPLE: Mrs. G.

Mrs. G. was a Hispanic woman in her middle sixties. She was in fair health but was prohibited from strenuous activity because of a heart condition. Mrs. G. was a widow and lived in a small house in a neighborhood where most residents were poor. She lived with her 9-year-old granddaughter, Anna. Her primary source of income was SSI and old age pension, which totaled $430 per month. Mrs. G. also received food stamps. Mrs. G.'s daughter (Anna's mother) had three other children and received an Aid to Dependent Children (ADC) allowance for all four children. She gave a small amount of money to her mother every month to help with Anna's care. The department of social services had become aware of the presence of Anna in her grandmother's home. Mrs. G. contacted Legal Aid because she was afraid the department would take Anna away. A Legal Aid representative called the agency to request assistance with Mrs. G.'s case. A Legal Aid attorney stated that, even though it was a common practice among Hispanic families to allow a child to live with a grandparent in need of assistance, the department of social services had removed a number of these children, and the homes had been determined to be "unfit." In some cases the parents had been charged with neglect. The Legal Aid representative agreed to work with the worker and Mrs. G. to try to secure a satisfactory resolution to the situation.

*Worker Interventions*   Mrs. G.'s first meetings with the worker focused on her fear that the public welfare department would attempt to remove her granddaughter from her home. She was also afraid that the department of public assistance would file against her daughter for fraud, because she had been receiving an ADC allowance for four children while one of them was living with Mrs. G. The worker contacted a department of social services worker known to be a client advocate, and with the assistance of Legal Aid and a number of Hispanic associations, Mrs. G. was able to work out an adequate arrangement with the department of social services. Mrs. G. was involved in all aspects of the issue, including speaking to the membership of three Hispanic organizations and at meetings of agency representatives. The situation was resolved in a way that would assist others who faced the same problem. The worker encouraged Mrs. G. to attend meetings at the activity site in her neighborhood and later to become the representative from that site to the CCSO. Mrs. G. became a strong advocate of Hispanic causes. At first her interest was focused mainly on issues concerning the elderly, but it gradually became broader. A few years later she helped lead an effort to elect a number of Hispanic representatives to the school board. On several occasions Mrs. G. persuaded her grandson, who was the leader of a small Hispanic rock band, to give her the microphone during nightclub engagements so that she could encourage the audience to sign petitions or to participate in certain civic events. As a member of the CCSO, Mrs. G. became acquainted with Mrs. B., Mr. F., and Mrs. E.

## CASE EXAMPLE: Mrs. E.

Mrs. E. was a 71-year-old retired schoolteacher. She lived with and cared for her 78-year-old husband. He was a retired steelworker who suffered from increasingly severe dementia. He had been tentatively diagnosed as suffering from Alzheimer's disease. Mrs. E. had participated in (Methodist) church activities as well as some AARP programs, until her increased caregiving responsibilities precluded it. Mrs. E. had two children, one of whom lived in the city and was the mother of three teenaged children. Mr. E.'s deteriorating condition had been a source of increasing stress and bewilderment for Mrs. E. and her daughter. He had recently left home without supervision and had been lost for several hours. They had discussed nursing home placement, but Mrs. E. was hesitant to make such a decision. The worker was called by Mrs. E.'s daughter, who stated that she thought Mrs. E. might benefit from discussing the matter with a gerontological professional.

*Worker Interventions*   Mrs. E.'s early encounters with the worker included discussions of the guilt, anger, and despair she felt over her husband's situation and her own. She eventually made the decision to place her husband in a nursing home. Not only was this a difficult and emotional decision, but it also negatively affected her financial situation. In addition, she had numerous difficulties with the care her husband was receiving in the nursing home. The worker arranged for Mrs. E. to join a group of caregivers who were in similar situations, and over time Mrs. E.'s interest in social action increased. She also began to attend CCSO meetings regularly.

## CASE EXAMPLE: Mutual Activities of Mrs. B., Mr. F., Mrs. G., and Mrs. E.

Over a period of five years, each of these individuals participated in empowerment-oriented groups and activities. They became acquainted and developed their friendship through their mutual social action concerns and activities. Mr. F. and Mrs. E. provided transportation. Mrs. B., Mrs. G., and Mrs. E. were all articulate spokespersons and, because they represented different constituencies, were very effective with county officials and other decision makers. The four elders also offered personal support to one another when health problems, family crises, and other personal problems surfaced.

*Worker Interventions*   The worker strongly supported the engagement of these individuals in activities related to the personal, interpersonal, and political aspects of their life concerns. This support included sharing of information regarding resources, helping each person to begin problem assessment and problem-solving processes, and raising questions that challenged each person to engage in critical thought concerning the common nature of their problems. She also provided important links with resources, including government agencies and civic groups, and facilitated the development of relationships among the clients and between each person and others in similar circumstances. By maintaining contact with all the clients and encouraging them to critically analyze their experiences with service providers, the worker formed a partnership with each of them in order to accomplish the tasks of gathering information, brainstorming strategies, finding ways to develop support systems, working out transportation problems, and developing other resources. In addition, the worker provided information and consultation to the CCSO and small group leaders, worked resolutely to develop a network of social workers in other agencies who implemented empowerment-oriented practice, and generally assisted the efforts of the agency and the CCSO.

The worker was able to raise questions that encouraged the clients to explore the common aspects of their problems with other elderly persons of different racial and economic backgrounds. The worker was also able to increase the elders' awareness of the commonality of their circumstances with those of other oppressed populations. One strategy particularly effective in this respect was providing examples of the similarities between their struggles and those of women on public assistance (ADC) or of younger disabled persons. Overall, the worker played an active role by working in partnership with a large number of clients in pursuit of common goals.

In these case examples, the worker facilitated, linked, supported, and encouraged activities and attitudes that provided clients with opportunities for collective problem solving. As suggested in Chapter 2, powerlessness derives from individual loss, the perception of powerlessness, and environmental constraints, and from an interactional process among these three factors, which creates surplus powerlessness or compounded powerlessness (Maze, 1987). Empowerment-oriented practice combines individual, interpersonal, and institutional elements, according to Gutiérrez (1989), who also argues that focusing on any one of these elements is insufficient—empowerment must encompass all three.

## *The Empowerment Process*

Since empowerment is a process through which individuals become strong enough to participate in, share in the control of, and influence their own lives, it cannot be viewed as an end state or a plateau at which they arrive. Rather, it is the engagement of individuals in actions that challenge or change the personal, interpersonal, or political aspects of their life situations. Empowerment-oriented practice is not social service delivery in which an "empowered social worker" anoints or gives power to the "powerless elderly"; instead, empowerment-oriented practice is that in which both client(s) and worker are involved in mutual assessment and partnership and in which they together define and solve problems on behalf of the client group and society in general. No one person can empower another; workers can only facilitate activities that educate clients, foster the engagement process, and enable both clients and worker to become more empowered to act.

To enhance understanding of the empowerment process and its components, we provide the following summary of the available literature, based on our own thinking as well as that of Gutiérrez (1990), Kieffer (1984), and Torre (1985). The empowerment process contains four key components:

1. *Attitude, values, and beliefs.* The psychological attitude developed through the empowerment process comprises *self-efficacy* (production and regulation of events in one's life), a *sense of self* that promotes action on one's behalf, a *belief in self-worth,* and an *internal locus of control.* In psychological views of empowerment, this attitude set is frequently the sole component, and achieving it is a predominant goal in social service intervention. However, it is most easily achievable through engagement in the other components of empowerment.

2. *Validation of collective experiences.* Through the empowerment process, individuals recognize that experiences are not unique but shared. The collective view of experiences tends to reduce self-blame, increase the tendency to look for causes other than personal failure, and bring about a sense of shared fate and consciousness raising. Schaef (1981) argues that the first step in working with oppressed, devalued groups is to provide an opportunity for members to tell their "story" to others in similar circumstances and to have those stories heard and validated by others. A sense of collectivity and group consciousness develops out of mutual validation. Although face-to-face group interaction is perhaps the most desirable medium for achieving collective validation, this process can also take place through one-to-one work, through networking strategies such as telephoning and newsletters, and even through media and literature.

3. *Knowledge and skills for critical thinking.* Through the empowerment process, individuals become able to think critically about the internal and external aspects of the problem. They are able to identify macro-level structures and their impact as well as explore the ways in which their own values, beliefs, and attitudes have been acquired and how they affect the problem. Becoming empowered includes learning to think critically, acquiring the skills needed to access information and

to take action, taking action, and reassessing. The process of placing problems in a sociopolitical context results in a reduction of self-blame and helps individuals see that, to one degree or another, their problems have roots in the wider social environment. Through consciousness raising, individuals come to view their problems as similar to those of many others and begin to recognize common experiences that help them collectively to understand and take action.

4. *Action.* Through the empowerment process, individuals are able to develop action strategies and cultivate the resources, knowledge, and skills necessary to influence internal and external structures. Psychologically, they learn to assume responsibility for action. Behaviorally, they become willing and able to act with others for the attainment of common goals and social change.

These four components are considered necessary to the empowerment process, but no linear relationship among them is assumed, nor is one considered a better place to begin with the elderly than another. Because most services for the elderly are available only through medically oriented programs, however, many service contacts with this population are made in a one-to-one context, and the collective validation component may be the most elusive. Initially, none of the clients in the case examples thought of either causes or solutions to their problems as being outside themselves. Interactive experiences increased their problem-solving domains to encompass the acquisition of knowledge and new skills and action.

The empowerment process is most often area-specific. That is, engagement in the process in one area of one's life may or may not transfer to another area. For example, an older person may engage in all four components in a struggle to effect change in the area of health care but not engage in any in the area of housing. An organization such as the CCSO encourages a comprehensive view of late life survival and helps to connect the various arenas of problem solving.

## Defining Empowerment-Oriented Practice

When a social service worker engages with clients in the empowerment process, some behaviors and attributes of helping differ from those used in traditional social work practice. The relationship between worker and client is different; the traditional expert/nonexpert relationship is discarded in favor of one of collaboration and mutual responsibility. The client must experience a personal sense of power within the relationship with the worker and must be actively engaged in the change process itself. Empowerment is clearly not something that is done *to* another person, but a process that must be engaged in by mutual effort. Clients become active helpers, not only of themselves but of others as well.

***Principles and Strategies***    The following are principles and strategies of empowerment-oriented practice (Cox, 1991; Gutiérrez, 1989, 1990; Maze, 1987; Parsons, 1991):

- Basing the helping relationship on collaboration, trust, and shared power
- Utilizing collective action
- Accepting the client's definition of the problem
- Identifying and building upon the client's strengths
- Raising the client's consciousness of issues concerning class and power
- Involving the client in the change process
- Teaching specific skills
- Utilizing mutual support and self-help networks or groups
- Experiencing a sense of personal power within the empowerment-oriented relationship
- Mobilizing resources or advocating for clients

These principles are interwoven into the practice model presented in this book.

Perhaps the most intriguing aspect of empowerment-oriented practice is that the focus is not exclusively on the personal or the environmental aspect of problem solving, but rather on the connection and interaction between the two. As outlined in Chapter 2, the environmentally imposed propensity for elderly people to experience powerlessness may result from physical decline, economic stress, loss of support networks, and loss of social status through role changes that accompany the aging process. Unfortunately, social policy and social services' response to policy often increase powerlessness. Late life brings challenges that require gaining new knowledge and mastering new skills. This combination of events mirrors the dual aspect of problems—personal and environmental.

# ELEMENTS OF THE EMPOWERMENT-ORIENTED PRACTICE MODEL

The practice model presented here draws not only from the social work literature, but also from the literature of other disciplines. A large number of practice models were developed in social work during the 1970s and 1980s; Johnson (1989) summarizes twenty-seven such models, which represent only a fraction of those developed. In addition to full practice models, there is an even larger array of intervention strategies for social work practice, including, for example, brief therapy modalities, self-help education, mutual support groups, mediation, advocacy, and brokerage activities.

The difference between an intervention strategy and a practice model is not always made clear. An intervention strategy is simply an action or technique used by a social worker to assist a client. A social work practice model must include a *value base, sanction for intervention,* and a *theory base. Together, these determine practice guidelines for worker/ client relationships, problem definition and assessment, goal setting, and the choice of intervention strategies and techniques* (see Figure 3.1). The empowerment-oriented practice model will be presented in terms of these components. Like all models, the empowerment-oriented practice model will fit actual situations in which social workers find themselves with varying degrees of usefulness.

Models of social work practice that have been especially helpful in the development of the empowerment-oriented practice model include Germain and Gitterman's (1980) life model of social work practice, Compton and Galaway's (1989) problem-solving model, Maluccio's (1981) competency-oriented model, Galper's (1980) radical social work model, Schwartz's (1974) mediating model, and Middleman and Goldberg's (1974) structural approach to social work practice.

## Value Base

The values guiding the empowerment-oriented model, like those underlying all social work practice models, incorporate the basic values of the National Association of Social Work's Code of Ethics. Of particular importance to empowerment-oriented practice are several commitments outlined in the code. First is the effective engagement of client and worker

## Figure 3.1   Components of a Practice Model

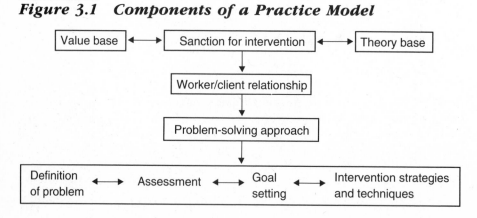

in the *creation of an environment compatible with human needs,* which is congruent with social work's commitment to promote social justice. The professional commitment to *self-determination* stressed in the code is also of key significance to empowerment-oriented practice (Compton & Galaway, 1989), as is the value of *self-actualization*. The involvement of elderly people to the fullest extent possible in planning for and controlling their lives creates an opportunity for them to utilize untapped abilities and develop themselves to their fullest potential in their late years.

The predominant values that guide empowerment-oriented practice are

- Fulfillment of human needs
- Promotion of social justice
- More equal distribution of resources
- Concern for environmental protection
- Elimination of racism, sexism, ageism, and homophobia
- Self-determination (the fullest possible participation in decisions that have an impact on one's life, both personal and political)
- Self-actualization

Incorporation of most of these values into practice can be seen in the case examples.

## Sanction for Intervention

Sanction for empowerment-oriented practice is drawn from the values discussed in the preceding section and is the basis for social workers' assumed right to engage with clients and pursue goals that will assist them to solve their problems and improve their life situations.

Sanction for empowerment-oriented practice is derived from a number of additional sources, including laws, rules and regulations of organizations, personal values, and client requests. These sources often do not sanction the same actions, however, and may be in direct conflict. For example, the beliefs of elderly clients about their rights to health care may conflict with the regulations of a specific agency or a social policy provision. Empowerment-oriented workers who work in agencies are often concerned about the goals sanctioned by their agency—or the *lack* of sanction for specific resources or activities that are proscribed by agency rules and regulations. For example, many home health care agencies restrict the number of visits that can be made to an elderly client. Also, agencies may not allow workers to support clients' efforts to engage in the political aspects of solving their problems.

The sanction bases found in an organizational setting vary in strength, as Figure 3.2 illustrates. It is important for practitioners to assess the strength of organizational support for any of their activities. Often

Written rules  – –  Administrative  – –  Administrative  – –  Accepted  – –  Individual
and regulations    guidelines              discretion          informal        staff decisions
                   (written)                                   behaviors

Strong ◄──────────────────────────────────────────► Weak

## *Figure 3.2  Relative Strength of Organizational Sanction Bases*

empowerment-oriented workers and their clients find themselves
challenging agency rules and regulations because these rules and regulations do not promote the goals of empowerment-oriented practice (for
example, to counter ageism or to create a more egalitarian distribution
of resources). It is not uncommon for agency regulations based on a goal
of shortsighted cost efficiency to conflict with the needs of client constituencies, social work values, and the principles of empowerment.
Consequently, empowerment-oriented workers must take a position based
on the overall values of empowerment-oriented practice. Chapter 4
addresses interventions aimed at the service delivery system itself.

Sanctions or acceptance of values by society in general is often
reflected in the status of an issue. Figure 3.3 shows the relative strengths
of various societal sanction bases. If an issue or client need is perceived
to be legitimate by only the client and/or a small group, the worker and
the client are operating with a very weak sanction base. If a larger group—
for example, the Older Women's League—is a proponent of a specific
need, a stronger societal sanction is apparent. Empowerment-oriented
workers and their clients will find that exploration of the sanction base
with respect to the issue they want to address is an important aspect of
critical thinking as well as strategy development. In the case examples,
the presence of the CCSO provided the agency-based worker with an
alternative avenue for strategic intervention. A multipurpose senior center
usually has broader sanction bases than more narrowly focused agencies do. Connecting to community organizations is key to empowerment-
oriented practice.

## *Theory Base*

Both social and general systems theory and developmental theory
have provided the bases for many contemporary social work practice
models (Compton & Galaway, 1989; Germain & Gitterman, 1980; Pincus
& Minahan, 1973). The empowerment-oriented practice model utilizes
both of these theoretical bases: in line with developmental theory, aging
is viewed as a normative developmental process; systems theory provides
the basis for understanding the status and role of elders in a modern

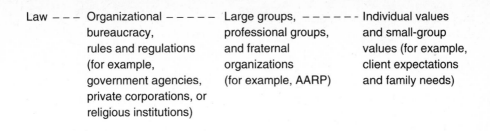

Law – – – Organizational – – – – – Large groups, – – – – – – Individual values
bureaucracy, professional groups, and small-group
rules and regulations and fraternal values (for example,
(for example, organizations client expectations
government agencies, (for example, AARP) and family needs)
private corporations, or
religious institutions)

Strong ← —————————————————————— → Weak

***Figure 3.3*** **Relative Strength of Societal Sanction**
 **Bases**

capitalistic society. Empowerment-oriented practice is also rooted in the
political-economic perspective, which assumes that society consists of
groups with varying degrees of power and conflicting interests. It does
not assume an ultimate goodness of fit between different groups' needs,
expectations, and resources. Instead, it assumes that empowerment is,
in part, a process of struggle to bring needs and resources into compatibil-
ity (Gould, 1987).

## The Worker/Client Relationship

Most social work practice models are in agreement that the relationship established between worker and client is key to the success of any
intervention. In traditional relationships with clients, the worker assumes
roles that are appropriate to the process of assisting the clients to achieve
mutually agreed upon goals. The worker views his or her part in the relationship as involving a conscious selection of role that allows the realization of professional expertise. Maluccio (1981) suggests that the
worker/client relationship must be redefined appropriately to fit the
competency-based model, particularly in terms of mutuality and authen-
ticity. Clients are to be redefined as partners in the helping process and
resources rather than as simply carriers of problems. Galper (1980) also
emphasizes the need for an egalitarian relationship between client and
worker in order to achieve the goals of social work practice.

An *egalitarian relationship,* or *balanced partnership,* with clients
is a critical aspect of empowerment-oriented practice. The worker's focus
is not on assuming roles but on bringing knowledge and skills into a
mutually collaborative relationship. This relationship is based on the
assumptions that the client is a resource and that, in the context of
understanding private troubles as public issues, the client's long-range
goals (social justice) are also the goals of the worker. When addressing

powerlessness, social workers must avoid authoritarian relationships and demystify expertise whenever possible.

It takes time to achieve a partnership. Socialization of clients and workers, including professional education, can serve to reinforce workers' belief that their expertise must be a factor that serves to give them a higher status than their clients. The empowerment-oriented model views expertise as simply knowledge and skills that the worker brings to a problem-solving situation. The client is also seen as a source of knowledge and skills (expertise) that can be added to the worker's contribution to aid in their mutual effort. In one of the case examples, Mrs. G.'s knowledge regarding Hispanic families contributed to the ultimate solution of the problem.

In the circumstances under which workers and clients meet, a number of factors come into play that affect the process of achieving an egalitarian relationship. The following are among the most important:

- Preconceived perceptions of roles
- Values and beliefs concerning power and status
- The ability of the worker and the client to identify and appreciate each other's strengths
- The ability of the worker and the client to accept and respect diversity
- The ability of the worker and the client to overcome judgmental interpretations regarding weaknesses perceived in each other
- Interests shared by the worker and the client concerning the political dimension of the problem or issue addressed

Preconceived perceptions of roles may include the belief that the professional holds all the knowledge and therefore is superior or should take responsibility for the solution of the problem. The belief that seeking help with a problem is a sign of weakness—or any of a number of beliefs based on the medical model or on academic or other hierarchical experiences of the client or the worker—may hinder the achievement of an egalitarian relationship. The worker may have been socialized through traditional training to assume the role of helper assisting a helpee and may find it difficult to accept a more equal relationship.

Values and beliefs regarding status and power are closely related to perceptions of professionalism. Power in the egalitarian relationship must be understood as the *collective* power to achieve goals, both personal and political, rather than power *over* each other . The client and the worker cannot allow status concerns to interfere with the equal exchange of ideas and mutual efforts toward achieving the goals of the social work process. Specifically, action must not be determined by authoritarian worker/client relationships.

Identifying strengths in each other requires sharing experiences and knowledge about subjects of mutual concern. The worker must be aware of the context and history of the problem, the cultural factors involved, the daily struggles of the client or group, local relationships, and many other aspects of the situation that only the client has access to, as well as the formal training and skills the client may have. The client will benefit from the worker's formal training and work experience. The key lies in remaining open to these possibilities. In the case example about Mrs. B., the worker had knowledge about problems other people were having with service agencies and solicited advice from Mrs. B. about necessary changes in service policies.

Respect for diversity includes recognition of each other's strengths and nonjudgmental approaches to each other's apparent weaknesses. It grows from sharing experiences as worker and client proceed toward the realization of mutual goals.

A common interest between worker and client regarding the political dimensions of a problem becomes clearer as the consciousness raising proceeds and the political dimensions of specific personal problems become more apparent. Many political interests common to workers and clients and related to personal problems are readily apparent in work with the elderly and their families. For example, the impact of the lack of an adequate national health care system that addresses long-term care needs of the elderly on them and their families is often clear.

Although this discussion outlines some of the important issues faced by empowerment-oriented workers as they struggle to develop egalitarian relationships with their clients, other important issues continually emerge and are addressed as workers and clients engage in this process. Task-focused activities requiring the use of the knowledge and skills of both client and worker in order to achieve goals can be a powerful means of enhancing mutual respect and fostering mutual learning.

Finally, one of the most frequently encountered challenges to the development of egalitarian relationships is the onset of dementia and other problems that affect mental functioning in elderly clients. Special attention, especially careful and continuous assessment, is required in attempting to develop balanced relationships with individuals suffering from these problems. The primary guidelines for practitioners engaged in this type of worker/client relationship call for giving mutual respect, paying careful attention to changing conditions, and making a commitment to allow or mobilize the fullest possible participation of all clients in decisions affecting their lives.

## Problem Definition and Assessment

**Assessment as Consciousness Raising**   In empowerment-oriented practice, the client and worker join together to gather and evaluate data and to formulate a joint, ongoing assessment of the internal and external components of the problem. The strengths and weaknesses of the client and environmental factors are considered in the effort to address the client's problem situation. Interaction between the client and the worker allows not only definition of the problem, but also selection of the data considered relevant to solving it.

This assessment process considers sources of problems from personal to external (or structural) and from historical to contemporary, thus opening up the personal and political dimensions for consideration. Both Schwartz (1974) and Galper (1980) visualize the worker and client as involved in a dialectic process for the purpose of mutual formulation of the problem. The assessment process of these two authors most closely resembles that of the empowerment-oriented model. Their models, as well as that of Longres (1990), rely on worker and client working as partners, both taking action and both reviewing the action to better understand the problem and plan further strategies.

***Addressing Expertise***   The transfer of knowledge about aging from "expert" to client is crucial to an elderly person's sense of control. In empowerment-oriented practice, client and worker join together to share their collective expertise in an attempt to understand the problem. For example, knowledge about the physical, psychological, and sociopolitical aspects of aging is often considered to be the turf of professional gerontologists, or "experts." Empowerment-oriented practitioners operate on the principle that knowledge applicable to a client's situation should be shared with the client. The emphasis is on the development of critical thought processes.

***Multilevel Emphasis***   Analysis of the involvement of micro systems (small systems such as individual, family, and peer group) and macro systems (service delivery agencies and political institutions and structures) with the problem at hand is essential. For example, the worker and client may approach a reticent service provider with a variety of tactics, then together they will review the results of their approaches to assist them in better understanding the service delivery process and in planning further actions. Traditional assessments for social work have focused on the individual's intrapersonal dynamics and immediate environmental supports. Assessment in the empowerment-oriented model goes beyond immediate systems to the broader environment and includes the interrelationship of personal and political aspects of a problem. Assessment is in effect engagement in a process of critical thinking and consciousness raising concerning all dimensions of the problem.

***Reflection and Action***   Consciousness raising requires both reflection and action and is continuous throughout the intervention process. For example, in an effort to assist low-income hotel dwellers whose housing was constantly threatened by neighborhood renovation or health standards violations, both workers and clients participated in a day-today political assessment of the situation. This assessment allowed them to identify strategies and proposals that might result in progress toward the preservation or replacement of the housing. Without this daily experiential learning and mutual struggle, an awareness of the political nature of the process would have been impossible. Also, their political awareness helped the clients understand their emotional response to the helplessness they felt in the situation. No static definition of the problem existed, and different levels of systems were focused on as new information allowed reformulation of the assessment. The problem required research (data gathering) on actions taken in cities throughout the nation in order to formulate a strategy for pursuing a local solution. In the earlier case example, Mrs. B.'s consciousness was raised with respect to service delivery issues in general, and the scope of her concern was expanded.

In summary, worker and client function as a team to gather information, assess the information, formulate strategy, prepare suggestions, and so on. The critical factor in empowerment-oriented practice, however, is that the process becomes a learning experience, an empowering process for both worker and client. Figure 3.4 displays the components of the assessment process.

## Figure 3.4  Components of a Practice Model

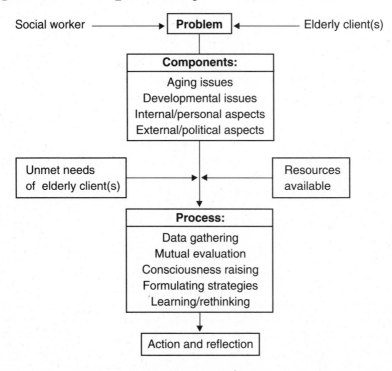

## Goal Setting

Goals are an important part of empowerment-oriented practice. In problem-solving models the goals of intervention are based on the decision of the client, with some assistance from the worker, and focus on the particular set of circumstances under consideration. In exploring how to help a teenaged son remain in school, for example, or how to gain control over an alcohol problem, the client's perception of success is critical to goal setting. Appropriate actions to solve an agreed upon problem become the essential focus of the interaction between worker and client.

Empowerment-oriented practice views long-range structural changes in society as essential and of immediate concern to clients and social workers alike. It stresses to clients the benefit of an ongoing engagement with others in order to build and sustain a positive environment. The empowerment-oriented practice model stresses the importance of struggling for the actualization of values that guide both consciousness raising and action. The basic assumption is that individual empowerment is inherently tied to group empowerment, which requires social justice and a safe environment. In the case example, the goals of Mr. F. were focused on his immediate need and on the problem of obtaining housing and caregiving assistance for elderly in situations like that of him and his sister. In summary, goal setting in empowerment-oriented practice expands the personal to the interpersonal and then to the political and meshes with values inherent in social work practice.

## Intervention Strategies

The interventive methods of most practice models—including the problem-solving model, competency-based model, radical practice model, and life model—are applicable to various sizes of client systems and directed toward goal achievement. These methods include individual one-to-one intervention, family intervention, group intervention, organizational strategies, community strategies, and national campaigns. The same is true of the empowerment-oriented practice model. The system level appropriate for intervention is determined by the assessment; however, increased emphasis is placed on the political and economic factors in empowerment-oriented practice.

Compton and Galaway (1989) note that carrying out a plan toward problem alleviation requires the social worker to apply the same knowledge and skills as in other aspects of assessment and planning: communication, development and use of relationship, development and use of resources, and use of self. They further suggest that activities may include encouragement and enhancing clients' awareness of their own behavior (for example, clarifying, confronting, and informing). Empowerment-oriented practitioners may use similar strategies, but they are seen as being equally appropriate for clients to use in the context of an empowerment-oriented relationship.

Strategies used in group work and community organization are also invaluable to empowerment-oriented practice. The key to using intervention strategies from the perspective of a social work practice model is the fit of a given strategy with the basic premises and value orientation of the model. For example, the common social work functions, or roles, of mediator, broker, advocate, counselor, enabler, and so on can be appropriate for empowerment-oriented practice but must be evaluated within a framework that emphasizes the creation of opportunities for clients to achieve empowerment for themselves. Consequently, the goal of intervention actions becomes twofold: (1) to achieve results relative to the immediate situation and (2) to teach clients the knowledge and skills necessary to perform these interventions for themselves and others. In empowerment-oriented practice the worker as advocate serves as a role model in training the client as advocate.

Solomon (1976) notes that the "practitioner must demonstrate an understanding of the dynamics of powerlessness and its consequences in order to develop expertise in the utilization of practice skills in the service of empowerment" (p. 26). She suggests that empowerment-enhancing interventions often have at least one of the following four goals:

1. Helping the client to see himself or herself as a change agent relative to problems
2. Helping the client to use the practitioner's knowledge and skills
3. Helping the client perceive the practitioner as a partner in the problem-solving effort
4. Helping the client perceive "powerlessness" as open to influence

Solomon's view reaffirms the importance of the value context in which specific interventions are implemented.

Maluccio (1981) suggests a number of specific approaches that contribute to competency-based interventions. These interventions, which include the strengthening of natural helping networks, the use of structured groups and skills development workshops, and education regarding lifelong learning processes, are also frequent tools of empowerment-oriented practice. Development of competency is an integral part of empowerment because a sense of competency in one area of one's life often facilitates risk taking and new learning in other areas.

The use of mutual aid groups similar to those suggested by Gitterman and Shulman (1986) is another intervention frequently used by empowerment-oriented practitioners. Gitterman and Shulman (1986) suggest nine processes that become available within mutual support groups and can have empowering outcomes for group participants. These processes include:

- Sharing data
- Dialectical process, entering taboo areas
- All-in-the-same-boat phenomenon
- Mutual support
- Mutual demand
- Individual problem solving
- Rehearsal
- Strength-in-numbers phenomenon

The use of mutual aid groups in the context of empowerment-oriented practice can be a key intervention strategy. Other intervention strategies for the empowerment-oriented practitioner include community organization activities and the development of opportunity structures (Matura, 1986) and/or the strengthening of mediating structures (Berger & Neuhaus, 1977), as well as the development of vehicles for collective empowerment in groups, organizations, institutions, or protest movements. In the earlier case examples, support and mutual aid groups helped the clients find solutions and assistance, as well as provided them with the motivation to become involved in the CCSO.

In summary, interventions that may be effective in empowerment-oriented practice are many and diverse; the key is the philosophy and value set within which the activities occur. Each intervention must pass a value screen: Does this action or activity assist the client to engage in the empowerment process? Will the client be better able to cope independently or participate in social change activities with the worker and with peers?

## INTERVENTION ON FOUR DIMENSIONS

For purposes of explication, empowerment-oriented practice may be conceptualized on a continuum of focus that ranges over the personal, interpersonal, environmental, and political aspects of the problem at hand. Focus on the problem may fluctuate from personal to political and from political to personal; however, all dimensions are critical to the empowerment process. The goal of empowerment-oriented practice is the most comprehensive analysis and approach possible for each problem-solving situation. Table 3.1 summarizes empowerment-oriented interventions relative to the four dimensions of focus. These interventions represent activities that are focused on client systems from individuals to larger sociopolitical systems, depending on which dimension is most appropriate to the situation at hand. Levels of focus may be related to describing the effects of the problem or issue in the personal, interpersonal, and political perspectives *or* perceiving causality, which often ranges from a personal causality to a political causality.

## Dimension 1

Interventions on Dimension 1 consist mainly of initial work with individual clients who have been identified by outreach or intake workers as being in need of assistance or who have sought assistance. The presenting problem can be related to lack of resources, interpersonal conflicts, emotional problems, specifically defined environmental problems, or any other concern of the client. The initial task with any client is to establish a working relationship and assess needs and resources. If indicated, as was true for Mrs. B. in the case example, securing of entitlements is a first step in the helping process. An initial assessment must be done at this level in order to determine need and direction for action. At this initial stage of helping, clients' consciousness of the global aspects of their conditions and circumstances may be very limited, or it may be obscured by an immediate need for resources. The problem is likely to be viewed by the elderly client and his or her family as a personal problem and a private trouble, as was the case with Mrs. G. The assessment includes soliciting the client's view of the problem, evaluating the level of awareness about such problems in both the client and the family, and gauging the client's perception of powerlessness or power to manage the problem.

## Dimension 2

Interventions on Dimension 2 are designed to provide knowledge and skills necessary to master the tasks of late life survival in general and to solve the identified problem in particular. Late life survival tasks include developmental tasks related to common transitions of aging: retirement, loss of members of one's support group, economic decline, and physical decline. These late life tasks often constitute the substance of presenting problems, but few elders have acquired basic knowledge about the aging process. Physical, social, and economic changes occurring as part of the aging process often come as a surprise to older couples and individuals. A number of organizations, including academically sponsored gerontology programs, offer training for older Americans regarding the aging process and methods of coping with changes and finding necessary resources.

The methods suggested for the second dimension of interventions include conferences, workshops, courses, small-group formats, newsletters, telephoning, and videos for shut-in clients. The use of an ongoing small group has the advantage of allowing the formation of support

## Table 3.1 Four-Dimensional Conceptualization of Focus of Interventions

| Dimensions of Focus | Consciousness Raising and Problem Assessment | Primary Problem-Solving Activities | Primary Actors | Primary Targets for Change |
|---|---|---|---|---|
| *Dimension 1: Personal* Individual needs, difficulties, values, and attitudes | Increase the development and use of critical thought, including the ongoing analysis of internal and external aspects of political-economic pressures (oppression) | Establish worker/client relationship and meet immediate needs: link individuals and families with existing services, secure information about how to locate and access resources, begin consciousness-raising process | Individuals Families (primary network) Worker | Individual or family (primary network) |
| *Dimension 2: Interpersonal* Common problems and personal strengths and weaknesses | Increase the development and use of critical thought, including the ongoing analysis of internal and external aspects of political-economic pressures (oppression) | Develop knowledge and skills for self-help, personal growth, and problem solving: access information on aging issues (such as age discrimination) and the physical, social, and psychological aspects of aging; develop new skills in advocacy, mediation, and mutual problem solving; use group process to address common problems; learn self-help through helping others | Individuals Families Small groups (immediate community) | Individual or group situation or common problem |

| Dimension | Goal | Objectives | Target systems | Target systems |
|---|---|---|---|---|
| *Dimension 3: Micro environmental and organizational* Problems with service delivery | Increase the development and use of critical thought, including the ongoing analysis of internal and external aspects of political-economic pressures (oppression) | Secure resources and assess and change middle-level systems: gain knowledge about organizations, develop skills in communicating with professionals and bureaucrats and in organizing for change, participate in activities to change organizations and join decision-making bodies, create or join self-help groups or organizations | Individuals Families Small groups Large groups Problem-focused networks (such as AA or Arthritis Association) | Individuals Agencies Organizations |
| *Dimension 4: Macro environmental or sociopolitical* Political systems and social policy | Increase the development and use of critical thought, including the ongoing analysis of internal and external aspects of political-economic pressures (oppression) | Engage in social action for political and social change: articulate the political nature of personal problems, gain knowledge about political and economic systems and issues, participate in state and national senior organizations (such as OWL and NCOA), develop skills in negotiating and mediating, engage in activities for change (such as letter-writing or phone campaigns, lobbying, and picketing) | Individuals Small groups Large groups Communities Local and statewide organizations National organizations | Large groups Communities Legislative and administrative bodies at local, state, and national level Social policies |

networks of elderly individuals. Group members often discover strength in their common interests and have their perceptions and experiences validated by one another through discussions of the content of the training. The responsibilities of empowerment-oriented workers include identifying and organizing educational materials. Acceptability of content, format, and delivery of materials are dependent on the background and current environment of the specific elderly target population. Acceptability also varies according to the needs and interests of the population members. Consequently, educational experiences designed without input from the target population risk failure. Educational programs designed for the elderly must also take adult learning styles into account. In second-dimension interventions, problem definition becomes broader, and the assessment of the power dynamics begins to use larger systems. Causality of problems may still be viewed as private or internal, but clients can see that these problems are common to many others. This comprehension of a problem as a "common issue" often leads to self-help and collective action. In the case example, Mrs. E. had to learn about the emotional trauma of nursing home placement and, through that education, became more politically aware not only of her situation, but also of that of others in the same situation.

Self-help approaches to empowerment require participation of the elderly in groups focused on alleviation of a shared problem. Problems such as alcoholism, illness, poverty, fear of crime, and housing difficulties are examples of issues that are frequently addressed through self-help groups. Mrs. E.'s participation in a self-help group of caregivers created energy for expanded social action.

The knowledge gained through participation in self-help activities has as its primary source the collective intelligence of the group. Knowledge gained from individual and collective experiences is combined with academic knowledge. Most often this knowledge is made available through affiliation with local, state, or national networks or from individual group members. For example, the National Stroke Association has developed materials that are used by self-help and support groups throughout the country. Family members of persons with Alzheimer's disease receive support in coping with the caregiving situation through the Alzheimer's Disease and Related Disorders Association.

A key factor in self-help is the action role assumed by group members. The essence of this action is described by Reisman (1965) as the helper-therapy principle. Members of the self-help group seek not only to assist themselves in overcoming or coping with a problem, but also to assist other members of the group in their struggle. Individuals appear to benefit greatly from the helping process. Development and use of interpersonal skills such as counseling, listening, and advocacy are often required for such participation. At this level, consciousness of the public nature of the problem and of the political nature of causality begins to emerge.

Mrs. B. and Mr. F. were able to assist each other, thereby providing needed help and also gaining the satisfaction of playing a helping role.

## Dimension 3

Interventions on Dimension 3 are focused on change or mediation within the client's immediate environment. Learning about social service and health care resources and how to access them is one key activity. Another is the development of knowledge about professional helpers and about ways to communicate with them effectively. This dimension of focus often follows from the ongoing consciousness-raising process by which clients and workers continue to explore the impact of the environment on personal problems. For example, an older woman concerned about employment may engage in training programs and support groups as Dimension 2 activities and engage in job development and/or exploration of age discrimination processes and sanctions as Dimension 3 activities.

## Dimension 4

Interventions on Dimension 4 focus on involvement of clients in the political aspects of their problems. This focus includes social action or other collective efforts to affect environmental forces that contribute to individual problems. The knowledge base comes from a combination of the collective intelligence of the participants involved and formal knowledge from sources such as national social action groups and academic institutions. For example, participation in the Older Women's League (OWL) enables an elderly person to address health care issues from an informed base of social action. OWL, as a national organization, disseminates materials to its members regarding current social policy of interest to elders. In addition, local chapters offer training in the skills necessary for social action. In the case examples, the CCSO provided a broad base for addressing common issues.

## Interrelationship of the Dimensions

The dimensions of focus for intervention outlined in Table 3.1 are not mutually exclusive. Tasks in all dimensions may proceed simultaneously. For example, while in the stage of relationship development, worker and client may become involved in a discussion of national organizations for seniors or may attend a social action event. Also, it is important to note that although joining support groups (Lee and Swenson, 1986) is a useful strategy, many of the tasks and activities that enhance empowerment can be accomplished on a one-to-one basis if for some reason the group medium is not feasible. The function of one-to-one relationships in the empowerment process will be described in Part Two of this book.

We do not suggest here that these dimensions of focus are linear or necessarily sequential. Intervention with elderly clients may begin in *any* dimension, and each enhances the others. Most traditional social work practice has been done in Dimensions 1 and 2. The goals of empowerment-oriented practice include the development of critical consciousness and engagement in political activity (Dimensions 3 and 4) even though not every client will be willing or able to participate in activities in these dimensions.

Understanding personal problems as political issues is a principle that guides consciousness raising in all four dimensions of intervention. The worker seeking to facilitate empowerment assists elderly clients to understand their difficulties as problems frequently experienced by elders and to see the relationship of these problems to society as a whole. Problems of financial insecurity, for example, are common to many elderly and have their roots in the economic structure and values of American society. Through Dimension 1 interventions, elderly persons may be able to find ways to alleviate financial problems to some extent by finding and securing entitlements. Through Dimension 2 interventions, elderly persons may participate in discussion groups concerning rental costs in their housing unit and learn about housing alternatives. Through Dimension 3 interventions, a group of elderly individuals may set up and participate in a communal garden or a craft co-op to help alleviate financial woes. Through Dimension 4 interventions, elder groups or individuals are encouraged to identify links between personal problems and societal dynamics and to participate in actions that oppose detrimental political or policy changes such as decreases in pensions and other entitlements.

The worker serves as a catalyst by raising questions about the relationship between private problems and related public issues, then challenging the group members to come to their own conclusions. This type of education raises consciousness and awareness of the continuum from private trouble to public issue. A key assumption that links the quest to help elderly clients comprehend their private problems as public issues and the consequent increase in critical consciousness is stated by Gil (1987), who notes that consciousness and its communication are "potential means for reflecting upon established ways of life, criticizing them, and initiating changes in them" (p. 7). For those practitioners who believe that a change in individual consciousness is the first step toward fundamental change in society, linking individuals to groups in which their common needs and problems can be collectively explored is crucial. Empowerment is often a by-product of this process.

Comprehension of the environmental aspects of one's struggles is often a first step in gaining control over some aspects of one's life situation.

However, consciousness-raising activities must also focus on the internalized aspects of the problem in order to facilitate empowerment. An elderly person may be inhibited in productive problem-solving activity by personal beliefs or values that appear to others involved in the situation to be nonfunctional. Often the person is unaware of the source of the difficulties or is acting on ideas that have never been challenged. Group participation frequently allows the individual the opportunity to reassess beliefs or ideas in the light of new information. Such new information may be related to changes in the environment or a better understanding of the sources of the ideas that guide one's behavior and beliefs.

The task of consciousness raising also requires that individuals seek to understand the external aspects of the problem, such as age discrimination, lack of jobs in the economy, and so on. Participation with others in coming to a collective understanding of these conditions and group activities aimed at their alleviation are very helpful. In summary, both aspects of the problems faced by elderly clients must be explored in order to facilitate empowerment.

As noted earlier, the essential goal of the interaction between worker and elder is to achieve a partnership in the mutual quest for the solution of the problem at hand and subsequently a better society. The practitioner may engage in numerous activities in the development of this partnership, including teaching, advocacy, consultation, mediation, and other common activities of social workers. An essential aspect of empowerment-oriented interventions is that the client learn these skills whenever possible. For example, it is important that elders learn to be advocates for themselves and others regarding the large organizations that affect their lives.

The most important functions of the worker throughout his or her work with client populations is to assist individuals to identify links between personal problems and societal dynamics. The worker is responsible for raising questions that help clients to understand their situations in relation to social justice, which is a goal of empowerment-oriented practice. Specifically, where possible, the worker seeks to emphasize the reality of common human needs and engage clients in a conscious struggle to create an environment governed by the values of empowerment-oriented practice.

## *SUMMARY*

The empowerment process involves critical review of attitudes and beliefs about one's self and one's sociopolitical environment, validation of collective experience, development of knowledge and skills for critical thinking and action, and engaging in action for personal and political change. These components are all necessary in empowerment-oriented social work practice.

A social work practice model consists of values, sanction, and theory base, which determine worker/client relationship, problem identification, assessment, goal setting, planning strategies, and interventions. The empowerment-oriented practice model includes these components but in the context of the empowerment process.

Interventive strategies are conceptualized on a continuum of focus that ranges from personal to political with consciousness raising and education as an ongoing theme. There are four dimensions of focus for interventions. Dimension 1 activities include contact (which can occur in any dimension but often occurs as a Dimension 1 activity), problem identification and assessment (consciousness raising regarding the presenting problem), and securing provision of basic services. Dimension 2 activities include ongoing consciousness raising regarding the problem and the group dimension of the issue (such as values held by the family or community, the nature of the discrimination the group is experiencing, and so on), as well as acquiring knowledge and skills for coping with both the identified problem and other late life developmental tasks. Dimension 3 activities include ongoing consciousness raising concerning services, health care resources, interorganizational networking, service provision issues, and strategies of action related to these issues. Dimension 4 activities include consciousness raising regarding political aspects of presenting problems, including social action and collective efforts.

The four dimensions are interrelated rather than mutually exclusive. The practitioner should be engaged in a continuum of consciousness raising and action taking with the client, not in place of the client. Education is an inherent component of service delivery across these dimensions.

## REFERENCES

Berger, P. L., & Neuhaus, R. J. (1977). *To empower people: The role of mediating structures in public policy.* Washington, DC: American Enterprise Institute for Public Policy Research.

Compton, B., & Galaway, B. (1989). *Social work processes* (4th ed.). Belmont, CA: Wadsworth.

Cox, E. O. (1988). Empowerment interventions in aging. *Social Work with Groups, 11*(3/4), pp. 111–125.

Cox, E. O. (1991). The critical role of social action in empowerment-oriented groups. In A. Vinik & M. Levin (Eds.), *Social action in group work.* New York: Haworth.

Galper, J. H. (1980). *Social work practice: A radical perspective.* Englewood Cliffs, NJ: Prentice-Hall.

Germain, C. B., & Gitterman, A. (1980). *The life model of social work practice.* New York: Columbia University Press.

Gil, D. G. (1987). Individual experience and critical consciousness: Sources of social change in everyday life. *Journal of Sociology and Social Welfare, XIV*(1), pp. 5–20.

Gitterman, A., & Shulman, L. (Eds.). (1986). *Mutual aid groups and the life cycle.* Itasca, IL: F. E. Peacock.

Gould, K. H. (1987). Life model versus conflict model. *Social Work, 32*(4), pp. 346–351.

Gutiérrez, L. (1989). *Empowerment in social work practice: Considerations for practice and education.* Paper presented to the Council on Social Work Education, Annual Program Meeting, Chicago.

Gutiérrez, L. (1990). Working with women of color: An empowerment perspective. *Social Work, 35*(2), pp. 149–154.

Johnson, L. C. (1989). *Social work practice: A generalist approach* (3rd ed.). Newton, MA: Allyn and Bacon.

Kieffer, C. H. (1984). Citizen empowerment: A developmental perspective. *Prevention in Human Services, 3*(Winter/Spring), pp. 9–36.

Lee, J. A. B., & Swenson, C. R. (1986). The concept of mutual aid. In J. Gitterman & O. Shulman (Eds.), *Mutual aid groups and the life cycle.* Itasca, IL: F. E. Peacock.

Longres, J. F. (1990). *Human behavior in the social environment.* Itasca, IL: F. E. Peacock.

Maluccio, A. (Ed.). (1981). *Promoting competence in clients: A new/old approach to social work practice.* New York: Free Press.

Matura, R. C. (1986, April). *Opportunity structures for the aged.* Paper presented at the North Central Sociological Association, Toledo, OH.

Maze, T. (1987). Empowerment: Reflections on theory and practice. *Aging Network News, 9*(5), p. 1.

Middleman, R. R., & Goldberg, G. (1974). *Social service delivery: A structural approach to social work practice.* New York: Columbia University Press.

Parsons, R. J. (1991). Empowerment: Purpose and practice in social work. *Social Work with Groups, 14*(2), pp. 27–43.

Pincus, A., & Minahan, A. (1973). *Social work practice: Model and method.* Itasca, IL: F. E. Peacock.

Reisman, F. (1965). The helper-therapy principle. *Social Work, 10*(2), pp. 27–32.

Schaef, A. W. (1981). *Woman's reality.* Minneapolis, MN: Winston Press.

Schwartz, W. (1974). Private troubles and public issues: One social work job or two? In R. Klenk & R. Ryan (Eds.), *The practice of social work* (2nd ed.). Belmont, CA: Wadsworth.

Solomon, B. (1976). *Black empowerment: Social work in oppressed communities.* New York: Columbia University Press.

Torre, D. (1985). *Empowerment: Structured conceptualization and instrument development.* Unpublished doctoral dissertation, Cornell University, Ithaca, NY.

# EMPOWERMENT-ORIENTED INTERVENTIONS APPLIED TO LEVELS OF PRACTICE

# EMPOWERMENT AND THE ARENA OF SOCIAL POLICY

In the idealized progression toward understanding personal problems as political issues, participation in the policy arena is the ultimate goal of the empowerment process for most clients. It is important to note here that the empowerment-oriented social worker is, in most cases, working with clients who have an ongoing relationship both with the worker and with one another. Frequently, before turning their attention to the social policy aspects of their problems, these clients have been members of mutual support or empowerment groups and therefore have been active in self-help and self-education efforts.

Furthermore, the policy arena lends itself readily to the forging of a balanced partnership between worker and client. Very often worker and client are affected by the same social policies and have a clearly defined *mutual interest* in changing specific policies. The two parties thus find themselves sharing a struggle for the achievement of a common goal. This situation allows for collective effort and use of the knowledge and skills of both worker and clients, thereby enhancing the empowering effect of shared participation in policy-changing activities.

Social work practitioners are faced with a dual task in their effort to facilitate empowerment in the policy arena—the need to *empower themselves* as agents for social change and the need to *help clients become empowered* with respect to those social policies that affect their lives.

Chapter 2 briefly described the disempowering effect that social policy in the United States has on those dependent on social services for survival resources, and Chapter 3 emphasized the key role that participation in social action plays in the empowerment process. This chapter provides an overview of the challenges faced by empowerment-oriented workers as they struggle to engage their elderly clients in the development and change of social policy. Strategies to overcome resistance to participation, as well as to increase the knowledge and skills of both worker and clients, are suggested. Issue-based efforts to change policies at the national and state levels are highlighted. Organizational and agency-level policies that address social service delivery will be discussed in Chapter 5.

## *SOCIAL POLICY PRACTICE: AN OVERVIEW*

The 1980s and early 1990s have witnessed a growing recognition of the concept of "social policy practice" within the social work profession (Cox, Erlich, Rothman, & Tropman, 1987; Haynes & Michelson, 1986; Wyers, 1991). Prior to this era, curricular attention to social policy in schools of social work focused primarily on learning about existing policy, understanding the policy-making process, and analyzing policy. Little emphasis was placed on affecting social policy, especially at macro levels, except in community organization courses.

Five policy-related tasks important to the empowerment-oriented worker are as follows:

1. Overcoming workers' and clients' resistance to involvement in the policy process
2. Obtaining and sharing information regarding existing policies, pending policies, and implementation of policies
3. Gaining and sharing knowledge about the policy process and policy makers
4. Developing and testing frameworks for understanding and analyzing policy
5. Acquiring and sharing practical knowledge about how to change policy

Empowerment-oriented workers often find themselves engaged in the above tasks for their own needs as well as for their clients' (Pierce, 1984). Such activity on the part of workers is a reaction to the severe frustrations inherent in their daily efforts to assist clients in finding adequate resources to meet basic needs. The reality that many elderly clients find themselves without access to basic health care, adequate income, appropriate housing, and other survival resources continues to spur social workers' need to participate in social action. Often client and worker share a need for the resources sought through policy action. For example, an adequate national health care system would benefit both workers and clients.

The policies to be given priority by a particular group are determined by the primary concerns of the seniors involved. These concerns can be related to policy at one or more levels—state or service agency administration, landlord/tenant relations, local government, and/or federal regulations or funding. It should be noted that even though the worker

**Leadership requires courage and willingness to act.**
*(Photo courtesy of Senior Resource Center, Wheatridge, Colorado)*

becomes involved in social policy practice as a partner with clients, the worker remains responsible for stimulating and facilitating the overall activity until client leadership is developed. Throughout the empowerment process, however, the worker and the elderly participants share their knowledge, energy, and skills.

## OVERCOMING RESISTANCE TO INVOLVEMENT IN THE POLICY PROCESS

Apathy and a sense of powerlessness characterize many elderly individuals, as well as people of other ages (Harding, 1990), despite a considerable amount of discussion in the popular press about the growing political power of older Americans (Pollack, 1988; Wallace, Williamson, Lung, & Powell, 1991). Many elderly individuals have restricted their policy-influencing activity to voting. Others believe that even voting is futile. The complexity of policy issues and the rapidity of policy changes seem beyond the control of most citizens. In this highly technological society, the implicit claim of various experts to be the only well-informed decision makers tends to cause many individuals to give up and "let the experts handle it." The empowerment-oriented worker must frequently counter these apathetic attitudes.

The worker is often able to overcome some of the resistance to involvement by first assisting clients to articulate their personal problems and become aware of others who share these problems and then providing information that facilitates the process of connecting these personal concerns with public issues. Once elderly clients develop a clear understanding of the ways in which specific social policy issues directly affect their lives, resistance to involvement in the policy process often lessens.

In one empowerment-oriented group, for example, identifying age discrimination as a common experience helped individual members limit self-blame and feelings of inadequacy and uselessness. This change in perception led to the involvement of some group members in efforts to change employment policies at an organizational level, and ultimately resulted in their joining a national senior lobbying effort to eliminate forced retirement and to enforce the civil rights of older people with respect to fair employment.

In addition to apathy, a common obstacle to motivating both workers and elderly clients to take policy action is their assumption of powerlessness: "What difference does it make what I think?" "No one will listen anyhow." "Only the rich get their way." These and similar comments are frequently heard among seniors and younger people. An increasing sense of powerlessness has also been noted among human service helping professionals (Burghardt, 1982).

## *Strategies*

*Role modeling*—active involvement by the empowerment-oriented worker in the policy process—is a significant way to help clients counter the feelings of powerlessness that prevent their participation in policy-changing activities. Another effective strategy is for the worker to present examples of successful policy manipulation by senior groups or other groups with similar interests. Further motivation often comes from within the client group itself, as group members encourage each other to participate in the policy arena.

Overall, the most effective stimulant of policy action is active participation—clients taking part in change activity, especially in the companionship of others concerned with the same issues, and seeing the results. Long periods of inaction spent discussing and studying the problem or planning actions can often result in disengagement in the process of policy change. Some actions, such as letter-writing campaigns targeting legislators, if not followed up by other activities, can even lead to discouragement. This is especially true if a long time passes without response or if responses are noncommittal.

Sustaining active client participation is key to a successful outcome. In one project designed to organize senior advocacy teams in eleven council areas of a large western city, enthusiasm ran high during the initial meetings as new groups were called together to identify problems. Continuation of the groups was difficult, however, because of a lack of staff to attend follow-up meetings, a time lag before completion of a time-consuming plan of action, and a lack of response by officials to letters, calls, or other forms of communication issued by the newly formed groups (Chimento, 1987). Therefore, it is important for the empowerment-oriented worker to have knowledge of a wide range of policy-changing strategies.

## Values

Commonly held values related to social welfare benefits represent another source of the resistance to involvement in the policy process that is frequently encountered at the motivation stage. For example, elders may express ambivalence regarding their right to entitlements. Many elderly people have a fear of government intervention, a reluctance to seek help, and a tendency to blame themselves for a lack of resources. The use of political consciousness-raising interventions, such as group process, to identify common problems and to bring about an understanding of society's role in their occurrence can help overcome the resistance of elderly individuals to policy-related activity in support of increased social welfare benefits. The role of the social worker in this case is to provide both the opportunity for consciousness raising to take place and the relevant information. The following sections suggest some of the kinds of information that will be helpful.

## OBTAINING AND SHARING INFORMATION ON POLICIES

The first task related to obtaining information about policies is closely related to motivation: the necessity to establish a belief in one's right to "meddle" in policy making and implementation. As noted earlier, one barrier to participation in the policy-making process is the assumption by many laypersons of their own ignorance. The idea that policy decisions are made by "wise persons" and "experts" is not uncommon. Along with other professionals, gerontological social workers share this appearance of expertise, created by their serving as "experts" at hearings and meetings, their publications, and their positions in academic institutions. Empowerment-oriented practice does not negate the value of knowledge gained from experience, academic study, or other sources. However, the empowerment-oriented worker's task is to convey to elderly clients that knowledge and ideas are potentially available to everyone. In order to gain significance, such knowledge must be tested by lay constituencies through application to their daily lives.

It is important to keep in mind that, regardless of the social acceptance of expertise, individuals with high levels of formal education are seldom the key decision makers. Empowerment-oriented workers can point out to clients that decisions are most often made by lay individuals holding positions of power, with input from a large variety of sources. Certainly, key decision makers in Congress, state legislatures, and local governments are often without expertise in many areas that their decisions affect.

Demystification of policy issues through analysis as well as through exposure of the value-based nature of most decision making—whether that basis is economic self-interest or philosophical preference or both—is another important part of affirming each individual's right to participate in policy decisions. When the fear of being "less professional" than other participants in the policy arena is alleviated, elderly citizens may begin to seek information about policies on their own.

The need for information on which to base policy decisions is shared by both workers and their elderly clients. Seeking this information can be a joint venture. Information concerning policy areas of concern to the elderly is often conflicting, so the worker must (1) *discover the most effective sources of information* in each area of concern and (2) *learn how to use these sources*—for example, how to get on the appropriate mailing lists and where to find numbers for legislative hotlines. Many hours of work are usually required to identify good sources of information.

## *Sources of Policy Information*

Sources for information on state and local policies vary from state to state and change over time. Key national organizations (such as AARP, NARFE, NCOA, NCSC, and OWL) collect and disseminate information regarding national policy issues of importance to elders. These organizations also campaign for legislative support on issues, which requires the assistance of local groups and individual social workers and their clients. Each of the organizations has special priorities and constituencies. However, the overall effect of their active lobbying efforts, legislative research, information publishing, hotline maintenance, organizational meetings, and high-quality legislative staff has been to provide invaluable resources for the policy actions of older people and their advocates.

The AARP, for example, annually prepares a document that provides a review of federal policy issues and guidelines for state legislative committees. Content areas include:

- Economic and budget policy
- Tax policy
- Retirement income policy
- Employment and worker equity policy
- Health care costs
- Quality of care and access
- Long-term care
- Low-income assistance
- Human services
- Education and training
- Housing and energy
- Consumer protection
- Personal and legal rights
- Protecting government integrity

Although the AARP assumes a politically moderate stance on most issues, its research efforts and its presence in decision-making arenas make it an invaluable source for all advocates interested in human services issues. Another senior organization, the NCSC, has not only a general interest in the legislative issues outlined by the AARP, but also a special interest in and information on senior employment.

Many other senior advocacy groups address the policy concerns listed above. Some of these advocacy groups tend to challenge traditional approaches to social services more than others. The empowerment-oriented worker's task includes motivating and assisting clients to take a critical look at the different perspectives of these groups.

State and local chapters of national organizations, where they are well organized, are excellent sources of information on state and local legislation. Most states have "silver-haired," or senior lobby, organizations that keep an ongoing account of state issues. Both the AARP and NARFE have active state legislative councils in most states. In 1987, NCSC had a network consisting of 33 state councils, 37 area councils, and over 4,800 clubs in 50 states. The fact that most of these organizations are, in large part, operated by seniors themselves is often inspirational to other seniors who are just becoming involved in the policy arena.

In many areas, local councils or commissions on aging can be excellent sources of information on city and county issues. These groups are frequently the outgrowth of the Older Americans Act (OAA), which provides for a designated office of aging in each state. Additionally, in most states, area agencies on aging constitute a source of policy information for designated regions within the state. These agencies compile data regarding the elderly, their needs, and available services, as well as issuing evaluation reports and other documents specific to policy implementation. Most states and local areas also have senior newspapers that offer valuable coverage of policy issues. The Administration on Aging (the national administrative office for implementation of the OAA) sponsors a number of specialized resource centers. Data useful for advocacy efforts can frequently be retrieved from these centers.

## Access to Information

The empowerment-oriented worker's role includes facilitating the compilation of a list of state and local resources and providing links between clients and these resources. Part of this linking process may involve helping clients set up networks to ensure the timely receipt and transmission of information from these sources. Access fees, membership dues, and costs for various publications can often be shared, or material can be secured without cost. Active members of various senior advocacy organizations are often available to attend group meetings in order to explain their organizations and distribute relevant materials. In some instances, where there is a strong common interest or shared goal for the empowerment group and the senior advocacy organization, the empowerment group may decide to become a local chapter of the organization.

Additional sources of policy information to which the worker can initiate access are formal workshops, conferences, and university-based classes or continuing education programs. Very often elders can attend such events or classes for a minimal fee or at no charge.

## The Contextual Perspective

The identification of sources of policy information and the access to selected data comprise only a part of the information-gathering process that the worker can facilitate. Discussion of the historical, political, social, and economic contexts of policy making is a valuable reinforcement for understanding the personal-as-political aspect of social policy. Such discussion can also shed some light on aspects of policy making and implementation that might go unnoticed without this background. For example, the struggle in the state of Colorado to establish an adequate protective services program for elderly individuals is better understood in light of the fact that most of these services were mandated by the federal government in the early 1970s. Without this contextual perspective, many older people might be influenced by the accusations of the program's opponents that the proposal is a pipe dream of its advocates.

Provision of a historical context for understanding current policy issues can not only give elderly individuals a feeling of mastery over the issues, but can also help demystify some of them. Often older participants have lived through the historical events that are discussed and can add important perspectives. Overall, because it enables elders to integrate their life experiences into the policy framework, the historical perspective plays a very important part in the development of their policy analysis skills.

# KNOWLEDGE ABOUT THE POLICY PROCESS AND POLICY MAKERS

In order to become effective participants in the policy arena, empowerment-oriented social workers and clients must understand the *decision-making process* pertaining to the policy of significance to the client constituency. The policy of concern may be public policy, organizational policy, or, as Pierce (1984) has suggested, a policy of some small group or individual. Also, it should be noted that the development of knowledge about the decision-making process is another opportunity for a joint effort between empowerment-oriented workers and their clients.

## The Formal Decision-Making Process

Understanding the formal decision-making process on any level requires considerable ongoing research. Basic information that defines the structure of government and outlines the ideal decision-making process is available in many forms. Civics books, videotapes, slide shows, and other media presentations are available through the seniors organizations mentioned earlier. State AARP and NARFE legislative chapters often conduct workshops on the subject of the legislative process. These resources can be located in any area of the country simply by making a few phone calls. Some city governments and state and federal agencies offer speakers on the subject, as do political party organizations. Such basic information is a good starting point for understanding the public legislative process at all levels of government.

## Informal Aspects of Decision Making

Informal aspects of decision making are as important as the formal process. Learning about the impact of various interest groups or about different philosophical perspectives on issues may be critical. Timing is also important in that there may be certain times at which it is best to contact decision makers. In addition, individuals and groups interested in legislative change must learn the power structure in a specific legislature and the many power strategies used by decision makers, such as killing bills by allowing them to lie dormant in committee until the close of a legislative session and appointing like-minded members to legislative committees.

Many state and national seniors organizations, as well as local interest groups and agencies, hire lobbyists who are experts in the field of legislation. These resource persons are involved in the policy-making process on a day-by-day basis and will often share their knowledge in either a presentation or a private interview.

An important part of the lobbyist's repertoire of knowledge is information about the individuals who have decision-making authority. Frequently, working with individual legislators on a regular basis is the only way to learn their philosophies of government, value bases, constituency concerns, and other characteristics—information advocates must have in order to attempt to win legislators' support. General information about the voting records of individual legislators is often reported by senior advocacy groups. This type of information is usually more readily available at the state level than for local decision makers.

It must be realized, with respect to the process of decision making as well as the decision makers themselves, that both the *content and strategies* of political issues and the *individuals involved* are constantly changing. Therefore, only ongoing involvement can ensure accurate information. Novices who stick to their task often find that they have become "experts" after what seems to be only a short period of time.

## DEVELOPING CLIENTS' SKILLS IN CRITICAL POLICY ANALYSIS

The empowerment-oriented worker is challenged to foster critical thinking by clients with respect to the analysis of policy. If elderly clients have become accustomed to using the group process as a medium for analyzing personal problems as well as for finding approaches to solutions, it is often a relatively easy step to engage them in policy analysis as a group. Also, policy analysis tasks such as research and evaluation can be facilitated by the group process. As mentioned earlier, the worker is encouraged to take responsibility for providing educational materials related to policy analysis. At this critical juncture, it is up to the empowerment-oriented worker to simplify and demystify as far as possible the policy analysis and decision-making process.

The following are key elements that workers should include in any attempt to help clients develop policy analysis skills:

- Definitions of social policy and aging policy, including their level and scope

- The historical context of current policy directions and debates
- The critical role of values in policy making and implementation
- A brief overview of several frameworks for policy analysis, accompanied by practice in formulating questions about policy issues
- Exploration of a wide range of policy alternatives, including those that challenge predominant societal values, and comparative analysis of the policy positions of various advocacy groups as well as the perspectives of those who oppose most human services–oriented legislation
- Discussion and implementation of action steps (because only through actual attempts to change policy can a realistic understanding of the process be attained)

The responsibility of the empowerment-oriented worker to assist clients in comparing the values inherent in policy decisions with the basic values supported by empowerment-oriented practice is key to all aspects of policy analysis.

## Definitions, Level, and Scope of Policy

The purpose of exploring various definitions of social welfare policy is to better understand the political significance of each variation, especially when it determines the focus of one or more interest groups. There is a wide range of definitions for social welfare policy. Many analysts focus their concerns on middle-level policies such as those concerning social security or Medicare. Others believe that all public and private policies that affect the quality of life of people in society are within the realm of social policy and should be the legitimate concern of those involved with social issues, including issues affecting the elderly.

Gil (1987) provides an excellent discussion on this topic, noting that many authors tend to equate social policy with social services or the policies that shape social welfare programs. He argues that this narrow conception tends to encourage constituencies to avoid focusing on issues within the important areas of economic policy and defense policy, both of which have a powerful impact on social welfare considerations. The same narrow view also tends to reinforce categorical conceptions—for example, the emphasis on the need for health care for the elderly rather than health care for all people.

The exploration of these kinds of ideas provides the empowerment-oriented worker with the opportunity to raise the level of concern of clients from issues of middle-level policy to elements of the political-economic system that affect middle-level policy. This elevated level of concern is particularly significant to understanding the political-economic perspective of aging, which is well articulated by Minkler and Estes

(1984, 1991). However, ongoing attention to the concerns or emergent needs of all members of the client group relating to policy at all levels is critical to maintaining their interest and motivation. Galper (1980) cites Leonard's excellent summary of this point:

> In working to integrate political education in daily efforts, we must be conscious of the requirements for any effective educational effort. In particular we must start within people's experience. There is little to be gained in presenting a complex theoretical analysis of the fiscal crisis of the state to a person whose overriding concern is to obtain a specific benefit. (p. 117)

## Historical Context of Current Policy Issues

The importance of viewing social issues within a historical context was discussed earlier in regard to helping clients gain a sense of mastery over issues and in terms of demystifying aspects of these issues. In addition, the historical context of social policy—including the history of the struggle for adequate income, housing, and health care in this society—aids the development of the ability to think critically about today's policy dilemmas. It is suggested, however, that the historical overview be presented only as the occasion arises rather than in a planned curricular fashion. A helpful tool for linking historical policy approaches to today's policy debates is the comparison of the current positions of different advocacy groups with those of groups in the past concerned with similar issues.

Elders who are just becoming active in the policy arena may be motivated by an understanding of the struggles of the past and the diversity of approaches suggested by current debates. The obvious lack of consensus and the political nature of the policy-making process may stimulate elderly clients to seek their own solutions and to explore a wide range of policy alternatives.

## The Critical Role of Values

In all interactions with client groups, the overriding significance of values in policy making must be stressed. A key part of policy analysis (which elderly clients can explore within a group) is *identifying and comparing* the predominant values reflected in proposed and established policy—for example, examining the difference between developing a stronger private pension system and establishing a universal public retirement fund.

Another strategy, which can assist the development of critical thought processes, is encouraging clients to interview decision makers. Asking legislators, city council members, and others what criteria they use to evaluate proposals can be very enlightening with respect to the important role values play in the policy-making process.

# Frameworks for Policy Analysis

Studying different frameworks for policy analysis in order to illustrate the relationships between the value priorities of different analysts can be especially useful for client groups. One effective approach to the discussion of frameworks is the presentation of four or five frameworks, or models, for analysis. Morris (1985), Gil (1987), Gilbert and Specht (1974), and Pierce (1984) offer models for policy analysis that pose insightful questions that can guide inquiry into policy. At the same time, these models can be used to illustrate the different emphases or values that guide the analysis of various analysts. Dye (1981, p. 19) identifies five major functions of policy models:

1. To simplify and clarify people's thinking about politics and public policy
2. To identify important aspects of policy problems
3. To help people communicate with one another by focusing on essential features of political life
4. To direct people's efforts to better understand public policy by suggesting what is important and what is unimportant
5. To suggest explanations for public policy and predict its consequences

Once they have provided information about various policy analysis frameworks, workers should give clients the opportunity to experiment with developing their own set of questions that will guide their review of specific policies of concern to them and their research into facts concerning these policies. Identifying the values underlying each specific framework for analysis is crucial. The application of several of these frameworks to one policy of great interest to the group can be helpful in illustrating the value differences (Cox, 1991).

## Exploration of a Wide Range of Policy Alternatives

Facilitating the review of a wide range of policy alternatives on issues that concern clients is a key role for the worker. Current policy debate often does not include alternatives that go beyond moderate modification of the status quo. Reviewing the positions of the AARP, NCSC, OWL, and other social action groups on a single controversial issue can be a useful process for individuals and groups learning about policy analysis. Also, comparing the voting patterns of different income groups or ethnic groups with respect to certain policy issues can be enlightening. This activity further illustrates the role of values in policy formulation, and it provides valuable knowledge about potential sources of support for or resistance to policies on which clients wish to focus.

For example, on the issue of the affordability of prescribed drugs, a proposed policy may provide for increasing the client co-payment in an effort to develop new resources to pay for medications for those most in need. The worker can introduce alternative approaches for discussion—such as urging the government to cap the cost of medication or to adopt a national medical system that pays for all medication. In other words, the worker can play an instrumental role by suggesting policy alternatives that are compatible with the values of empowerment-oriented practice. Such alternatives stress the values of egalitarian distribution of resources, full participation in making decisions about policies that affect one's life, collective effort, nondiscrimination, concern for natural resources, and the use of wealth to meet the needs of all people rather than the economic goal of a free market. Specific examples of the establishment and implementation of alternative policies in other countries are often useful in showing that other approaches do exist.

The overall goal of using frameworks, providing historical information, exploring a wide range of alternatives, and the other knowledge development strategies presented above is to *encourage, challenge, and develop the critical and analytical skills of clients* and thus facilitate their empowerment in the policy-making arena. In summary, in order for empowerment-oriented workers and their clients to participate effectively in policy action from an empowerment perspective, they must master conceptual skills, values clarification skills, political skills, interactional skills, and position-taking skills, as suggested by Jansson (1984) for understanding policy. Recognizing the value bases of policies, identifying the trade-offs underlying various decisions, exploring policy alternatives, assessing the political climate, introducing policy alternatives in the most positive manner, knowing the decision makers, and developing constituencies are key skills that can be developed by clients as both individuals and group members. The primary function of empowerment-oriented workers is assisting in the learning process, which involves the collective processes of seeking knowledge, locating sources of information, testing strategies, and evaluating outcomes of activities. In addition to these skills, reviewing the ideas of as many groups and individuals as possible is very helpful to clients who are new to policy analysis.

## KNOWLEDGE AND SKILLS FOR INFLUENCING POLICY

The final area of policy work that the empowerment-oriented worker must address is the development by clients of practical skills that will help them have an impact on the policy decisions that affect their lives.

*Collective action builds networks and brings results.*
(Photo courtesy Senior Edition, Denver, Colorado)

As clients gain interest, knowledge, and motivation, they become more likely to take action on the policies that they have determined to be the most significant to their lives. Many of the senior advocacy organizations discussed earlier have developed excellent policy intervention strategies. The Villers Foundation's ASAP legislative hotline and OWL's Mother's Day messages to legislators are two effective examples. AARP has not only been extremely active in negotiating on policy issues with members of Congress by means of its lobbying efforts and community education strategies, but has also developed a wide range of educational materials, which include packages that impart knowledge and skills for social action. Only after they have attempted to affect policy themselves will clients be able to integrate their knowledge of the policy-making process with the reality of their lives.

## Policy-Influencing Strategies

The following areas of content are among those suggested in the Massachusetts Association of Older Americans' *Advocacy Training Manual* (Curley, Mendelsohn, & Astreen, 1984) as important for efforts to affect policy:

- Planning from issues to action (defining and assessing issues, running a first meeting, choosing leaders, planning additional meetings, and evaluating group activities)
- Understanding the political system (how governments work— federal, state, county, and city bureaucracies and other organizations)
- How a bill becomes a law (state and federal)
- Budgeting processes (governments and private organizations)
- Taking action steps (letters, telegrams, phone calls, meetings, public hearings, petitions, rallies, demonstrations, boycotts, and picket lines)
- Using the media (television, radio, newspapers, newsletters, and so on)

These topics are specifically related to the legislative process and have been well received by older people in Massachusetts.

## Usefulness of Advocacy Organizations

A great number of the skills required for successful involvement in policy making are basic community organization skills, which have represented a well-defined area of social work practice since the mid 1960s. The 1970s saw the growth and development of advocacy organizations concerned with social welfare issues. Moreover, many of the social welfare issues of interest to the grass-roots organizations that were products of the 1970s are of concern to senior groups today.

There is an ever growing number of resources that can be used by empowerment groups in their efforts to develop policy intervention skills. The search for these resources, when they are not readily available within the group, can be facilitated by contacting advocacy organizations. A good place to begin is with any of the well-known senior action or advocacy organizations. The knowledge and skills that these organizations have developed can be of great value to empowerment-oriented workers and their clients.

Advocacy organizations include multi-issue organizing groups (for example, Metropolitan Organizational People, Families U.S.A., and Common Cause) and a number of groups that focus on specific social welfare issues. (Well-known examples include Greenpeace, Committee to Save Social Security and Medicare, National Center for Policy Alternatives, Economic Policy Institute, Association of Community Organizations for Reform, and the National Low-Income Housing Coalition). Such organizations can be of great assistance to empowerment groups in both their research and their efforts to choose and carry out policy intervention strategies.

# SUMMARY

Facilitating clients' engagement in social action to influence policies at the local, state, and national levels is crucial to the empowerment process. Five important components of this facilitation are overcoming resistance to involvement in the policy-making process; obtaining and sharing information regarding existing policies, pending policies, and implementation of policies; gaining and sharing knowledge about the policy process and policy makers; developing and testing frameworks for understanding and analyzing policy; and acquiring and sharing practical knowledge about how to influence policy.

Overcoming resistance to participation in the policy process requires both increased knowledge and action (experience). Furthermore, a worker/client partnership, or mutuality, in developing and sharing knowledge and skills related to policy change is effective for engaging clients in the process. The use of national and state organizations as information sources is helpful for policy analysis and intervention.

# *REFERENCES*

Burghardt, S. (1982). *The other side of organizing.* Rochester, VA: Schenkman.

Chimento, T. (1987). *Evaluation report: Denver senior advocacy team program.* Unpublished manuscript.

Cox, E. (1991). The critical role of social action in empowerment-oriented groups. In A. Vinik & M. Levin (Eds.), *Social action in group work.* New York: Haworth.

Cox, F. M., Erlich, J. L., Rothman, J., & Tropman, J. E. (1987). *Strategies of community organization* (4th ed.). Itasca, IL: F. E. Peacock.

Curley, M., Mendelsohn, R., & Astreen, B. (1984). *Advocacy training manual.* Boston: Department of Elderly Affairs of Massachusetts, Massachusetts Association of Older Americans.

Dye, T. R. (1981). *Understanding public policy* (4th ed.). Englewood Cliffs, NJ: Prentice-Hall.

Galper, J. (1980). *Social work practice: A radical perspective.* Englewood Cliffs, NJ: Prentice-Hall.

Gil, D. G. (1987). *Unravelling social policy* (3rd ed.). Cambridge, MA: Schenkman.

Gilbert, N., & Specht, H. (1974). *Dimensions of social welfare policy.* Englewood Cliffs, NJ: Prentice-Hall.

Harding, V. (1990). *Hope and history.* Maryknoll, NY: Orbis Books.

Haynes, K. S., & Michelson, J. S. (1986). *Affecting change: Social workers in the political arena.* New York: Longman.

Jansson, B. S. (1984). *Theory and practice of social welfare policy*. Belmont, CA: Wadsworth.

Minkler, M., & Estes, C. L. (1984). *Readings in the political economy of aging*. Farmingdale, NY: Baywood.

Minkler, M., & Estes, C. L. (Eds.). (1991). *Critical perspectives on aging: The political and moral economy of growing old*. Farmingdale, NY: Baywood.

Morris, R. (1985). *Social policy of the welfare state* (2nd ed.). New York: Longman.

Pierce, D. (1984). *Social policy for the social work practitioner*. New York: Longman.

Pollack, R. F. (1988). Servicing intergenerational needs, not intergenerational conflict. *Generations, 12*(3), pp. 14–19.

Wallace, S. P., Williamson, I. B., Lung, R. G., & Powell, L. A. (1991). In M. Minkler & C. L. Estes, *Critical perspectives on aging: The political and moral economy of growing old*. Farmingdale, NY: Baywood.

Wyers, N. L. (1991). Policy-practice in social work: Models and issues. *Journal of Social Work Education, 27*(4), pp. 241–250.

# SOCIAL SERVICE DELIVERY: AN ARENA FOR EMPOWERMENT-ORIENTED PRACTICE

The formidable challenge to empowerment-oriented practitioners is to enable clients to participate effectively in the use of services and the re-creation of a health care and social service system. This chapter examines the disempowering nature of health care and social services that are targeted at elderly people in this country and suggests effective strategies for the empowerment-oriented social worker. A review of the status and availability of health care and social services is followed by an examination of the relationship of this situation to the powerlessness of elderly recipients of these services. The impact of professionals and their methods of intervention on elderly clients is then discussed in terms of fostering empowerment. Finally, empowerment-oriented strategies directed toward both clients and organizations are presented.

## THE CURRENT STATE OF SOCIAL SERVICES FOR THE ELDERLY

The current state of social services for the elderly can only be understood through analysis of the nature of and the change in general social policy in the United States. Setting the context of the challenge to empowerment-oriented practice are the following considerations:

- The dramatic cutback in social services
- The inadequate and confusing state of health care
- The as yet undocumented impact of privatization of many health care and social services

Little progress has been made since the 1960s. Kahn (1979) cited a 1968 report from the Gerontological Society of America, which stated that no community in the United States had developed a comprehensive network of services for the aging and the aged. Comparing conditions ten years later, he pointed out that, although a bit improved, things were much the same. The meager headway that was made toward a universal system of services for the elderly, initiated by the Older Americans Act and advocated by a number of voices in the late 1960s, was almost obliterated by the pro-market privatization strategy of the Reagan era (Binstock, 1990; Estes, 1989). Today, services and programs available to the elderly in most U.S. communities are even scarcer and more difficult to locate. Binstock (1990) notes: "Little has been done in recent years to focus on seriously ameliorating the situation of those among the aged who remain extremely disadvantaged" (p. 91).

Current concerns among the social services community include:

- The ongoing search for a better way to *access* services
- The rhetorical call for development of a community-based long-term care *system*
- A "new" emphasis on deploying the resources made available by the Older Americans Act to those *most in need*
- A continued emphasis on *use of alternatives to* long-term care institutions for the elderly
- The possible transformation of the *home* into a new institution in the coming decades
- A great increase in competition among many programs for *fewer resources*

These issues, reflecting today's uncertainty, are indicative of the lack of an adequate system of health and social service for elderly citizens (Binstock, 1990; Estes, 1989; Huttman, 1985; Monk, 1990).

The social worker seeking to assist elderly clients in today's service market experience many frustrations. The program environment is characterized by numerous barriers to service:

- The large number of public and private, for-profit and not-for-profit agencies, coupled with the lack of a comprehensive directory to aid in locating them
- A complex eligibility system that varies from program to program
- Varying receptiveness among programs to working with Medicaid and Medicare payment systems
- Little or no information regarding the quality of service available through programs such as home health agencies
- An increasingly two-tier service system, as the gap in paying power between the wealthy and the poor widens
- Rapid turnover in agencies' staffs
- The rise and fall of agencies themselves

*Original art courtesy of Keith Tillery*

- Constant changes in services available through agencies once eligibility has been established
- Increasing out-of-pocket costs, such as for co-payments and deductibles for health care and professional fees, resulting in an increase in services paid for directly by clients
- Extremely limited supply of some critical services and resources, such as mental health services, moving services, low-cost housing, and transportation

These barriers to service evoke a sense of powerlessness in both workers and elderly clients. Furthermore, there have been well-documented criticisms of the lack of responsiveness on the part of social and health care services to the needs of older women, older members of ethnic minority groups, poor elderly, the very frail elderly, and other special-needs groups (Kravitz, Pelaez, & Rothman, 1990; Waxman, 1990). Rather than innovation and development of programs and services to meet the needs of an increasing number of at-risk elderly, the past decade has witnessed a string of cutbacks and a struggle to hold onto already inadequate programs.

Three other characteristics of current social and health care programs are especially relevant to the sense of powerlessness that may be felt by potential beneficiaries of these programs: (1) the increasing stigma attached to the use of public resources by elderly people, (2) the domination of social services by the biomedical model, and (3) the strong social control aspect of the existing programs and services.

## The Stigma of Receiving Public Assistance

An increasingly negative view of expending societal resources on the elderly is imposing a new barrier to service development. The popular press has increased its lamentations about the heavy use of public health care and social services by older Americans during the past decade, thereby contributing to this stigma. Furthermore, the generational equity movement has raised concerns among many that the elderly are using up resources at the expense of youth (Hewitt & Howe, 1988). This perspective, coupled with the regressive move from universal to means-tested programs as a cost-containment strategy, has laid the groundwork not only for more resistance to funding programs for the elderly, but also for a more negative attitude toward the recipients of those services.

## Domination of the Biomedical Model

Biomedical domination of most services that still carry the label "social services" has been assured by two factors: (1) the progressive dismantling of the community-based social services that existed, though to a limited degree, in the 1960s (supported by funds available through the Social Security Act, the Economic Opportunity Act, the Older Americans Act, and so forth), and (2) the increasing allotment of resources to the medical enterprise through Medicare and Medicaid. As a consequence, the social work profession has, to a large extent, lost control of social services. Empowering components of social service programs—such as self-help, social action, community development, advocacy, and many family and group interventions—have been eliminated or severely reduced. Such strategies were empowering in that they enabled clients and their families to gain more control over their lives, their communities, the health care and social services, and the larger political environment. Although a few social services remain intact, these are primarily funded by shrinking governmental contributions and foundation grants, which are extended at the discretion of boards, usually on a year-to-year basis. Token funding for some social services in the 1980s and early 1990s has been gleaned through "bending" or stretching of medical funding sources to include social service positions or programs that are critically needed.

Allocation of public resources as a key factor in establishing biomedical domination of services is emphasized by Estes and Lee (1985):

> The bias toward medical care in the allocation of public resources for the elderly has resulted in the "medicalization" of services, as exemplified in the high proportion of publicly financed health expenditures allocated to hospital and physician coverage, as opposed to community, in-home and other social services. (p. 21)

These authors note the preference for acute care interventions, which are more professionally and economically rewarding for the medical profession.

The medical model of intervention assumes dependency of elderly clients and affords very little opportunity for increasing their power over any aspect of their lives. The social services forged from medical sources of reimbursement tend to focus primarily on adjustment-oriented activities or on access to meager survival resources that will enable clients to move or to sustain themselves in circumstances that require less costly levels of care (for instance, receiving home care rather than extended hospitalization). Few of these services are aimed at prevention or at enabling clients to take control over their lives (Estes & Binney, 1991).

## The Social Control Aspect

A growing literature documents the way social policy regarding late life entitlements perpetuates the classism, racism, and sexism experienced in American society and adds to the oppression of the elderly (Axinn, 1989; Dowd, 1980; Minkler & Estes, 1984; Torres-Gil, 1987). The overall shift toward the market system as the provider of the resources necessary for late life survival (including health care and social services) has severely reduced the economic rights of many older Americans. During the 1980s and early 1990s, health care and social services that were previously provided by the government as a matter of right based on citizenship or need have been cut back. The loss of these services has made elders who were receiving them or who are now in need of them dependent on private charity and other unreliable sources. Inability to command the financial resources and services necessary for survival has greatly increased the sense of powerlessness among elderly people. The control of social programs and private charities over the lives of older people who need their assistance has likewise increased. For example, in one state the cutback in funds for a public program that allowed low-income elders to hire family members or other providers of their choice to furnish needed home care left these individuals either at the mercy of private charities and other programs that give clients no choice regarding who provides the service or, in many cases, without care at all. In sum, faced with needs that far outweigh the availability of services, older citizens who previously were able to meet their needs through state-supported programs (entitlements developed in the 1960s) are left without recourse or are forced to appeal to private charity.

In addition to the loss of their right to services and of control over services, many elderly persons experience the social control aspect of social services through the onset of disability. The social control aspect of most social services available to the elderly in the 1990s is strongly reinforced by their administration through medical model programs. Clients are seen as "patients," and their primary responsibility in the process of receiving services is *compliance*. Within the worker/client relationship in this context, the emphasis is on expertise and helper/helpee activity.

Many elders are in need of both economic support and service support to accomplish the tasks of daily living. In defining vulnerability multi-dimensionally, Longino and Soldo (1987) state that nearly 90% of frail elderly people are not simply disabled but are also socially, economically, or environmentally impoverished. In summary, the current state of social services is, in large part, diminishing the opportunity of elderly clients to control the practical details or the social context of their lives. What about the role of professional gerontologists in this situation? Are the helping services helping?

## THE ROLE OF PROFESSIONAL KNOWLEDGE IN FOSTERING EMPOWERMENT

Social work practice has historically been concerned with oppressed populations. The elimination of racism, sexism, and other forms of discrimination has been an overall goal of the profession. Despite this common commitment, great diversity in approaches to practice and choice of guiding theories has been evident within the profession. This diversity has taken on different emphases during different historical periods. Even during specific periods, however, the various schools of thought within the profession have led to diverse methodologies of practice. The following is a brief comment on some of the recent patterns.

## Challenges to Traditional Practice Approaches

In the 1960s and early 1970s, many criticisms were leveled at the practice approaches used by professional social workers. Such criticism, in an era of human rights movements, supported empowerment-oriented interventions as opposed to interventions that stressed adjustment to an oppressive system or environment. Furthermore, it came from several quarters—the poor, ethnic and racial minorities, feminists, radical practitioners, radical social scientists, gay and lesbian groups, and, somewhat later, advocates for the elderly and handicapped populations. These groups challenged both the social science theories on which helping professionals were basing their interventions and the nature of the interventions themselves (Bailey & Brake, 1976; Frank, 1979; Galper, 1975; Milwaukee County Welfare Rights Organization, 1972; Morales & Shaefor, 1977; Solomon, 1976). Predominant themes of these challenges to professional practices included concerns about (1) practitioners' lack of knowledge of the "real world" and the life-styles of diverse groups, (2) the general bias of human behavior theories toward middle-class white Americans and the status quo, and (3) assumptions about normal functioning derived from these theories. Even systems theory came under close scrutiny and was criticized because of practitioners' tendency to use it in a prescriptive manner—to describe how things should be—rather than as a tool to observe how things were working (Evans & Williamson, 1984).

Radical social work practitioners and members of the antipsychiatry movement challenged the tendency of social workers to assess the problems of their clients through a strictly psychological lens, rather than placing balanced emphasis on the political, historical, economic, cultural/social, *and* psychological aspects of a client's situation. These critics also provided useful insights into the way professional practice embodied the same forms of discrimination and prejudice found in the larger society. Finally, they documented the social control aspect of professional practice. Prior to this challenge, social workers had not been made critically aware of the disempowering aspects of many apparently benevolent interventions (Bailey & Brake, 1976; Frank, 1979; Galper, 1980).

These challenges had some impact on the profession of social work—an impact that continued, in varying degrees, into the 1980s. Examples of the outcomes include increased program content concerning special populations within curricula of social work schools and more focus by some academics and practitioners on competency-based activities and other empowerment-oriented approaches (see, for example, Galper, 1980; Maluccio, 1981; Norman & Mancuso, 1980). The contemporary-based (or social change–focused) practice suggested by these authors and others has been strongly reinforced by the flourishing self-help and social support movements (Gartner & Riessman, 1984; Riessman, 1976; Whittaker & Garbarino, 1985). The extent of its impact on professional social work as a whole, however, has yet to be assessed but does not appear to be dramatic.

## The Impact of Social Gerontological Theories

The health, social work, and psychological professions have demonstrated an increased interest in gerontology during the past two decades. This has led to intensified study of the physical, social, and psychological aspects of aging by professionals from a number of disciplines. Training based on the theories generated by these studies has been made available to more and more practicing professionals. Advocates for the elderly have lobbied professional associations and encouraged educational institutions to expand their offerings related to gerontology. Overall, there has been an increase in many professionals' understanding of the aging process and of the needs of the elderly. As is typical of any knowledge development process, however, questions have arisen regarding the strengths and weaknesses of the conclusions generated by research. Criticisms of social gerontological theories are of special interest to empowerment-oriented practitioners because many social work interventions are based on these theories.

Important criticisms have been raised concerning the nature of the dominant social gerontological theories of aging. Estes, Swan, and Gerard (1984) summarize these criticisms:

> Social gerontological theories, however, have focused largely on individuals and their role loss, economic dependence, adjustment and isolation in old age . . . such theories give little theoretical and empirical attention to the social creation of dependency through forced retirement and its functions for the economy, or to the production of senility and the economic, political, and social control functions of such processes. (p. 27)

Strongly supporting these criticisms, Evans and Williamson (1984) describe the issue as follows:

> For the most part theories of aging have focused upon individual adjustment to problems associated with aging, not on the structural creation of the problems. Gerontologists have shown even more reticence in aggressively investigating, analyzing, and unmasking the insidious social control element involved with medicalization, institutionalization, and decarceration of the elderly and in exposing who ultimately benefits from these trends. (pp. 67–68)

An important area of analysis for empowerment-oriented workers and their clients is *the effect of social gerontological theories on professional practice.* Accordingly, the interventions of professionals who subscribe to theories of aging that emphasize individual deviance should be scrutinized closely. The chance of misdiagnosis is great if sociopolitical factors are ignored in the assessment process. Pointing to the structural creation of problems, some observers suggest that poverty in old age is the primary cause of lack of stimulation, dependence, illness, inadequate health care, and an overall shrinking of opportunities. Moreover, others observe that the indignities and role deprivation suffered as soon as one retires are quite sufficient to warrant the anger, despair, and confusion that psychiatrists routinely diagnose as mental illness (see, for example, Brown, 1990; Dowd, 1980). These observations illustrate the need for careful examination of the assumptions of professionals who may have neglected social, political, and/or economic realities in their assessment process.

The emphasis on the psychological reactions of individuals to the situational problems of poverty and to their needs for health and social care resources supports an intervention model that has, at best, a helper/helpee nature. At worst, the outcome is provision of services in a reluctant manner born of the belief that the recipient should not need the service.

In summary, professional knowledge and interventions are critical factors in discouraging or fostering empowerment. Social work practice is adversely affected when it medicalizes the problems of the elderly, focuses on adjustment-oriented strategies, and/or views or assesses individual elders through the lens of social-psychological theories that emphasize deviance and place blame primarily on the individual (Estes & Binney, 1989; Kane, 1989; Relman, 1987; Rose & Black, 1985). Therefore, it is essential that empowerment-oriented practitioners be able to understand and recognize when these theories and practices are guiding the work of professionals with whom they are involved.

# EMPOWERMENT STRATEGIES AND SERVICE DELIVERY

As the preceding discussion has made clear, both the current state of social services and the traditional roles of professional knowledge and interventions present serious challenges to empowerment-oriented social workers. With respect to the empowerment-oriented goal of enabling clients to participate in the social change process, many of the strategies and activities suggested in Chapter 4 for work in the social policy arena are also applicable at the service delivery level. A corollary is that issues generated at the service delivery level often inspire activities directed at changing macro policies.

Both empowerment-oriented workers and their clients need to understand how the way services in this country are provided affects the elderly. This impact involves not only the actual receipt of the service or resource but also the social-psychological effects of the context in which it is delivered. For example, stigma attached to a particular service may cause anxiety and withdrawal from social support resources or other negative reactions, as is the case with many elderly people who are eligible for food stamps yet hesitate to use this resource because of the visibility of its use. Utilization of a service or potential resource may be low because of these kinds of reactions.

A negative attitude toward receiving assistance is not found only among seemingly independent members of society; it is often strongly ingrained in the value system of elderly people who find themselves in need of services (Binstock, 1990). Consequently, the focus of the empowerment-oriented worker is on changing not only the service delivery system, but also the beliefs and attitudes of potential consumers. In terms of empowerment-oriented strategies, the use of groups can be extremely valuable in providing the context for a consciousness-raising experience centered around clients' perceptions of their *right* to available services and resources.

As discussed earlier, the transmission of knowledge and skills to client populations constitutes another major empowerment-oriented strategy. Relevant knowledge for working with service delivery issues includes understanding the following areas:

- Local service delivery systems, or nonsystems
- Organizations and bureaucracies
- Professional helpers and service providers
- The organizational policies that guide service delivery

A closer look at each of these areas follows.

## Local Service Delivery Systems

The changing and elusive nature of health care and social service provision has been discussed above. One key strategy for empowering elders who are potential clients of such programs is transmitting to them knowledge about how to find available resources. A social worker can often find a number of directories or information hotlines with which to acquaint clients, but it is important that the worker involve the clients themselves in a mutual effort to locate key resources. A starting point for elders who wish to identify services both for themselves and for others is developing familiarity with key organizations—for example, United Way, public social service programs, Area Agencies on Aging, and large multi-purpose centers that serve as clearinghouses for information about all programs that provide services and resources for the elderly. In general, the goal of the empowerment-oriented worker is to acquaint the members of a group or individual elders with methods for finding resources.

Involving clients in the tasks of supplementing existing resource directories with updated and additional information and identifying major gaps in service provision represents another important collective educational process. Furthermore, these activities also allow for identification of key areas in which self-help efforts could supplement existing services or supplant ineffective services and toward which change efforts should be targeted. It is important to emphasize that, because of the fluid character of many resources, the search for resources constitutes an ongoing task. The overall task of acquiring expertise regarding the service delivery system can be empowering not only to group members who may need services, but to other seniors with whom group members are in contact.

## Organizations and Bureaucracies

Knowledge of organizational structure and interorganizational relationships constitutes another important strategy for facilitating empowerment at the service delivery level. Therefore, another educational task of the empowerment-oriented worker is to assist the group or individual in learning about the operation of organizations and bureaucracies. The basics of organizational theory—how organizations work and strategies for dealing with them—can be packaged for dissemination and discussion in client groups. Usually, elderly people have considerable life experience working in various levels of organizations; their experiences can be valuable in their collective effort to understand the functioning of the social welfare organizations that are impinging on their lives.

Hasenfeld (1984) provides a valuable "organizational map" that directs social workers in gathering significant information about organizations, including interorganizational relationships and the political economy of their environment. Internal features of organizations—such as structure, technology, scope, clients, and resources—are also outlined for exploration. This comprehensive framework for organizational analysis will, no doubt, be modified by empowerment groups in their attempts to understand specific organizations, but it is useful for identifying critical aspects of organizations.

Understanding the informal decision-making process in agencies, as well as the values and commitments of workers, is also valuable. As the empowerment-oriented worker and the clients study and analyze an organization in which they have an interest, they will learn how to provide relevant information to the organization that will encourage it to take immediate action on issues that concern them. Identifying key points of impact and ways in which clients can become involved in the decision-making process of the organization should be stressed throughout the process.

How-to strategies for influencing organizations and their environment are also valuable skills for late life empowerment. Advocacy is a particularly effective strategy; therefore, *the transmission of advocacy skills to client populations is critical.* Moreover, to gain efficacy in accessing services and resources, elders must learn basic advocacy skills—skills frequently taught in schools of social work. The process of teaching advocacy skills to elderly clients is discussed further in Chapter 7. The group context is an excellent setting for learning these skills and practicing them, relative to one's own needs or to those of other group members.

Other important skills that can be transmitted by the empowerment-oriented worker include:

- Strategies for locating and accessing public information about organizations
- Strategies for getting on boards and advisory committees
- Ways to be an effective board member
- Ways to develop client support groups, self-help groups, and communication networks
- Strategies for presenting concerns about organizational functioning to various levels of organizations, their boards, and funding bodies
- Ways to develop feasible alternative proposals

Several senior organizations such as OWL and the Gray Panthers make available useful training packages regarding these skill areas.

In conclusion, understanding organizations and acquiring the skills needed for influencing them are key empowerment-oriented strategies for addressing service delivery issues. The empowerment-oriented worker can offer assistance to senior groups or individuals in the form of knowledge about the nature of organizations, interorganizational relationships, basic operations, and the internal features of particular organizations and can also impart various strategies for influencing these entities.

## Professional Helpers

Another key area of activity for the empowerment-oriented practitioner is preparing clients to manage their relationships with professional helpers. A number of strategies have been developed to empower clients in their interactions with professional helpers. It is especially important that clients know their rights in order to offset the power differential that is often present in the client/professional relationship. The welfare rights movement, the women's movement, and the civil rights movement called attention to the critical importance of knowing and standing up for one's rights when dealing with oppressive and discriminating systems. Later chapters of this book that focus on specific practice settings (such as nursing homes) or resource areas (such as income or housing) will demonstrate that knowing and/or struggling to establish rights is a key component of empowerment. The empowerment-oriented worker can play a central role in educating clients or potential clients as to what their rights are in various situations that may confront them.

As suggested above, elderly clients can be given the opportunity to become familiar with the various theoretical knowledge bases, value orientations, and beliefs that underpin professional interventions. This kind of knowledge serves to demystify much of the worker's thinking and helps the client to understand interventions.

Also of great importance to clients in managing their relationships with professional helpers is the need to learn about the problem area of concern. Whether the specific problem is a medical one, a behavioral issue, or an economic one, increased knowledge on the part of the client can help to balance the worker/client relationship. Consumer rights movements and peer support groups that stress development of self-knowledge and self-care in selected arenas of physical and mental health are already organized (examples are the Alzheimer's Association and the Association of Mental Health Consumers). These organizations and movements often involve their members in decision making and political action that can influence relevant policies and programs. Identifying these programs and linking clients to them can have an empowering impact with respect to receipt of services.

Knowledge about the helping process and helpers is also valuable in overcoming the feelings of inadequacy that the worker/client relationship may instill in some clients, especially when the worker's approach is authoritarian in nature. It is interesting to note that psychotherapists who work with the elderly have found that educating clients about the therapy *process* is a necessary prerequisite to their effective participation (Knight, 1986). The use of a group context for transmitting knowledge and skills about how to relate to professionals from various disciplines is especially fruitful when some group members have had considerable experience with professionals and the agencies that employ them.

The use of social support from other group members to facilitate service for one member has been proven effective in a variety of health and mental health–related settings (Gottlieb, 1983; Whittaker & Garbarino, 1985). Regardless of the specific task of the group or the degree of structure used by workers, the common experience of group members appeared to reinforce individuals' determination as they dealt with the problems (or the professionals and systems) affecting their lives (Whittaker & Garbarino, 1985). For example, in an empowerment group composed of elders dwelling in single-room-occupancy hotels, the worker noted that members not only shared an ongoing analysis of the service delivery systems and the strategies for coping derived from their experiences, but also provided personal support to those who had failed in efforts to influence systems or professional/client relationships, which encouraged those members to persist and succeed.

In general, the empowerment-oriented worker can play a very important role in enabling elderly clients to manage their relationships with service providers by developing (1) a curriculum that describes clients' rights in the client/professional relationship, (2) a professional knowledge base and practice approaches, and (3) how-to skills regarding communication with professionals. Attention can also be given to developing clients' skills in helping each other with these interactions.

## *Organizational Policies*

Empowerment-oriented social workers often occupy administrative positions that afford them special opportunity to have an impact on organizational policies. Based on observations of the staff at Denver University's Institute of Gerontology, the following characteristics of programs or program components stand out as important to the empowerment of clients:

- Transfer of knowledge and skills useful in self-care to clients, their families, and communities
- Transfer of expertise to clients that will increase their competence in gaining needed resources from, or changes in, their environment (for example, training in how to be an advocate or a mediator, information on social and political systems, and training in methods of effective political participation)
- Use of intervention strategies that help clients understand their personal problems in a broader perspective as public issues (thinking and acting in terms of the personal as political alleviates self-blame and helps individuals understand the internalized aspects of powerlessness)
- Provision of training and motivation for clients to critically analyze their life situation and encouragement of consciousness-raising exercises and experiences
- Emphasis on cooperative and interdependent activities for accomplishment of mutual goals
- Provision of respected societal roles for elders
- Establishment of worker/client relationships that essentially represent partnerships, or are egalitarian in nature
- Enabling clients to develop or maintain personal support networks
- Enabling groups to take more active roles in decision making that affects their environment (place of residence, organizations that affect their lives, neighborhoods, communities, and country)
- Evaluation of service provision in terms of its contribution to the realization of the goals of empowerment-oriented practice (outlined in Chapter 3)

Empowerment-oriented workers can take leadership roles in the development of programs that stress these characteristics. Such program development would enable workers in agencies to provide empowering interventions as part of their daily mandate. Empowerment-oriented workers may also assume roles that allow them discretion in the hiring of staff or in the training and supervision of staff. Such roles afford the opportunity not only to question theoretical assumptions and intervention strategies that are not empowering, but also to promote alternative frameworks for practice.

## SUMMARY

The inadequacy and complexity of the health care and social services systems available to older Americans make it imperative that empowerment-oriented workers assist such clients to become knowledgeable about and skilled in accessing and advocating for change of these systems. Workers and clients must educate themselves regarding the values, practice models, and funding issues that have an impact on needed services. For example, the current domination of the medical model over social services must be understood. Empowerment-oriented practitioners must guide a process of understanding political and professional aspects of the health care, social service, and other types of organizations that affect the lives of their elderly clients.

Clients must also develop specific skills in accessing information, becoming effective on boards and advisory committees, and communicating with organizations and professionals. It is incumbent upon empowerment-oriented workers to employ a range of strategies in assisting clients to gain these skills. Small groups provide a useful format for learning and testing communication skills and other self-help strategies.

## REFERENCES

Axinn, J. (1989). Women and aging: Issues of adequacy and equity. In J. D. Garner & S. O. Mercer (Eds.), *Women as they age*. New York: Haworth Press.

Bailey, R., & Brake, M. (1976). *Radical social work*. New York: Random House.

Binstock, R. H. (1990). The politics and economics of aging and diversity. In S. A. Bass, E. A. Kutza, & F. M. Torres-Gil (Eds.), *Diversity in aging*. Glenview, IL: Scott, Foresman.

Brown, A. S. (1990). *The social processes of aging and old age*. Englewood Cliffs, NJ: Prentice-Hall.

Dowd, I. I. (1980). *Stratification among the aged.* Pacific Grove, CA: Brooks/Cole.

Estes, C. L. (1989). The future of gerontology: Golden purpose or tarnished promise. *The Connection, A*(2), p. 6.

Estes, C. L., & Binney, E. A. (1989). Biomedicalization of aging: Dangers and dilemmas. *The Gerontologist, 29*(5), pp. 583–584.

Estes, C. L., & Binney, E. A. (1991). The biomedicalization of aging: Dangers and dilemmas. In M. Minkler & C. L. Estes (Eds.), *Cultural perspectives on aging.* Farmingdale, NY: Baywood.

Estes, C. L., & Lee, P. R. (1985). Social, political, and economic background of long-term care policy. In C. Harrington, R. J. Newcomer, & C. L. Estes (Eds.), *Long-term care of the elderly.* Beverly Hills, CA: Sage Publications.

Estes, C. L., Swan, J. H., & Gerard, L. E. (1984). Dominant and competing paradigms in gerontology: Towards a political economy of aging. In M. Minkler & D. L. Estes (Eds.), *Readings in the political economy of aging.* Farmingdale, NY: Baywood.

Evans, L., & Williamson, J. B. (1984). Social control of the elderly. In M. Minkler & C. L. Estes (Eds.), *Readings in the political economy of aging.* Farmingdale, NY: Baywood.

Frank, K. P. (1979). *The anti-psychiatry bibliography* (2nd ed.). Vancouver, British Columbia: Gang Press.

Galper, J. (1975). *The politics of social services.* Englewood Cliffs, NJ: Prentice-Hall.

Galper, J. (1980). *Social work practice: A radical perspective.* Englewood Cliffs, NJ: Prentice-Hall.

Gartner, A., & Riessman, F. (1984). *The self-help revolution.* New York: Human Sciences Press.

Gottlieb, B. (1983). *Social support strategies.* Beverly Hills, CA: Sage Publications.

Hasenfeld, Y. (1984). Analyzing the human service agency. In F. M. Cox, J. L. Erdler, J. Rothman, & J. E. Tropman (Eds.), *Tactics and techniques of community practice.* Itasca, IL: F. E. Peacock.

Hewitt, P. S., & Howe, N. (1988). Generational equity and the future of generational politics. *Generations, 7*(3), pp. 10–13.

Huttman, E. D. (1985). *Social services for the elderly.* New York: Free Press.

Kahn, A. J. (1979). *Social policies and social services* (2nd ed.). New York: Random House.

Kane, R. A. (1989). The biomedical blues. *The Gerontologist, 29*(5), pp. 583–584.

Knight, B. (1986). *Psychotherapy with older adults.* Beverly Hills, CA: Sage Publications.

Kravitz, S. L., Pelaez, M. B., & Rothman, M. B. (1990). Delivering service to the elderly: Responsiveness to populations in need. In S. A. Bass, E. A. Kutza, & F. M. Torres-Gil (Eds.), *Diversity in aging.* Glenview, IL: Scott, Foresman.

Longino, C. F., Jr., & Soldo, B. J. (1987). The graying of America: Implications of life extension for quality of life. In R. A. Ward & S. S. Tonkin (Eds.), *Health in aging: Sociological issues and policy directions.* New York: Springer.

Maluccio, A. N. (Ed.). (1981). *Promoting competence in clients.* New York: Free Press.

Milwaukee County Welfare Rights Organization. (1972). *Welfare mothers speak out.* New York: W. W. Norton.

Minkler, M., & Estes, C. L. (1984). *Readings in the political economy of aging.* Farmingdale, NY: Baywood.

Monk, A. S. (1990). *Handbook of gerontological services.* New York: Van Nostrand Reinhold.

Morales, A., and Shaefor, B. (1977). *Social work: A profession of many faces.* Boston: Allyn and Bacon.

Norman, E., and Mancuso, A. (1980). *Women's issues and social work practice.* Itasca, IL: F. E. Peacock.

Relman, A. S. (1987). The new medical industrial complex. In H. Schwartz (Ed.), *Dominant issues in medical sociology.* New York: Random House.

Riessman, F. (1976). The self-help movement has arrived. *Social Policy, 6,* pp. 63–64.

Rose, S. M., & Black, B. L. (1985). *Advocacy and empowerment.* Boston: Routledge & Kegan Paul.

Solomon, B. B. (1976). *Black empowerment.* New York: Columbia University Press.

Torres-Gil, F. (1987). Aging in an ethnic society: Policy issues for aging among minority groups. In D. E. Gelford & C. M. Barresi (Eds.), *Ethnic dimensions of aging.* New York: Springer.

Waxman, H. A. (1990). The forgotten catastrophe: Financing long-term care. *Journal of Aging and Social Policy, 2*(1), pp. 11–13.

Whittaker, J. K., & Garbarino, J. (1985). *Social support networks.* New York: Aldine.

# 6 EMPOWERMENT-ORIENTED INTERVENTIONS WITH GROUPS AND INDIVIDUALS

Working with individuals and working with groups are common ways to intervene in problems of the elderly. When empowerment is a goal of social work practice, the ways in which a practitioner approaches individual and group work change. This chapter discusses how an empowerment-oriented focus changes the nature of work with groups and individuals, gives specific strategies and processes to employ in working with groups and individuals, and provides examples of empowerment-based group work and individual work.

## THE GROUP AS A MEDIUM IN EMPOWERMENT-ORIENTED PRACTICE

Many authors who write about empowerment perceive the group as a critical vehicle for facilitating the empowerment process (Cox, 1988; Gutiérrez, 1989; Kieffer, 1984; Parsons, 1988; Staples, 1987). Group work lends itself to a broad range of problem solutions. Schwartz (1974) stresses the importance of group workers assuming a holistic approach—one encompassing both private troubles and public issues—when assessing the perceived problems of clients. Mutual aid is a powerful dynamic for facilitating both self-esteem and problem resolution. The self-help and social support movements emphasize mutual helping as a powerful tool in the maintenance of mental and physical health, as well as in an individual's struggle for self-empowerment (Lee & Swenson, 1986).

Empowerment-oriented practice relies heavily on consciousness raising, for which the group process is potentially the most productive medium. Consciousness raising is a process of interaction with others. In his explication of radical practice intervention, Galper (1980) suggests that oppressed people internalize their oppression and that this internalization needs to be examined if people are to become free enough to deal with the oppressive forces. He further states:

> Some radical therapists have suggested that a group process is more valuable than one-to-one relationships in pursuing the aims of empowerment because it encourages sharing, which is crucial when people confront their sense of isolation and their responsibility for causing their own problems. (p. 146)

Other empowerment theorists see the group process as integral to allowing isolated individuals to discover that their problems are shared by many others. One frequent and important result of realizing the commonality of problems is the lessening of guilt among oppressed individuals. Blaming oneself for failures that are often beyond one's control can have a very disempowering effect on every aspect of one's life.

One-to-one interaction with a worker may be ineffective for a self-blaming client, especially if the client perceives the worker as an authority or even "the enemy"—that is, part of the oppressive environment. The sharing of experiences within a group can often produce critical insights for individuals with similar problems much more quickly than one-to-one interactions can, especially when an individual shares a problem that others are experiencing but denying.

A group provides a milieu in which the individual members can demonstrate that they and others who share their life status are able to achieve successes essentially without outside help. For example, when the entire group is engaged in finding resources, the group members learn not only about the availability of resources, but also about the process of finding and accessing those resources. Members also experience self-initiated problem definition and problem solving.

## Group Processes for Empowerment

There are a number of processes of empowerment-oriented groups that must be promoted by the social worker or by leaders within the group. These include:

1.  *Identifying and sharing common problems, needs, and goals.* Members often see themselves and their concerns as unique. Discovering that their problems are more common than unique tends to build group identity.

2.  *Exploiting the group's collective intelligence through sharing of facts, experiential knowledge, and ways of coping.* Members discover that they possess a wealth of resources and knowledge that can be shared.

3.  *Providing mutual support and assistance.* Mutual support, as opposed to helper/helpee relationships, is facilitated by group work. Workers can model and participate in mutuality both by

sharing resources and by expressing needs for more information.

4. *Participating in consciousness-raising experiences regarding the personal and political dimensions of the issues being considered.* Understanding the interconnection of the personal and the political helps the group better perceive their mutuality.

5. *Facilitating the egalitarian relationship sought by empowerment-oriented workers.* When group members share common concerns, perhaps have common backgrounds, and are involved together in an effort to bring about change, workers more easily become mutual participants.

6. *Encouraging participants to believe in their own abilities.* Yalom (1975, p. 81) speaks of the "installation of hope" as an important strength of the group process, allowing members' confidence in their own abilities to be increased.

7. *Trying out new behaviors with the support of others and sharing the success of new behaviors.* When members feel safe in a group, they will risk adopting new behaviors both inside and outside the group.

8. *Supporting and practicing proposed activities such as confrontations with medical providers or family members.* Again, a cohesive group provides safe surroundings in which to practice behaviors needed for outside problem solving.

9. *Providing ongoing personal support and a network for collective political action.* Mutual assessment of outcomes, mutual support in the event of negative outcomes, and mutual decision making about new strategies provide the necessary support for further action.

10. *Accomplishing goals as a group that cannot be accomplished by individuals alone.* Such goals may include resolving landlord/tenant disputes, combatting neighborhood crime, obtaining a change in procedures for service delivery, or initiating a new bus stop.

11. *Opening up topics previously thought of as taboo.* Safe groups tend to encourage members to share taboo topics, such as abuse by a family member and fear of dying, which often results in the group members' discovering additional commonality.

12. *Engaging in social action activities.* Such activities might include rent strikes, petition-signing campaigns, and participation in coalitions, which increase group cohesion.

Overall, the group format allows empowerment-oriented workers to facilitate discussion and activity among elderly participants on common

***Group power is the combined strength of committed
individuals.*** *(Photo © Bill Aron/Photo Edit)*

problems, individual attitudes and beliefs, and political issues. Empowerment-oriented groups often have multiple foci; that is, they deal concur-
rently with all dimensions of an issue. A group may have health care
education as its primary focus, for example, but individual members may
introduce problems they have in securing benefits or communicating with
medical provider systems. These concerns can lead to individual or collective action. The group not only serves as a vehicle for education, but
also provides support to members for engaging in personal or social
action.

Empowerment-oriented groups for the elderly often serve as personal support networks for members who are otherwise isolated. Isolated
elders often believe that they do not have anything in common with other
older people, that their problems are unique. Once group members begin
to appreciate the commonality of their concerns, they often change their
minds about their lack of similarity to others. This is an important step
in the empowerment process.

In order for the empowerment process to be facilitated, the group
has to be led in a way that promotes interaction, sharing, and learning.
This type of leadership means that the worker has to let go of the expert
role and take a more facilitative role. In this role the worker facilitates
problem exploration and definition, goal setting, and action among the
members.

## CASE EXAMPLE: Empowerment-Oriented Work with Groups

In a project targeted at hard-to-reach elders in a metropolitan downtown area, graduate students were trained to create empowerment-oriented groups in residential hotels, apartment buildings, and senior high-rise buildings. The project, sponsored by the local mental health center, the state department of mental health, and the University of Denver Institute of Gerontology, was designed to reach elderly citizens who had "fallen through the cracks" of the service delivery system and who were in need of basic survival skills and mental health services. The goal of the project was to reach these isolated elders through the use of groups in order to connect them with needed services.

The project involved a professional team from the mental health center, composed of a social worker and a nurse, and an outreach team made up of social work graduate students supervised by their professors. The outreach team went into downtown hotels and apartment buildings to establish empowerment groups among the elderly residents. The first task of the outreach team was to gain the permission and cooperation of the housing managers so that the team members would have access to the buildings and the residents in them.

Once access was obtained, the outreach team contacted the elderly residents to inform them about the groups and what they might expect from them and to assess their interest in such groups. The team explained that the groups would be established for the purpose of determining the needs of the residents and generating group solutions for ways to meet those needs. At first, many residents were reluctant to admit that they had any problems or difficulties or, for that matter, anything in common with the other residents. A frequently heard comment was something like "other people here seem to need such a group, but I don't—I get along just fine." The outreach team spent ample time getting to know the residents individually and gaining their trust, as well as that of the management. Team members assessed the needs of the residents by talking to everyone in the buildings. Eventually a time and place were set for weekly meetings. The groups were led by students on the outreach team.

After the initial organizing meetings, outreach workers determined the kinds of information and resources the residents as a whole seemed to need in order to cope with their situations. A curriculum was developed that could be used in each group to educate the residents with respect to normal aging processes, aging issues, and available resources. (Description of this curriculum can be found in Chapter 7, where this type of educational intervention is described in more detail.) The curriculum was used when deemed appropriate for each group. Each group lasted approximately three years, during which time there were some changes in leadership among the students on the outreach team. Below is an account of the activities of one of the empowerment groups during a year in which the group was involved in relocation as a result of the demolition of their hotel to make way for a new convention center.

*The Ford/Montgomery Group*　This group was called Ford/Montgomery because it began in the Ford Hotel and later moved to the Montgomery Hotel, where most of its members had been relocated. The original group consisted primarily of 16 members, all elderly individuals who had long histories of mental illness and/or alcoholism and who had for the most part been longtime residents of the Ford Hotel. When the group was first organized in October, the common problem concentrated on by the members was the lack of safety in their own building; they brought up issues such as locks and security procedures. The worker and the group members collaborated with hotel management to improve building security, and some satisfactory changes were brought about.

Plans for the construction of a new convention center in central downtown, however, seemed likely to doom the hotel to destruction. Most of the year's activity focused on the traumatic nature of this event; it provided a crisis around which the group could rally and organize. The worker served as facilitator, advocate, educator, and partner during that year of decision making and coping. The worker also provided intensive crisis-oriented casework for individual residents.

*Pre-move Group Activities*　Once it was confirmed that eventual destruction of their hotel was a certainty, the group's behavior centered around dealing with the issue of a forced move. In early-January meetings, discussion focused on rumors that the Ford's owners might buy a motel outside the downtown area, the pros and cons of living in the downtown area, and the relative value of moving together as a group. During mid-January meetings, members talked about their past experiences in housing, what they wanted from new apartments, and what area of the city they wanted to live in.

Because pressure was brought to bear on city officials to assist the residents with moving costs, many city representatives became involved in the lives of the residents. A late-January meeting involved a trip to look at alternative housing and a discussion of eligibility, resources, and potential actions. The rules, regulations, and structure of the alternative housing facilities were seen as a barrier by several group members. City officials came into the hotel to interview elders about their needs. Rumors concerning resources that might possibly be provided for the move and how they could be obtained were rampant.

The intensity of the crisis provoked emotional responses in the elderly group members. Many of them felt angry and powerless in the wake of this invasion of strangers and the lack of dependable information about alternatives. The anger and anxiety provided some of the impetus needed to motivate speakers from the group to attend a city council meeting, where testimony was to be heard regarding selection of a site for the new convention center. Three group members volunteered to speak, and other members helped them put together the relevant information and outline the points to make with respect to the group members' plight. Most of the group attended the council meeting, even though only two members were allowed to speak. Speaking before city council proved to be a significant educational experience. Time limitations due to a crowded agenda and a large number of speakers on other topics prevented council members from focusing on the relocation issue. Group members found the experience somewhat discouraging but a valuable lesson in social action. Group members' testimony, however, did lend support to the city's plans to appropriate funds for relocation assistance.

The group format allowed both the members and the worker to deal with the relocation task itself and the emotional aspects of the crisis. Late-January and early-February meetings provided a forum for the discussion of financial aspects of the move and the process required to obtain the resources appropriated by the city to assist the group members. The worker brought in outside resource people to explain how to access the city's moving reimbursement funds. The members all agreed to take charge of planning their own moves and to assist others in making decisions about their moves. Individual members had personal crisis periods, and the worker often provided one-to-one support and advocacy between meetings; group members helped each other whenever possible. One member was placed on a 72-hour mental health hold. This situation was central to the mid-February meeting, when a discussion arose about how to handle the high stress of the move and how to help each other get through the crisis.

Members expressed feelings of severe loss; some cried and talked of other losses in their life and how they had coped with them. Mutual support was encouraged and was forthcoming.

As the moving date approached, group activity further intensified. The last meeting in February was again used for emotional support. Members expressed their anger, loss, and sadness and comforted each other. An early-March meeting focused on accessing resources for the move and planning the details of the move. A city social service representative attended the meeting to act as liaison and set up moving times for members. The group members met again on moving day in mid-March to help each other with final packing tasks and provide mutual support during the evacuation. Individual dilemmas were debated, and emotional frustrations were vented. Nine of the Ford group moved to the Montgomery Hotel, only a few blocks away; others located nearby. A few moved greater distances away, and some residents disappeared.

*Post-move Activities*    The next phase of group life involved reorganization following the crisis of the move. The late-March meeting at the Montgomery was a lively celebration for those who had moved there and to locations nearby. The next two meetings were spent helping members obtain their relocation monies and organizing an attempt to locate other former Ford residents, which included trips to other hotels. Group members initiated an aggressive effort to find and communicate with everyone who had moved to see whether they had received all of their entitlements and whether their moves were satisfactory. Also on the group's agenda was getting acquainted with the new neighborhood. Members created a map as they took walking tours and filled in pertinent information about shops, grocery stores, and convenience stores. April activities of the group included knocking on doors in the Montgomery Hotel to invite new people to the group. This period was also a time of reflection for all group members.

With the moving crisis over, the group turned its attention to more general concerns of the members. In May a number of educational topics from the empowerment curriculum were chosen by the group. One important topic was the significance of work in American society and the effects of unemployment. The group expressed feelings of rejection related to their not working; they felt as if they were being discriminated against. Members generally focused the discussions on their personal experiences, and they continued to help each other get settled in. Once the intense group interaction surrounding the move subsided, members began to distance themselves somewhat from the group; they began to note differences among group members' wants and needs. Many of the members were very frail or had hearing problems or decreased mobility. Others had serious alcohol problems. Attendance and participation fell off.

The new location changed the nature of the group. Members had a different attitude about the manager at the Montgomery, who was somewhat less supportive of the group than the Ford's manager had been. The viability of the group was temporarily in jeopardy. The moving process had included many educational experiences and social change actions. Members had become educated regarding their rights and the laws and policies relevant to their lives; they had testified at the city council meeting. As they became aware of their rights as tenants, they began as a group to ask the hotel manager to respond to their needs. The cohesion built by the activities involved in the move provided strength for the group to pull together again and act as a whole. Members adopted new attitudes toward management and toward themselves as tenants.

During June, July, and August, the group focused on educating themselves. The members examined health care issues, discrimination against the mentally ill, their rights as mental patients, and legal aid. Meetings continued to provide mutual support and a forum for the expression of feelings and for solving individual problems. Training activities to develop individual skills were conducted.

Meetings held during September, October, and November continued discussions of topics in the educational curriculum, including how to deal with the health care system and an update on retirement entitlements. Friendship was identified by the group as an important concern and became the topic of a lively discussion. As fall reached an end, members dealt with holiday issues, discussing the "low" of holidays and planning activities to help each other through the period. At the end of December, the members evaluated the group process and began to plan for future activity.

*An Individual Member's Participation in the Group*   The growth and development of the Ford/Montgomery group was an ongoing process. Although individual participation varied, the group was a viable means for initiating and sustaining the empowerment process within its members. Mr. C. is one example.

Mr. C. was a divorced male in his late sixties. He was a veteran of World War II and had spent much time in a POW camp in the Philippines. According to Mr. C., he had had difficulty most of his life "fitting into" regular society. He had been married three times and had spent a good portion of his life driving trucks. He admitted to having difficulty at times controlling his alcohol intake. As an original member of the group at the Ford Hotel, Mr. C. had the opportunity to participate before the relocation crisis began. When the relocation was announced, he began to drink more heavily and had frequent outbursts of anger during meetings. At this time, he was told he could not come to the meetings if he had been drinking.

The crisis of relocation along with his relative noninvolvement with the group may have driven Mr. C. away. In early February, without speaking to anyone, he checked out of the Ford Hotel. The worker's subsequent contacts with him were mostly limited to finding him about once a week on the street, in meal lines, or at the senior center, usually intoxicated. His physical state appeared to deteriorate rapidly during this time. The group was meeting at a neighborhood restaurant at that time, and Mr. C. made a point of walking by the group each Thursday morning, usually refusing to join it. When he did join, he resisted discussing his rights to financial remuneration for the relocation and would leave midway through the meeting, very angry.

Mr. C. did not move with the group but later rejoined it. In March the majority of the group relocated to the Montgomery Hotel. Mr. C. had moved to another hotel six blocks away. Group members found Mr. C. and invited him to a meeting at a member's apartment in the Montgomery. Mr. C. started coming each week, and gradually he began to ask for assistance. With help from group members, he received the reimbursement due him from the city. In the spring he found a small basement apartment on his own. He gained more and more control over his drinking. The group started meeting at his apartment every two weeks, at his invitation. Mr. C. began to take an active role in the group, giving genuine support to others and at times accepting support.

The group proved to be a valuable asset to Mr. C. In the fall he became quite ill with a respiratory infection. He had difficulty obtaining medical assistance, but together the group built a support network to get him to the doctor and help him recover. At Christmas, in a conversation over dinner, Mr. C. told the group that the one thing he could point to that got him through the last year was the group, and he thanked them all. He remained a vital part of the empowerment group.

*Summary of the Group's Accomplishments* During the year, the group provided important survival information for members and significant emotional support during the transitions imposed on them; it was also a source of personal and political growth. The worker encouraged members to use the group for support and knowledge exchange and as a medium for giving and receiving valuable assistance. The group acted as mediator between the individual members and the various environmental systems that impinged on them, such as the bureaucratic systems involved in the relocation. The city offered a number of choices regarding the move, none of which were appropriate for the needs and life-style of the group members. The group legitimized members' real needs and their right to strive for an acceptable alternative. Even though their efforts brought minimal success in some instances, the support of the group appeared to help individual members avoid the negative consequences of the relocation suffered by some of their nonmember counterparts.

The outreach worker's role in the empowerment process was a critical one. The worker acted as facilitator, counselor, partner in activities, advocate, educator, and liaison, as well as someone members could rely on during very turbulent times for the Ford/Montgomery group. The worker's focus was on encouraging group members and helping them to take charge of their own meetings, curriculum content, and activities. The worker was the motivator in the group's search for outside assistance and contributed knowledge regarding resources and services to the pool of information. The worker encouraged members to document sources of aid and information and share them with other group members and Montgomery residents who were not group members.

This empowerment group focused on the social, environmental, and personal aspects of the problems experienced by these elders. Although the group was not originally presented as a way to handle emotions and fears of aging and helplessness, as the members addressed their common problems, these personal dimensions were central to the group process. The group provided opportunities for work in all four dimensions of the empowerment-oriented model presented in Chapter 3, from initial assessment and linkage with resources to education regarding one's own circumstances, mutual aid, and organizing for social action. The Ford/Montgomery group organized in order to force the service delivery system to become more responsive. The members spoke to representatives from agencies and helped to educate students in social work about themselves and their needs. They organized testimony at the city council in an effort to halt the demolition of their building. Even though they were unable to accomplish that goal, they did have an impact on the city's decision to provide relocation assistance and reimbursement. The group provided a forum for recognizing the personal-as-political aspect of common problems and issues.

# EMPOWERMENT-ORIENTED STRATEGIES WITH INDIVIDUALS

This section discusses empowerment-oriented work with individuals and the strategies and skills that contribute to this approach. Perhaps there is some degree of paradox in applying to a one-to-one relationship a model based on mutuality, linking, networking, collectivity, peer aid, and the self-help strategies associated with the group process; however, even though most of these strategies are best applied in a group setting, not all elderly people who are in need of help can or will participate in a group. Many are socialized to "go it alone" and are not comfortable sharing their concerns, or particularly their frailties, with others. To do so may represent a loss of face and be perceived as a loss of independence. Moreover, many elders are too frail and physically incapacitated to go out to group activities. In such cases the task of the worker is to bring empowerment-oriented principles to the one-to-one situation. How can the empowerment-oriented model be applied to the helping format most common in human services with elderly clients—individual work?

## Principle Differences in Work with Individuals from an Empowerment Orientation

The employment of an empowerment-oriented approach in work with an elderly individual calls into question some of the traditional frames of reference for such work. Social work gerontological services are predominantly organized around one-to-one service structures, which can be found in home health care, hospital-based social work, nursing home social work, other community-based health care facilities, and even senior centers. Social work intervention via such structures is designed to help clients cope with their individual problems. An assumption often present is that problems are found in individuals, and that individuals therefore have to figure out how to resolve their own problems. This paradigm of helping comes from a medical perspective; that is, aging is viewed as medical dysfunction instead of as a normal developmental process, and problem solutions are viewed from a narrow medical model.

Empowerment-oriented practice with individual elders utilizes several nonmedical premises about aging and differs from the traditional approach in several ways.

**1.** *Problems are identified by the elder.* The initial identification of problems by elders themselves, not by the expert worker (Akins, 1985), is the first step in empowerment-oriented one-to-one work. As gerontology has become an increasingly popular field, many professional helpers have sought to become "aging experts." Although it is helpful to know as much about the aging process as possible, the assumption of the expert role by the worker does not adequately utilize clients' expertise concerning their own situations. In the empowerment orientation, expertise is shared by the worker and the client. Workers may offer what they know, have observed, or have been taught, but the final expert on any client's condition is the client.

**2.** *Elders' problems belong to immediate environmental systems.* Traditional approaches to one-to-one work with elderly people view the helping process as a narrow dyad involving elder and professional helper. The empowerment process builds upon existing resources, of both the client and the family and community, and mobilizes the elder to meet expressed needs. This approach emphasizes the social-environmental context of problems and solutions and thus tends to put the resolution of problems in a much larger arena than many traditional approaches do.

**3.** *The worker does not control the helping process.* The professional must relinquish control of the process and of the outcome of the intervention. All actions must be measured against the degree to which they provide the older adult with the opportunity to act on his or her own behalf. Workers must avoid "doing for" and "doing to" and learn to take cues from their elderly clients, listening to their definitions of their needs and serving as collaborators who help them link with others and with resources. The professional becomes the elderly client's partner, blending his or her professional knowledge with the client's wisdom, experience, self-knowledge, and insight.

**4.** *The worker assists the elder to take a broader view of his or her problem.* When a social worker meets with an elderly person in order to resolve a specific problem, the context of discussion is usually how the worker's agency defines its role and the presenting problem. Although it is very tempting to confine the helping process to these narrow parameters, empowerment-oriented practice calls for the worker to help broaden the elder client's perception and consciousness of the problem, to help the elder see the problem in a larger context. For example, clients who are depressed because of multiple losses and failing health would readily learn from a group of peers that their condition is common to quite a few others. Without benefit of that group setting, however, the empowerment-oriented worker must nevertheless bring that collective experience of being "in the same boat" to the individual elderly client. (Strategies for doing this are discussed in the next section.)

## *Specific Strategies for Empowerment-Oriented One-to-One Work*

Some strategies used in empowerment-oriented one-to-one work with the elderly are the same as those used in any other approach, and some are different. The following strategies have been employed successfully in empowerment-oriented work with individuals:

**1.** *Listening to the elderly person and thus helping him or her cope with the current situation.* Reminiscence and life review are common interventive techniques. Workers encourage clients to reflect on their lives, to remember and reconstruct other losses, depressions, or times of crisis and how they coped with them. Empowerment-oriented practice does not ignore the emotional or intrapsychic aspects of a problem. Elders must be listened to, validated, and helped to cope with their own issues in their own unique ways. Engaging and drawing out the emotions of elderly clients and helping them frame their situations in view of past experiences and events are effective listening techniques.

**2.** *Identifying skills for coping and for initiating change.* Elderly clients have many skills they can teach one another about coping with adversity. The worker might encourage elders to learn from other elders, as well as to provide teaching materials for others. Ways of doing this include encouraging clients to write or tell their life stories and articulate what they can tell others in similar situations about coping and making changes in the face of adversity.

**3.** *Bringing videotapes of groups of older people who are coping with and/or changing conditions similar to those of the client.* Videos of peers discussing how to cope with aging and what one can expect from the aging process are effective educational tools; they help to broaden the elder client's perspective of the problem. Such material may reduce the individual elder's perception of being alone in a situation.

**4.** *Bringing in newsletters or stories.* Newsletters and articles from newspapers and magazines providing, for example, information from a group of elderly people who have initiated service projects to others as a way to cope with loss or discussions of political issues of special relevance to elders demonstrate a sense of commonality.

**5.** *Providing links with others.* Older people in similar circumstances can provide mutual support and education through telephoning, letter writing, or newsletters. Clients in the most isolated of circumstances can benefit from links to others.

**6.** *Encouraging the client to contribute to others.* Lending a hand to others or participating, even in some small way, may create a feeling of productivity in elderly clients. Taping the reading of a book for children, providing reassurance by telephone to another elder, writing letters to or calling legislators or agency personnel to express opinions— all such activities make the client feel useful and contributory. In addition, some activities can enable the elder to better understand her or his problem and get a sense of the interpersonal and political nature of the situation.

***Individual spirit and talent are enhanced through participation.*** *(Photo © Paul Conklin/Photo Edit)*

# CASE EXAMPLE: One-to-One Empowerment-
                     Oriented Work

Mrs. S., in her eighties, didn't like to go out because she was prac-
tically immobilized by hip fractures. She was visited by the social
worker from the local senior center. All attempts to get Mrs. S. to come
to the center failed. She told the worker, "I like to talk to people and
I like to help others, but I just can't go out without a lot of trouble
and pain, and I don't want to be bothered to go out unless I have
to." The worker then asked Mrs. S. what kind of volunteer work she
could do at home. Mrs. S. took a long list of elderly people who were
shut-ins and began to call them on a weekly basis. She later was
able to get some of those on the list to call others in turn; that is,
she established her own telephone reassurance program from the
list given to her. Volunteer callers reported to her. In cooperation with
the senior center, Mrs. S. received referrals from callers and from
those being called. Because of her contacts, she began to go to the
senior center on the days she had doctor appointments to see some
of the staff and seniors she'd talked to on the phone.

Mr. D. lived alone and refused to come to any group activities, but he
had a keen interest in following the activities of the state legislature,
particularly regarding laws and bills relevant to the retired population.
The senior resource center worker asked him to follow legislation in
both the state and the federal legislature and to write down an account
of the progress of certain bills. She took Mr. D.'s research and printed
it in the resource center newsletter. He was so delighted to see his
research in print that he expanded the scope of his coverage.

Mrs. T., who was getting frail, had been married for a long time to
a verbally abusive man. He had begun to take many medicines, along
with alcohol, and was becoming more and more abusive to her. The
social worker helped Mrs. T. to assess her life, her options, the meaning of her current situation to her, and how she had coped in the past
with her situation and to weigh her alternatives. Because Mrs. T. was
not interested in going out to attend groups or other activities at the
senior center, the worker provided her with videotapes and reading
material about elder abuse, alternatives, and resources, and numbers
to call if she was in crisis. Through this information, Mrs. T. was linked
with other women in her situation, and they began a telephone support system, which helped Mrs. T. understand the problem she was
experiencing. In addition, the system enabled her to seek support
from and give support to others in her situation. She became less
depressed, began to blame herself less for the situation she was in,
and had less of a sense of powerlessness over circumstances.

Mr. G., who was retired from the military, was grieving the recent loss of his spouse and had begun to drink heavily, a coping response he had used in the past to deal with pain. The worker helped him identify the loss and grief issues, informed him about the grieving process, and discussed with him what his options were. Not wanting to join a group, Mr. G. agreed to begin writing down his feelings about the loss of his wife so others could benefit from his experience. He was encouraged to keep a journal. His job in the military had been to write a newsletter; with additional encouragement he began a newsletter for the agency on dealing with grief issues. Mr. G. communicated with the agency staff and, eventually, other elderly clients of the agency to obtain stories about loss, grief, and coping. He was able to curtail his drinking, and he told the worker that he felt useful for the first time since his wife had died.

## *Summary of Empowerment Principles in Individual Work with Elders*

In the case examples above, the workers were able to facilitate and encourage problem understanding, coping, and solving along the four dimensions of the empowerment-oriented practice model. The strategies included personal help, education about one's situation, mutual aid, and organized help for others. Older clients who initially saw their problems as personal, unique to them, and theirs alone to resolve were able to expand their vision and understanding to a broader view that encompassed others like them. Eventually, these clients were able to reach out to others and contribute to a common goal. Inevitably, mutual aid efforts resulted in increased strength and self-esteem. Individual work includes attention to the personal and political aspects of identified problems.

## *SUMMARY*

Empowerment-oriented practice utilizes the principles of self-help and mutual aid no matter what the level or medium of intervention. Clients are seen as competent potential helpers with their own strengths and expertise regarding their problems. Consciousness raising is a necessary component of empowerment. The traditional helping principles of "doing for" are called into question, and the worker must learn to share expertise and to facilitate the problem-solving abilities of elderly clients, whether through the group process or through one-to-one work.

Empowerment-oriented group work calls for the worker to identify common problems and goals, tap collective intelligence and contributions, promote mutual support, and facilitate consciousness raising and egalitarian relationships. Groups can provide an environment in which participants come to believe in their own abilities, try out new behaviors, provide mutual support, discuss taboo topics, and set and accomplish common goals.

Empowerment-oriented individual work includes encouraging identification of the problem by the elder, connecting the problem to the environment, sharing control of the helping process, and expanding the elder's view of his or her problems.

# *REFERENCES*

Akins, T. E. (1985). Empowerment: Fostering independence of the older adult. *Aging Network News, 2*(5), pp. 1–10.

Cox, E. O. (1988). Empowerment of low-income elderly through group work. *Social Work with Groups, 11*(4), pp. 111–125.

Galper, J. (1980). *Social work practice: A radical perspective* (2nd ed.). Englewood Cliffs, NJ: Prentice-Hall.

Gutiérrez, L. (1989). Empowerment in social work practice: Considerations for practice and education. Paper presented at the Council on Social Work Education, Chicago.

Kieffer, C. (1984). Citizen empowerment: A developmental perspective. *Prevention in Human Services, 3*(Winter/Spring), pp. 9–36.

Lee, J. A., & Swenson, C. R. (1986). The concept of mutual aid. In A. Gitterman & L. Shulman (Eds.), *Mutual aid groups and the life cycle.* Itasca, IL: F. E. Peacock.

Parsons, R. J. (1988). Empowerment for role alternatives for low income minority girls: A group work approach. *Social Work with Groups 11*(3/4), pp. 27–45.

Schwartz, W. (1974). Private troubles and public issues: One social work job or two? In R. Klenk & R. Ryan (Eds.), *The practice of social work* (2nd ed.). Belmont, CA: Wadsworth.

Staples, L. (1987). *Powerful ideas about empowerment.* Unpublished manuscript.

Yalom, I. (1975). *The theory and practice of group psychotherapy* (2nd ed.). New York: Basic Books.

# Three

## EMPOWERMENT-ORIENTED INTERVENTIONS: SELECTED PRACTICE EXAMPLES

# INCREASING KNOWLEDGE AND SKILLS FOR LATE LIFE SURVIVAL

Late life presents all people with new challenges, new experiences of the aging process, new utilization of service delivery systems, and new problems to solve. Conveying knowledge and skills for problem solving is one of the key components of empowerment-oriented practice. This chapter briefly examines educational needs arising from situations and experiences in late life that require new problem-solving strategies and describes the general educational needs of the elderly, as cited in the literature. Education for empowerment is then discussed in terms of phases of learning as well as program design. Finally, skill-based programs that have been successfully implemented are presented. The specific programs that have been included address late life survival skills, peer counseling, effective personal communication, conflict resolution, and advocacy.

## *EDUCATIONAL NEEDS FOR LATE LIFE SURVIVAL*

As the discussion in Chapters 1 and 2 suggested, there is enormous diversity among the elderly in reactions to adversity, coping strengths, and resources. However, there are clearly late life challenges that face all elders. These challenges are generated by an increased state of dependence based on the aging process, health problems, loss of significant others, financial readjustments, and an increased reliance on both informal and formal support systems.

### *New Challenges and Situations*

Independence is a highly valued state in our society. Circumstances encountered in late life call upon the elderly to acquire new knowledge and skills for coping with a less independent life-style. Some of the new challenges and situations that require late life learning are as follows:

- *Late life developmental changes* are common to all elders and can be frightening or depressing if they are mysterious or thought to be unique instead of normative parts of the aging process.

- *Increased reliance on informal support systems* (such as family, friends, and neighbors) for help may require elders to adjust their attitudes toward receiving help, to learn to ask for help, and to communicate their needs to others more clearly and effectively.

- *Increased need to provide help and support to other elders who are friends, family, or neighbors* also may call for increased levels of communication and problem-solving skills. Because elderly people may have been socialized to avoid conflict or differences, they may pull away from interactions with their support systems or with those they are attempting to help, rather than trying to work out differences.

- *Increased need to utilize formal helping systems,* particularly for health care, may give rise to conflicts with service providers and create a need for more information about, as well as skills in dealing with, the service delivery system.

- *The need and the desire to continue to make a contribution to society* may compel elders to acquire knowledge and skills in new areas in order to provide a service to others. Elders' desire and capacity for continued productivity, though varying widely, are well established. (See, for example, Herzog & House, 1991; Simonton, 1991.)

- *Identification of issues and concerns common to other people* creates new challenges in learning to work with others for mutual benefit.

## General Educational Needs: A Schema

The need for educational interventions with the elderly is a common theme in the literature on aging (Lowy & O'Connor, 1986; Pifer & Bronte, 1986). McClusky (1973), in his report for the Technical Committee on Education of the 1971 White House Conference on Aging, developed an educational needs schema for older adults that includes coping, contributory, influencing, and expressive and contemplative needs, as well as the need to transcend. Lowy (1988), elaborating on McClusky's schema, suggests that each category of need can be more completely described as detailed in Table 7.1.

## Table 7.1  Educational Needs Schema for Older Adults

| Need Category | Description |
|---|---|
| 1. Coping needs | How to manage:<br>• Daily tasks of living<br>• Health care<br>• Nutrition<br>• Income maintenance and management |
| 2. Contributory needs | How to further the general well-being by performing services including:<br>• Work in public and private service organizations<br>• Participating in legislative affairs<br>• Teaching in schools |
| 3. Influencing needs | How to exert some control over the world in which one lives by:<br>• Joining with others to bring about change<br>• Speaking, talking, and giving opinions about matters of concern |
| 4. Expressive and contemplative needs | How to engage in activities for the pure joy of learning:<br>• Learning new arts and crafts skills<br>• Learning new languages or dances<br>• Studying topics of longstanding interest such as history, religion, and mysticism |
| 5. The need to transcend | How to transcend the physical experience and to reach a higher, spiritual level of understanding |

From "Human-Services Professionals: Their Role in Education for Older People" by L. Lowy, in *Generations, 12*(2), 1987, pp. 33–34. Copyright © 1987 by the American Society on Aging.

In the empowerment process, the transfer of knowledge and skills encompasses the coping, contributory, and influencing needs of the schema. Lowy (1987) emphasizes that social workers must promote need-based learning as an integral part of social services. This empowerment-oriented perspective on working with elders promotes the utilization of their capacities, not only for the sake of their physical and mental health, but also for their own general betterment and that of others.

## EDUCATION FOR EMPOWERMENT

On an educational dimension, the process of empowerment involves discovering how one's own personal resources can be channeled and then pooled with those of others in order to create desired changes. The role of educator and trainer is suggested as central to the responsibilities of the empowerment-oriented practitioner (Gutiérrez, 1990; Solomon, 1976). According to Solomon, "it is the failure of the individual to learn the cognitive, interpersonal, and technical skills in the ordinary course of events that increases dramatically the probability that the professional change experience will be necessary" (p. 350). She suggests that a primary role of the social worker is that of teacher or trainer in a relationship in which basic skills for survival are taught and learned. Moreover, Solomon explains that the best help a client can receive is help to attain a useful and contributory role. Applying Reissman's (1965) helper therapy principle, Solomon suggests the need for more lay helpers. According to the helper therapy principle, people with a problem help other people who have the same problem in a more severe form. The helper usually gains more than the helpee through the process of learning and applying new knowledge, but both gain from the empowerment-oriented approach to a problem situation. Clearly, knowledge and skills may be shared not only between worker and clients, but also among clients and others like themselves. The last section of this chapter details programs through which knowledge and skills can be transferred to the elderly so that they may become helpers, teachers, and trainers themselves, as is implied by Reissman (1965).

### Phases of Learning

Self-help is a necessary part of the empowerment process according to Zimmer (1988). In her work with self-help groups at the Brookdale Aging Center, she identified the following three phases of learning associated with self-help:

Phase 1—Educational and skills training. Cognitive learning takes place as group members come for specific information about and instruction in dealing with the issues of late life.

Phase 2—Mutual aid and/or peer support. Experiential learning is employed to enhance understanding of the commonality of problems, the bonding of the group, and the movement from airing of stress toward reality testing and changing of behavior. Learning via mutual aid and/or peer support reflects Reissman's helper therapy principle, as group members receive help and in turn become helpful to others like themselves.

*Phase 3—Social action and advocacy.* This phase of learning involves group solidarity as a basis for action directed toward social change, however, not exclusively; several types of learning take place. For example, there may be a need for further cognitive skills as well as for experiential sharing and mutual aid.*

All three of these phases of learning occur during the empowerment process, but they need not take place in any particular order and may in fact occur simultaneously. These phases are congruent with the dimensions of problem definition and focus of intervention, which were presented in the empowerment-oriented practice model in Chapter 3.

In summary, late life survival education and education regarding specific problems or conditions are necessary in order for elders to feel empowered. A self-help group or networking experience through which elders' experiences are validated as they learn from others with common concerns and problems is also necessary. Ultimately, empowerment necessitates joining with others—through either coalitions or networks—to make changes in the environment on behalf of oneself and others. As an ongoing strategy, learning opportunities offer the potential to increase elders' sense of personal control and mastery over life, which is central to empowerment.

## Designing Empowerment-Oriented Programs

Adherence to the goals of empowerment calls into question not only traditional means of service, but also the traditional development of educational programs and presentation of content. Gutiérrez (1988) finds support in the literature for the idea that when teaching skills for empowerment, workers should take on the role of consultant or facilitator rather than that of instructor, so as not to replicate the power relationships that worker and client are attempting to overcome. This suggested style of teaching is congruent with the learning strategy most preferred by older people.

Lowy and O'Connor (1986) quote Rappaport when he warns against "policy which limits us to programs we design, operate, or package for social agencies to use on people" (p. 164). These authors also suggest that if education is to serve as a tool of empowerment, educators "must develop procedures which provide for maximum participation of older

*From "Self-Help Groups and Late-Life Learning" by A. H. Zimmer, in *Generations, 12*(2), 1987, p. 21. Copyright © 1987 by the American Society on Aging.

adults in the planning, development, execution, and evaluation of educational programs in which they participate" (p. 165). This means that older people must be given the opportunity to design their own learning experiences, rather than being expected to respond to educational programs already set up by agencies. At the least they should be given a chance to have input regarding desired content and the manner in which that content is presented. Because the elderly bring lifelong experiences into their late life years, they possess many skills that can be repackaged and rechanneled into new learning. Programs that encompass the concept of empowerment—such as the Institute for Retired Professionals, developed by the New School for Social Research in New York City—utilize their elderly participants as both students and teachers (Lowy & O'Connor, 1986).

In short, the principles that instructors should be facilitators and students should be teachers and that learners should have maximum participation are crucial to empowerment. Such principles have been applied in the creation of the programs discussed in the remainder of this chapter. These programs were designed to enable elders to develop expertise and become involved as helpers—to use Reissman's (1965) term—in empowerment-oriented practice.

## EXAMPLES OF EMPOWERMENT-ORIENTED EDUCATIONAL PROGRAMS

The following programs, which have education as a key component, have been demonstrated by social work professors and their students. Described in terms of need, content, and objectives and illustrated by specific case examples, these empowerment-oriented programs facilitate the role of student as teacher, encourage maximum participation, and apply the helper therapy principle.

### Late Life Survival Skills

*Need*  Perhaps the most crucial educational experience for elders falls in the category of coping. It might be called late life education, or perhaps survival education, because it is necessary for survival. A premise of empowerment is the importance of having basic information about oneself and one's situation. It is not possible to perceive oneself as having competency to solve problems and mastery over the environment without having information about one's situation. The aging process, if not understood, can frighten people, making them feel helpless and powerless. This is an aging society; that is, as discussed in Chapter 1, an increasing percentage of the population is over 65. However, Americans are informed as a society neither about the effects of aging nor about what is considered normal in that process. In order for elders to value themselves in their later years, they must understand the aging process itself.

**Objectives**   In terms of client expectations, common objectives for programs designed to transmit knowledge and skills for late life survival include:

- Understanding the normal aging processes, including physical, mental, social, financial, and emotional changes
- Recognizing common problems encountered by those in the aging population, such as loss, loneliness, depression, housing needs, political problems, lack of sufficient resources, age discrimination, stereotyping, and dwindling of resources
- Learning about resources for meeting the needs of older people, such as agency programs and funds, medical care, use of wills, benefits, housing alternatives, and wellness philosophy
- Becoming familiar with problem-solving skills, such as effective communication and assertiveness

**Content**   Educational programs that cover the following general areas in their curricula can be very effective in meeting the above objectives:

- Aging demographics—the changing statistics regarding the elderly
- Normal physical, mental, emotional, and social changes of the aging process
- Abnormal conditions of aging, such as chronic physical and mental illnesses
- Basic problems of living, such as financial problems and crime
- Social and political advocacy

Although many educational institutions have initiated such aging curricula, this content is not sufficiently available to the general elderly population, particularly not to elders who are clients of the social service delivery system. It is important to note that educational programs of this type can be offered in various settings, such as senior centers, hospitals, meal sites, and churches, and to keep in mind that older people can be both students and teachers of the content. Videotapes containing information regarding changes in sight and hearing, arthritis, memory loss, and other conditions that may accompany the aging process can be purchased. Such tapes, which serve as an excellent discussion tool, can be shown in any setting with a television and a VCR. It can be very empowering for elders to learn that conditions with which they are continuously dealing are common accompaniments to the aging process. Moreover, many elders can teach others about the common conditions of aging.

In order to feel the most basic level of mastery in their lives, elders must gain this kind of primary knowledge. Again, they cannot engage in a process of empowerment without understanding the situation in which they find themselves. Because they are living it, elders can be major contributors to one another's understanding of their condition.

## CASE EXAMPLE: Late Life Survival Program

For a program initiated with a grant from the National Institute of Mental Health, the client population was identified by the grantor as hard-to-reach, inner-city elders in need of mental health services. The elders were in relatively poor health, of low-income status, and isolated in downtown hotels; many were mentally or emotionally in need of services. They all perceived themselves as disempowered and were mistrustful of formal services. After a creative outreach team obtained entry, empowerment groups based on a structured educational program about aging and about the elders' own situations were offered to them in their places of residence. As the groups developed, the members began to talk about themselves and their individual situations. Thus, in a nonthreatening and empowering environment, the elders gained a better understanding of the normal aging process as well as of their common problems and needs.

The curriculum content outlined in Table 7.2 was developed with the input and guidance of the empowerment groups' members, with the intention that in the future it would be taught by elders themselves. These topics were presented and discussed in weekly meetings that lasted one to two hours.

Guest speakers or tapes (video or audio) prepared by selected professionals were used for the presentations. The content and language of the tapes were geared toward the layperson instead of the professional. In addition, participants were asked to give feedback on the tapes, which, in some cases, resulted in revisions. The structured curriculum served mostly as a springboard for discussion during the group meetings, and when the curriculum was tried with a new group, the members of the group were consulted as to (1) their interest in the topics, (2) whether the order was appropriate, and (3) what other topics were of interest to them. Care was taken not to "lay the curriculum on" the group but rather to solicit members' reactions.

Overall, the experience of learning about the common conditions of group members created a sense of identity and cohesiveness within

**Table 7.2  Curriculum on Normative Aging**

| Month 1: How to Cope with and Celebrate Growing Older | Month 2: Consumer Topics for Older People | Month 3: Healthful Hints for Older People | Month 4: Healthful Hints Continued | Month 5: Safety First for Older People | Month 6: Wrap-up Topics of Interest to Older People |
|---|---|---|---|---|---|
| 1. How do you feel about growing older? | 5. Managing your resources | 9. Life-style challenge (health overview) | 13. Sight problems of older people | 17. Crime prevention (part 1) | 21. Low-cost energy |
| 2. Facts/figures/fulfillment: A profile of older Americans | 6. Informed decision making concerning health services | 10. How the body ages | 14. Depression in older people | 18. Crime prevention (part 2) | 22. Social security and old age pensions |
| 3. Assertiveness and problem-solving techniques | 7. Consumer rights: Door-to-door and mail order transactions | 11. Hearing problems of older people | 15. Healthy diet for older people | 19. Safety in the home | 23. Social and political advocacy |
| 4. Age discrimination: How to recognize and overcome it | 8. Know your rights as a patient | 12. Arthritis and older people | 16. Medicines: Use and abuse | 20. Energy-efficient environments | 24. Grand finale: Certificates and celebration |

the group that enabled group members not only to begin to define problems specific to the group, but also to generate strategies for solving them. Many group participants said they did not know that all older people were experiencing what they were; knowing that it was more or less normal for these things to be happening to them made them feel better. Eventually, group members so thoroughly mastered information about existing resources and how to access them that, when new residents in the hotels or apartment buildings came to the meetings, members conveyed such information to them without the worker's involvement.

The following are quotes from group participants:

"I know the people in my building better."

"It feels like I am part of something that matters."

"I'm not afraid to say what I believe."

"I feel like I have helped someone."

At a state conference on empowerment in mental health settings, a member of one of the groups was a co-presenter with the social work professionals who had participated. He told the audience:

I was 79 years old and never had voted. I had never even thought about how politics affect me. After being in this group and learning how these things affect the older people, I said, Ben, it's time you exercised your right to vote, and I did, for the first time in 79 years.

Familiarity with the common conditions of aging increases an older person's awareness and consciousness about himself or herself and about aging in society. Often, when elders learn about the conditions of others, their desire to help is heightened. The next four programs offer elders the opportunity to help others and to help themselves in the process.

## *Peer Counseling*

One arena in which many older adults have first assumed the adult learner role, then acquired new skills, and finally become productive contributors to society is peer counseling. With respect to McClusky's (1973) schema of educational needs for elder adults, peer counseling programs clearly serve to fill the coping needs of elders and, in many cases, their contributory and influencing needs as well.

Peer counseling reflects a holistic and wellness approach to counseling rather than an intrapersonal focus. According to the peer counseling perspective, individuals are composed of mind, body, and spirit; therefore, they need not only medical and/or physical care, but also social, emotional, and intellectual supports. The focus of wellness is not on pathology, but rather on the empowerment of individuals to attend to the whole of their needs and not just their ailments. Based on the premise that older adults are valued ordinary people who are likely to experience normal but often difficult social, physical, and emotional adjustments, peer counseling programs show older adults how to take responsibility for their own physical, emotional, intellectual, and spiritual health.

Perhaps the most valuable aspect of a peer counseling program is the bond created when elders help elders. Many older people indicate that having a confidant is highly significant to life satisfaction. Peer counseling can also help elders prepare for and get through difficult adjustments and can encourage the development of new interests and skills, resulting in a renewed enthusiasm for life.

**Need** The need for peer counseling programs in the aging field has been well established. The projected increase in the percentage of the population that is elderly is in itself seen as substantiating the need for greater numbers of people to become involved in and informed about the mental health and late life satisfactions of elders. The number of professionals choosing careers in gerontology, however, does not match the projected increase in the need for such professionals. More and more, this society will need to utilize elders themselves to solve their own problems. This process of enabling elders to help themselves and their peers is obviously congruent with an empowerment-oriented practice model.

Peer counseling programs for the elderly initially evolved from a need for aging people to identify, access, and utilize personal and community resources for improving the quality of their lives. In time, peer counseling programs across the country were developed to address the following issues:

- Widespread depression
- Loneliness
- Inability to cope with crises
- Poor health resulting from unhealthy behavior patterns
- Overdependence on medical care

Elderly persons may, for example, be isolated and reluctant to reach out, or they may be having difficulty identifying and accessing available resources. The assistance offered by peer counselors can be as simple as providing a thoughtful, concerned listener to someone who is in pain or informing others of available resources and their right to utilize them. In this regard, counselors can serve as excellent links between community resources and self-help groups for the elderly, because they tend to know what the community has to offer. Moody (1986) suggests that perhaps the most exciting potential of self-help lies in the possibility of encouraging older people and professionals alike to transform their images of what "dependency or productivity in old age might mean" (p. 211).

Overall, peer counseling not only provides a good way to utilize the "thrown-away" skills and talents of many older people, but also serves as at least a partial answer to the increased need for basic services in the face of dwindling resources.

***Objectives***   Peer counseling programs usually have the following objectives:

- To enable older adults, through training and supervision, to master new skills or reawaken dormant skills so that they can give aid and comfort to other seniors—their peers—who are experiencing depression or lack coping skills
- To provide satisfying and meaningful counseling and teaching experiences for the trained senior volunteers
- To increase understanding and mutual respect between elderly clients and community health and other service professionals
- To increase awareness and associated behaviors among elder participants concerning disease prevention; medical self-care and control; management of loss, pain, and stress; the benefits of proper nutrition, exercise, and medication; and availability of community health-promoting resources and opportunities
- To increase wellness and self-esteem and to decrease the incidence of depression, loneliness, apathy, and other forms of emotional and physical debilitation among elders

***Content***   Training for peer counselors should provide information in three areas. The first area covers normal changes in the aging process:

- Physical changes
- Mental and emotional changes
- Social changes, including the issues of loss
- Changes in political priorities
- Changes in financial circumstances

The second area includes special topics in aging:

- Alzheimer's disease
- Caregiving
- Chronic pain management
- Nutrition
- Building networks

- Exercise
- Depression
- Housing resources
- Financial resources
- Self-help groups

The third area involves in-depth discussion of topics concerning the counseling process:

- Self-awareness
- Assertiveness
- Effective communication skills
- Building relationships
- The helping relationship
- Termination of helping relationships
- Record keeping
- Termination with clients
- Specific helping skills
- Loss and grief
- Family relationships
- Conflict management
- Confidentiality
- Case supervision

Peer counseling programs are based on the belief that, with training, laypersons can acquire at least a minimum level of what can be called "core conditions" of helping: empathy, warmth, and genuineness in interpersonal communication (Truax et al., 1966). Candidates for peer counselors include older adults who are retired from a helping profession, who, simply from living a long life, have acquired a repertoire of good basic skills, or who possess a good "sixth sense" about people, usually acquired from living and dealing with a wide variety of people. Such individuals have excellent potential for learning the core skills of helping.

More generally, peer counseling programs recognize the value of the wisdom, knowledge, and experience that elderly people have gained over the years. In turn, these qualities are used to launch participants into new challenges that reaffirm them as valued and spirited members of the society. During this empowering process, the mutuality of helper and helpee is confirmed. Thus, it seems likely that peer counseling programs have a substantially more empowering effect on elders than do programs in which young people advise elders on how to cope with conditions the young people have not experienced.

***Special Needs of Peer Counselors***   In any peer counseling program, the needs of the counselors are an ongoing concern. There must be regular and consistent supervision from a professional or someone with long-term experience in the counseling process. There should also be peer supervision to help the counselors understand that the problems and situations they encounter in the counseling process are common and that they can seek common solutions. Supervision provides a chance not only for peer counselors to obtain suggestions for dealing with specific situations, but also for them to grow and change personally and so become more aware and more confident as counselors. They themselves may be dealing with many of the issues raised in the counseling process, and they must have the opportunity to talk about those issues and to separate their feelings from those of the person they are counseling. Moreover, the peer counselors bring their own needs and experiences to the training and supervision arena, and these constitute relevant content for other elders. The peer counselors are experts and should be consulted as such in the development of the curriculum and ongoing supervision of the programs.

## CASE EXAMPLE: Peer Counseling Program

An elderly client from a peer counseling program wrote:

> The Peer Counseling Program at the Seniors' Resource Center is designed for those of us who have a problem with knowing our worth, sadness from days gone by, long-ago troubles that keep cropping up in our minds, and other thoughts and feelings that keep us from living up to our potential regardless of our age. . . . I have found that the benefits of Peer Counseling have so far helped free my mind of longtime hurts and sadnesses; it has relieved my body pain because, I am sure, it has allowed me to be more relaxed, handle stress better, and have the beginnings of a new outlook on life.

According to the helper therapy principle, the helper may receive as much help as the person being helped. Here is one example of the help an elderly peer counselor received from the counseling experience:

> You know, one never knows what is in store for them. You just cannot plan things. I am taking care of my two granddaughters, one 16 and one 20. Their mother, my daughter, is an alcoholic, and refuses to deal with them. I really have tried my best, but just haven't been able to reach them. They feel that I'm too old and removed from their world. The kids never shared their thoughts

or feelings with me nor their doings in school. However, since I joined the peer counseling program, I started to apply some of the things I learned on my own grandkids. Do you know that now we sit around the table at suppertime and talk! The kids are now interested in what I'm doing and learning. They think it's great! Imagine, at my age, going to school and learning new things! I believe they think grandma is not so stupid after all! They even told their friends about me. Believe it or not, they have started thinking of aging and the attitudes that surround aging, including their own. Isn't it great! This program is my salvation!

Peer counseling provides an opportunity for elders to contribute to the well-being of others, to develop new skills for coping with their own late life issues, and to build a sense of commonality among themselves and their peers.

## Effective Personal Communication

***Need*** Late life challenges often create a need for improved communication skills. Conflicts may arise with family members, service providers, neighbors, friends, or congregate living mates. Older people often are socialized to keep things to themselves. They may believe that showing feelings is impolite and uncalled for. They do not want to "cause trouble," so when a conflict arises, they may try to sweep it under the rug. This tendency can have many negative implications for elders.

First, when differences are not resolved among people, barriers build up, and the affected parties are inclined to leave one another alone. This distancing increases the possibility of an elder's being isolated, a problem already experienced by many elders. Furthermore, when differences are allowed to build up between elders, between elders and their families, and between elders and the service and support agencies, elders become more powerless to engage in problem solving. They lose not only a perception of mastery over their environment, but also confidence in their ability to solve problems; they may become angry and depressed. Clearly, learning effective communication skills, including how to resolve conflicts, is of particular importance when coping with the challenges of late life. Acquisition of effective communication skills can meet the coping, contributory, and expressive needs for late life learning (Lowy, 1988; McClusky, 1973). Cox and Parsons addressed this need through a training program for effective communication skills. The program was offered in conjunction with a program to train older people to be lay mediators, which will be described later.

***Objectives*** Participants in the effective communication training were expected to meet the following objectives:

- Understand the basics of effective communication, such as active listening, reflecting content and feelings, and demonstrating self-awareness
- Understand the nature and anatomy of conflict
- Increase awareness of one's own socialization and preferred styles of communication
- Learn creative ways of understanding problems and others' perceptions of problems

***Content*** Approximately twenty elderly volunteers were recruited and trained based on the above objectives. After receiving training, the volunteers developed their own training packages to train other elderly people. Divided into training teams, the volunteers went into nursing homes, senior centers, and senior housing. They were able to train 250 elders in effective communication skills for living and solving problems. The volunteer trainers developed their own training packages, based on their knowledge base and life and professional experiences as well as input from the elders they were training. Materials included creative video presentations and a training manual. Real-life situations provided the case examples through which the concepts were presented.

Training content consisted of the following:

- Ice-breaker exercises and introductions
- Nature of conflict
- Component parts of conflict
- Conflict resolution styles
- Basic communication skills—listening, active listening, and barriers to communication
- Steps in conflict resolution and negotiation

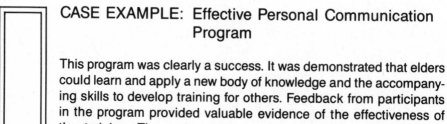

## CASE EXAMPLE: Effective Personal Communication Program

This program was clearly a success. It was demonstrated that elders could learn and apply a new body of knowledge and the accompanying skills to develop training for others. Feedback from participants in the program provided valuable evidence of the effectiveness of the training. These are some sample statements from program participants:

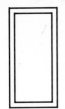

"The most important thing for me to realize was that I frequently made right/wrong judgments without any basis."

"I have become a better listener."

"Everyone has a point of view that must be considered."

"I teach I-messages to others, listen more effectively, and encourage self-solutions."

## Conflict Resolution

In response to the overcrowding of our judicial system, there has evolved a movement to use volunteers to facilitate alternative means of problem resolution in civil cases. The courts remain the principal milieu for resolving disputes, but many alternative structures—usually referred to as alternative dispute resolution (ADR) efforts—are being created. The services they offer are performed by a variety of individuals, including attorneys, social workers, and trained laypersons. The AARP has promoted an effort to train seniors to become mediators who assist in alternative dispute resolution. In addition to becoming mediators, elders can engage in other forms of dispute resolution, such as negotiation, arbitration, and the ombudsman process. Volunteers with skills in these areas are needed to assist with resolving the many disputes experienced in the senior community.

According to Pearson (1988), informal and formal service providers to the elderly have begun to explore ways

> . . . in which older persons' unfamiliarity with grievance procedures or power imbalances can be ameliorated. . . . Older persons without adequate resources or information often dismiss the thought of a formal lawsuit, recognizing that limitations of time, circumstances, and assets make such action difficult, and negotiation, mediation or arbitration can become appropriate alternatives. (p. 3)

The following areas outlined by Pearson (1988) encompass problems that may be resolved by alternative dispute resolution:

- Discrimination in housing
- Landlord/tenant disagreements
- Housing code violations
- Unfair evictions by landlords
- Noisy neighbors
- Homeowner warranties
- Small claims matters
- Civil rights violations
- Consumer issues

- Neighboring property neglect
- Family feuds
- Patients' rights
- Blocked driveway
- Petty thievery or pilferage
- Zoning changes or decisions
- Spousal support defaults
- Divorce negotiations
- Legal separation agreements
- Child custody defaults
- Community property disposition
- Property defacement or damage
- Loitering

Pearson (1988) makes the point that these kinds of problems often become exacerbated in the elderly, who consequently need to learn not only how to approach and resolve their own problems through effective communication and conflict resolution skills, but also how to serve as conflict resolvers for others. This need was addressed through a program that trained elderly volunteers to become volunteers in community conflict resolution. Through an ad in the newspaper, 55 elderly volunteers were recruited to be trained in conflict resolution skills, based on the following objectives, with particular emphasis on mediation and negotiation.

***Objectives***   The following were the objectives for participants in the training program for conflict resolution:

- Understand the basics of effective communication, such as active listening, reflecting content and feelings, using I-messages, and self-awareness
- Understand the nature and anatomy of conflict, its sequence, and its component parts
- Define the various forms of alternative dispute resolution, including arbitration, litigation, mediation, and negotiation
- Become aware of their own socialization and preferred style of conflict resolution and how that may differ from others
- Understand the steps in negotiation and mediation and the processes inherent in those steps

***Content***   The 30 hours of training in mediation and negotiation skills covered the following content areas:

1. Get-acquainted exercises
2. Introduction of content and processes of the training and demonstration programs
3. Generation of lists of conflict situations in the aging community
4. AARP slide show on elders' role in conflict resolution
5. Anatomy of a conflict and its component parts
6. What is conflict management?
7. Becoming aware of your own conflict management style
8. The cultural and age cohort basis of conflict management
9. Examining alternative resolution styles: power, suppression, denial, compromise, interest-based bargaining
10. Steps in interest-based bargaining
11. Techniques of interest-based bargaining
12. Processes of mediation and negotiation
13. Case application in mediation and interest-based bargaining
14. Defining problems and creating good solutions
15. Basic communication skills: listening and active listening
16. Basic communication skills: nonverbal communication, I-messages, and barriers to communication
17. Basic communication skills: brainstorming and video on mediation skills
18. Wrap-up, summarization, termination and planning, celebration

The basic training consisted of much practice.

### CASE EXAMPLE: Conflict Resolution Program

Examples of conflicts, provided by participants in the conflict resolution program, included the following types:

Family disagreements over nursing home versus community-based home care for elders

Cul-de-sac parking

Neighbors' barking dogs

An adult child wanting a more protective environment for his father than his father was willing to have

Smoking in senior residences

Noise and security issues in residential settings

Tenant/landlord disputes over safety

Feuds between nursing home roommates

Disputes between nursing home administrators and families

These conflict examples, which were very relevant to the participants' lives, provided case material around which role plays could be done.

Feedback from participants in the program was crucial in evaluating the effectiveness of the training. Here are some sample statements from program participants:

"I recently mediated a conflict with a business firm that in all probability would have gone to court had it not been for the mediation training."

"I have used the training to assist my children, certain friends, and church members."

"I have used mediation training to be more direct and up-front in expressing my own feelings."

"My mind thinks in compromise ideas instead of one idea being absolutely right in many situations. I have a new attitude."

The effectiveness of participation in this training program was evidenced in more indirect ways, also. For example, after completing their training, the volunteers divided into groups. Some served on *mediation teams,* which allied themselves with the city's Commission on Aging and initiated a Senior-to-Senior Mediation Service. Ongoing supervision was given to the volunteer mediators. The effectiveness of the elderly mediators was attributable to their understanding of the "senior" issues in the conflicts brought to them. In dealing with other elders in conflict situations, volunteer mediators quickly learned that many conflicts were deeper than simple disagreements. Beneath the conflicts that were presented there often lay issues involving isolated and needy elders who were not connected to basic services. The senior mediators discovered that they needed to familiarize themselves with information in a wide range of areas, from aging, dementia, and medications to tenants' rights, laws, and health services benefits and resources. Additional training in these areas was provided.

Although many of the elderly participants had been socialized to deny or suppress conflict, they readily learned new perspectives for looking at conflict resolution as a part of problem solving. The skills and strengths they brought to the learning and teaching process were an enormous asset to the program and a major factor in its success.

# Advocacy

The role of social work practitioners in advocacy has a long and interesting history. These historical roots include social action strategies, as exemplified by Dorothea Dix in her gallant struggle for the rights of mental health patients in the 1940s, and the comprehensive conceptualization of advocacy as a specific practice role, which was developed by a number of social work professionals during the late 1960s and the 1970s. During these two decades, advocacy programs were funded by the National Council on Aging and the Community Action Agencies that were funded by the Economic Opportunity Act. (Chapter 4 provides an overview of advocacy strategies and approaches that are helpful to elders involved in the social action process.)

From an empowerment perspective, it is evident that assisting disadvantaged individuals to gain resources or rights is an important contribution. This perspective is, however, tempered by the reality that even successful advocacy for others is far less effective in achieving the goals of empowerment-oriented practice than a strategy that engages individuals in successful *advocacy for themselves.* Consequently, the focus of empowerment-oriented practice is on the teaching or sharing of advocacy skills with target populations.

**Need** The need for advocacy skills among the elderly population is evident from the stories told by the elderly of their frustrations as they struggle to obtain basic services and have their basic rights honored. Both peer counselors and peer mediators have discovered the need for more advocacy skills in order to fulfill their roles of assistants to other elders.

This section briefly describes an approach to training elders as advocates, with an emphasis on the *case advocacy* aspects. Key elements of this framework are modified to more appropriately address concerns of the elderly.

Several factors are considered prerequisite to learning the specific knowledge and skills of advocacy. In order to further the goal of empowerment, advocacy skills must be learned within the context of empowerment-oriented principles and values. One of the most difficult tasks is to persuade the elders trained as advocacy volunteers to transfer the skills they have learned to those they are helping. Elders who have gained advocacy skills often find themselves in the role of helper and, like many professionals, find it difficult to change that role to one of partner in problem-solving efforts. Therefore, as part of any training effort, the philosophy and goals of empowerment have to be clearly addressed, and ongoing supervision must pay continuing attention to this aspect of advocacy.

***Objectives***   Consistent with empowerment-oriented practice, key objectives for participants in advocacy training are as follows:

- Understand the focus of advocacy (case and class advocacy) and, specifically, the meaning of advocacy in the context of empowerment philosophy
- Learn the basic resource systems for older Americans
- Review prior experience and identify prior styles of "advocating"
- Learn a framework for the implementation of advocacy, including skills in assessment of advocacy strategies
- Learn to know, identify, and implement a wide range of advocacy strategies

In addition to the emphasis on empowerment and incorporation of this philosophy into their work, all trainees must receive a comprehensive overview of services and resources appropriate to the needs of the elderly. The more knowledgeable one is regarding the resources available, the more effective one's advocacy attempts will be. As suggested above, resource training focuses not only on what is currently available, but also on the ways and means of identifying resources in an ongoing manner.

It is important to realize during this teaching and learning process that most individuals have previously established ways of handling the task of advocacy, that is, individualized styles. Styles and strategies in advocacy—such as telephoning public officials or using threatening approaches with employees of large bureaucracies—may be patterns that are hard to change in individuals who have found such tactics to be successful. These individuals need to see that some of the positive outcomes experienced from these techniques might have been accomplished with less intensive or less confrontational interventions.

The advocacy training therefore stresses thinking through a range of possible methods of intervention, targeting levels of intervention, and attempting to solve the problem at the lowest possible level of intervention with the least possible expenditure of energy. It is important for participants to realize that making a simple request for change or clarification is easier and many times more effective than filing a formal complaint or resorting to use of the legal system. A necessary part of training advocates is raising their awareness of their own personal styles and providing them with alternative ways to look at solutions.

Cox and Parsons have presented basic advocacy training to a number of different groups of elders, and the content has been modified to fit a range of formats, from 1-day, 6-hour sessions to 40 hours of training spread over 5 weeks. It was found that the more comprehensive training efforts yielded more successful outcomes.

***Content***   An outline of the content used for advocacy training is presented in Table 7.3. This content was based on (1) problem examples

## Table 7.3   Outline of Content for Advocacy Training

I. Definition of Advocacy and Examples
   A. Case advocacy
   B. Class advocacy
   C. Advocacy and empowerment
   D. Overview

II. Identifying Components of Advocacy
   A. Advocacy agent
   B. Client/beneficiary
   C. Primary source of the problem
   D. Objectives of the intervention
   E. Target of the intervention
   F. Sanction for intervention
   G. Resources
   H. Levels of intervention
   I. Strategies for intervention

III. Personal Styles and Strategies of Intervention
   A. Power orientation
   B. Conflict resolution styles
   C. Leadership and behavioral styles
   D. Communication styles and feedback
   E. Self-awareness as a change agent

IV. Resources for Elders and Their Families
   A. Social security and old age pensions
   B. American Association of Retired Persons
   C. Senior centers
   D. Senior lobbies
   E. Senior newspapers or newsletters
   F. Transportation services
   G. Meal programs
   H. Home health and other medical services

generated by the participants, (2) exercises to help individual participants identify their own style of advocacy, and (3) a number of exercises to develop and practice intervention skills. Elders bring so much strength and experience to the training that it is an enriching experience for all participants.

Elders trained in advocacy are able to provide others with valuable access to services and to train their clients in self-advocacy skills by example. They are also able to offer training in advocacy strategies to other elders. The empowerment-oriented worker plays a key role in reaffirming the importance of empowering the recipients of services, helping senior advocates continue to update their resources and skills, and assisting senior advocates to generate more permanent organizational sponsorship of their advocacy activities.

Advocacy skills are an important component in empowerment. Such skills enable elderly people to obtain resources and services as well as to work for social change. Engaging in advocacy meets the contributory, coping, and influencing needs described in Table 7.1.

## SUMMARY

Late life presents new challenges and experiences that require elders to acquire new coping skills. These challenges include the normal developmental processes of aging, increased reliance on informal support systems, the need to help friends and others in similar situations, increased utilization of formal support systems, the need and desire to continue making contributions to society, and the need to identify with other elders. Education is a critical component of empowerment-based practice with the elderly and encompasses skills training, mutual aid and peer support, and social action.

Five empowerment-based interventions focus on late life survival skills, peer counseling, effective personal communication, conflict resolution, and advocacy. Education for late life survival covers issues such as loss, loneliness, depression, housing needs, resources, age discrimination, stereotyping, political issues, and resource management. Peer counseling is an empowerment approach that draws on older people's strengths and skills for helping others deal with common situations, such as loneliness, depression, crisis management, declining health, and lack of medical care. Training in effective personal communication addresses communication skills needed to overcome late life challenges. Areas covered include understanding communication dynamics and one's own cultural socialization to communication as well as the development of new skills such as active listening and using I-messages. Conflict resolution training addresses such problems as housing and neighbor disputes, family conflicts, landlord/tenant disagreements, and other issues relevant to the elderly. Skills taught include effective communication, conflict analysis, and mediation and negotiation techniques. Training for advocacy is directed toward elders' own advocacy needs as well as their need to advocate for others. Skills taught include ones in the areas of understanding advocacy issues, learning resource systems, assessing systems and power issues, and being assertive.

## REFERENCES

Gutiérrez, L. M. (1990). Working with women of color: An empowerment perspective. *Social Work, 35*(2) pp. 149–153.

Herzog, A. R., & House, J. S. (1991). Productive activities and aging well. *Generations, 15*(1), pp. 49–54.

Lowy, L. (1987). Human-service professionals: Their role in education for older people. *Generations, 12*(2), pp. 31–36.

Lowy, L., & O'Connor, D. (1986). *Why education in the later years?* Lexington, MA: Lexington Books.

McClusky, H. Y. (1973). Education for aging. In S. N. Grabowski & M. W. Dean, *Learning for Aging.* Washington, DC: Adult Education Association.

McGowan, B. (1978). Case advocacy in child welfare. *Child Welfare, 57*(5), pp. 275–284.

Moody, H. R. (1986). Education as a lifelong process. In A. Pifer & L. Bronte (Eds.), *Our aging society.* New York: W. W. Norton.

Pearson, L. (1988) *Neighborhood dispute resolution: Seniors helping seniors.* Washington, DC: AARP.

Pifer, A., & Bronte, L. (1986). *Our aging society.* New York: W. W. Norton.

Reissman, F. (1965). The helper therapy principle. *Social Work, 10*(2), pp. 27–32.

Simonton, D. K. (1991). Creative productivity through the adult years. *Generations, 15*(2), pp. 13–16.

Solomon, B. (1976). *Black empowerment: Social work in oppressed communities.* New York: Columbia University Press.

Truax, C. B., et al. (1966). Therapist empathy, genuineness, and warmth, and patient therapeutic outcome. *Journal of Consulting Psychology, 30*(5), pp. 395–401.

Zimmer, A. H. (1988). Self-help groups and late life learning. *Generations, 12*(2), pp. 19–21.

# GENERATING
# SURVIVAL INCOME AND
# HEALTH CARE RESOURCES

**8**

This chapter discusses problems elderly people may encounter in their attempts to secure income, health care, and other survival resources and suggests empowerment-oriented interventions to assist them in their efforts to meet basic needs. Interventions focus on collective ways to increase income, such as income-producing projects, and on volunteer programs that allow for the accumulation of service credits. Group strategies for obtaining or expanding health care services are also suggested.

## RECOGNIZING INCOME AND HEALTH CARE NEEDS

### Income Concerns

Income concerns are a great burden for many older Americans. Although popular debate regarding the older population highlights its relative wealth, a review of demographic information identifies pockets of severe poverty and deprivation in its midst (Atchley, 1991; Bass, Kutza, & Torres-Gil, 1990). For example, in 1987, 33.9% of elderly blacks had incomes below the poverty line, as did 27.4% of elderly Hispanics and 10.1% of elderly whites (Bass, Kutza, & Torres-Gil, 1990). Despite progressive reports, approximately 20% of elderly Americans are either at the poverty level or within 25% of that level (AARP, 1991). Jakobi (1990) notes:

> The overall economic well-being of the "oldest old," historically the poorer cohort among the aged, is anticipated to improve over the next 50 years. This improvement will increase the economic gap between the majority of the aged and a minority who will carry their existing poverty into old age. (p. 85)

This situation has shown no signs of change. The 1990 census verified that income inequality among the elderly has increased; there is a wider gap between well-off and poor elders than occurs in any other age group (Kleyman, 1992).

No universal income program exists that provides an adequate income for retired older Americans. Social security, which is the primary source of income for many elderly citizens, was never intended to be the sole source of late life income (Morris, 1985). The personal savings, private pensions, and other forms of income that were the intended sources of additional income are not available to many people. Supplemental Survivors Insurance (SSI), an income supplement program (controlled by a means test) for poor elderly and disabled persons, keeps its recipients below the poverty line. Maximum awards from SSI in 1991 were $407 per month for one person and $610 for a couple (Social Security Administration, 1991).

Overall, the inadequacy of the SSI program, coupled with the low level of social security income (the only shield against poverty for millions of elderly people) and the often tenuous state of private pensions, leaves many elderly Americans either without adequate income or in great fear of losing their battle against poverty. Furthermore, the lack of a comprehensive health care system for financing long-term care imposes additional burdens on elders. Obviously, there is a continuing need for social workers to focus on survival resources for the elderly, regardless of the relative wealth of some segments of the elderly population. Assisting the many elders who are in dire circumstances of poverty to find ways to supplement their income is an ongoing challenge to empowerment-oriented social workers.

Social work practitioners often come into contact with elderly clients who are struggling to gain or maintain survival resources. Other professionals and society at large expect that social workers will have knowledge of a wide range of entitlements and services that can assist elderly persons. Knowledge of these services (whether they are publicly or privately provided) and of ways to access them is indeed important to social workers as they assist elders and their families with immediate concerns. The empowerment-oriented social worker inevitably finds, however, that the process of linking individuals to resources is far more complex than simply knowing about existing resources, eligibility requirements, agency protocol, and other nuances of the service delivery system. The quest for resources for survival involves the dynamic interplay of values, attitudes, and beliefs, availability, power relations, knowledge, and strategies.

## Health Care Concerns

Health care is also a source of worry for older Americans. Most middle-class older people either experience difficulty in securing resources to pay for health care or live in fear of the cost of a potential medical crisis. Although some provision is made for very low-income elderly, they must still worry about limited coverage for routine expenses (such as the costs of prescriptions) and the often substandard quality of services available to them.

The Medicare program provides universal health insurance for all Americans 65 and over; however, this program is not comprehensive. Also, the early 1990s have been witness to cutbacks in Medicare coverage and increases in premiums for all forms of medical insurance for the elderly. Rising costs of Medicare premiums and deductibles, rising premiums for Medicare gap programs, and expanding gaps in coverage make health care insurance a very expensive item for most elderly Americans. One critical gap in coverage is the failure of Medicare to cover long-term care in institutions (nursing homes) or in the community (home- and community-based services). Medicaid is a more comprehensive program, designed to provide health care for the poor. However, coverage and eligibility requirements for participation in Medicaid differ from state to state. Although nursing home care and other services not available through Medicare are provided by Medicaid, reimbursement is at a fixed rate that is often below the market price. In an overview of health care availability, Kutza (1990) notes that "in the matter of long-term care services, federal and state governments pay for about 47%; the remainder is the responsibility of older persons themselves or their families" (p. 106).

Overall, resources for health care are limited, and the specter of an unexpected need for intensive, ongoing care looms threateningly in the minds of many older Americans and their families. In addition, the continual changes in state regulations regarding eligibility for and level of Medicaid coverage make it a very tenuous resource for the poor.

## Values, Attitudes, and Beliefs

The values, attitudes, and beliefs related to how individual human needs should be met in society are a critical aspect of service delivery. Who should be responsible for the provision of income? Is it acceptable to need help? Is it right to expect one's children to help? What should the government's role be in the provision of health care? Should Medicare cover all long-term care needs? These and numerous other questions are relevant to the issue of seeking survival and health care resources. The value perspectives of society (what are believed to be the acceptable values of the times), elderly people, their families and friends, and helping professionals and their organizations are all important in the quest for resources. These value perspectives apply not only to how needs should be met but also to *what is considered a legitimate need*. What is considered to be adequate income, housing, medical care, and so on is also based on social and cultural values (Goodin, 1990).

The values of both workers and elderly clients determine the selection of strategies and approaches to be used for the acquisition of resources or services, as well as the decision about whether or not to seek specific resources. The sanction basis for intervention is an important consideration when thinking about an approach to helping clients acquire resources. Social sanction ranges from a *legal right* to receive a given resource or to have a particular need met to the *belief* of individuals, groups, or society that a given perceived need should even exist and/or be met. In short, the values one holds regarding one's right to receive help in case of need and the attitudes of society toward both the provision of help and those in need of help have an important impact on service provision.

## Strategies for Addressing the Needs for Income and Health Care

Numerous means—both legal and illegal—for the acquisition of survival resources or health care have been used by people in need. The empowerment-oriented practitioner is concerned with assisting clients to secure survival or health care resources in ways that preserve the clients' sense of personal efficacy and increase their sense of power over the environment. Although the problems encountered in attempting to access adequate resources will differ according to the client's economic status, needs arising from lack of resources—or *perceived* lack of resources—are common to many elderly people in this society.

Empowerment-oriented social workers assisting with the generation of survival or health care resources must exercise creativity in order to engage older clients in a range of activities:

- Consciousness raising regarding the issues, including exploration of their own perceptions of and attitudes toward the need and the methods of provision for addressing the need
- Learning how to use practical strategies for securing entitlements and charitable resources and for managing existing resources
- Securing employment in the face of age discrimination and other challenges
- Developing collective self-help efforts to meet needs for which individualized strategies fall short
- Participating in social action efforts dedicated to meeting needs through change in the social-political-economic system

The remainder of this chapter discusses the issues faced by elderly people in their attempts to obtain adequate income and health care and the strategies used by empowerment-oriented practitioners with respect to filling these needs. Although income level is often the key to adequate health care provision, special issues prevail in each area. Strategies emphasized in this chapter supplement the activities for resource acquisition suggested in the discussion in Chapter 5 of ways to influence the service delivery system.

## SECURING LATE LIFE INCOME

The problem of securing late life income has several aspects: values, attitudes, and beliefs; access to resources; management of existing resources; employment opportunities, and supplemental income.

### Values, Attitudes, and Beliefs about Income and Status

Perceptions of what constitutes an adequate late life income vary greatly. Sensitivity to the cultural significance of how much money one has cannot be ignored. As noted in Chapter 2, social policy related to retirement in American society does very little to equalize status among the elderly population. Class distinctions tend to be strongly reinforced throughout the aging process (Estes, Swan, & Girard, 1984; Lockery, 1988; Minkler & Estes, 1991). In addition, middle-class and lower middle-class individuals often find themselves losing economic ground, in a comparative sense, as health care costs and inflation take their toll on fixed incomes. Empowerment-oriented workers frequently meet elderly clients who feel shame at their decreased capacity to maintain the standard of living they feel is essential to their self-esteem—who are for the first time having difficulty providing for basic needs such as food, medical care, and housing.

**Perceived Need**   Exploration of elders' need for income and other resources requires stimulation of critical consciousness. Marcuse (1964) described the creation of "false consciousness" with respect to needs by modern consumeristic, material-oriented societies. His work elucidates the role socialization plays in shaping one's consciousness with respect to what one believes are one's basic needs. For example, the housing, neighborhood, clothing, automobile, and amount of money one believes one must have to be "happy" or "responsible" is strongly tied to socialization rather than to any finite measure of need.

Both one-to-one discussion and group process can be valuable in examining and clarifying perceived need in older individuals. Often one of the most empowering experiences people can have with respect to their daily living is to gain awareness of their ability to achieve and maintain a high quality of life at a reduced standard of living. Values clarification or consciousness-raising strategies can often be employed to help elderly clients deemphasize material possessions and find other meaningful dimensions of life. The group process is a useful format for helping individuals analyze their beliefs and think through how these beliefs affect their functioning in their current circumstances. For example, elderly individuals can focus attention on contributions they can make to their families, friends, and communities that do not require economic wealth.

---

### CASE EXAMPLE: Attitude Changes and New Insights

One elderly woman who was referred to Retired Senior Volunteer Program (RSVP) by a social worker commented on her experiences this way: "I spent a lot of time worrying about all the things I couldn't afford when I could have been busy living. Since I joined RSVP, I've been too busy and happy to think about those things."

An older client whom a worker had introduced to a food bank commented, "Joining this food bank keeps food on my table and other people's as well. I feel like my work really means something."

A number of elderly women who had lost their capacity for safe driving participated in a group designed to help them reassess their feelings about the significance of driving to their lives and to teach them to use public transportation and to assist other elderly people facing this problem to successfully deal with this loss. One participant commented, "I don't know why I thought the world would stop if I couldn't drive. I thought it meant I wouldn't be independent anymore."

---

*Feelings about Having Inadequate Resources*   Social workers report abundant examples of the following behaviors and feelings among elders who become subject to the need for resources:

- Denial of changed income status and efforts to cover up visible signs of a change in circumstances through cost cutting in areas such as food and health care, which are necessary to survival and quality of life
- Feelings of uselessness and depression arising from an inability to provide monetary assistance to children or other significant persons
- Feelings of shame about current income inadequacy which should have been prevented by lifelong work and savings patterns that were intended to provide security until death
- Refusal to apply for available income supports because of a feeling that it is "bad" to take welfare (many elders even include social security in their concept of welfare)

Elderly clients often report hiding their social security and/or old age pension checks, refusing to use food stamps, hesitating to use Medicare or Medicaid, and avoiding other forms of assistance. One 89-year-old retired schoolteacher stated, "When my resources run out, that's when I should run out too."

***Strategies and Interventions***   The empowerment-oriented social worker must assist individual elders to identify clearly their own values, attitudes, and beliefs and their levels of need and to challenge those that stand in the way of physical and/or mental health. Addressing these aspects has obvious political and personal implications and is very difficult for some individuals. The worker must ask elderly clients to engage in an ongoing process of assessing their beliefs about several important issues:

- Individuals' rights to benefits
- What is needed and what is superfluous
- What is fair and what is not fair with respect to the distribution of wealth
- Self-worth as a reflection of personal property (the perceived need for material possessions is critical to feelings of self-respect for many)

This process often entails the need to reassess and change value preferences in order to achieve a sense of power over one's current environment or situation. One's mental and physical health are often dependent on one's ability to engage in such a process.

A long struggle with consciousness raising may have to precede practical changes such as using the public transit system rather than a private automobile or providing companionship and love to children and friends rather than monetary support. Empowerment-oriented workers need to develop skills that encourage individuals to face their dilemmas and struggle for change rather than ignoring changing circumstances in their lives and feeling helpless. Consciousness-raising groups that directly address attitudes and values are a critical component of empowerment in the realm of survival resources. It is not always possible, however, to use peer learning experiences to this end. One worker reported his struggle to address such issues on a one-to-one basis with elderly people who were not able (or were unwilling) to engage in a group process:

> I spent a lot of time helping with small resource needs and getting to know each person; I tried to talk about their feelings of guilt or worthlessness about not having enough money whenever they brought it up. It was very difficult and the subject got changed a lot. Finally, I started leaving questions for discussion at our next visit. We pretty much followed the same format and issues for discussion the group did: What is an adequate income? What are my most important needs? What should be our basic

income rights as retired persons? Etc. Sometimes I try to use network support by introducing people to each other and encouraging one-to-one relationships between them. Of course, the big step for both the groups and individuals is to move from talking to acting.

The process of changing values and attitudes related to standards of living and perceived needs requires not only changing one's perceptions but also adjusting one's style of living. Lending support for these changes is often an important function of the worker and of the group and other significant members of an elderly person's support network. Examples of life-style changes that might be required in response to income strains include sharing a home, accepting food stamps, participating in a home equity conversion program, and giving up the use of an automobile. Whatever the interventions used to assist older individuals to empower themselves to deal with their financial situation, the importance of facing and dealing with values and attitudes regarding income adequacy cannot be ignored.

## *Access to Entitlements and Charitable Resources*

*Entitlements*  As suggested in the discussion in Chapter 3 of Dimension 1 activities, social workers must seek to make clients aware of all possible public or private entitlements. As noted in the discussions of Dimensions 2 and 3 (educational and self-help) activities and of empowerment work in relationships, however, it is equally important to encourage clients to learn how to identify and access resources for themselves and convey this information to other elders. In other words, individuals as well as groups and networks of elders must become their own information and referral experts.

---

### CASE EXAMPLE: Accessing Resources

In one senior high-rise apartment complex, a group of residents, who had first begun to meet in order to socialize, found themselves involved in information gathering and referral. Discussion of their daily experiences led to the identification of problems with transportation and health care availability. The group's subsequent research and sharing of information led its members to establish an ongoing resource-location and information-providing team. The worker's role consisted mostly of encouraging and assisting group members in their work. In one instance the worker provided a list of common income sources (including social security, public and private pensions well known in the area, state old age pension) and a list of persons who

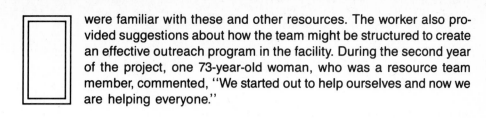were familiar with these and other resources. The worker also provided suggestions about how the team might be structured to create an effective outreach program in the facility. During the second year of the project, one 73-year-old woman, who was a resource team member, commented, "We started out to help ourselves and now we are helping everyone."

The task of gathering information about resources is difficult—and not only because of the elusive character of the provision system. According to one department of social services worker:

> It is sometimes important to suggest questions for resource gathering and for resource people. We even rehearsed or role played the activities before individual elderly began their data-gathering tasks. I still doubt if much would have happened if some people had not found entitlements early in the effort that they did not know they had a right to.

A worker assigned to a neighborhood center in a moderate- to low-income community reported the following effort:

> I got the group to come up with a list of all the possible income sources. . . . We divided them up to find out more about them, get brochures, etc. Then everyone listed what they were likely to be eligible for and everyone helped each other apply. It was amazing how much people had coming. We discussed problems people had with different agencies and workers and brainstormed different approaches. After we had dealt with most entitlements, we tackled the churches, civic groups, and other private charities to see if we could find money for dentures, home repairs, auto repairs, etc. I think when everyone was looking for resources for themselves and everyone else the stigma disappeared. The real problem is always keeping it going, being on the lookout for new resources or reliable sources of information. Although over 50 people benefited from this effort, only 6 or 7 people were constantly involved. They did a lot of work and began to be active in other senior groups in the city.

In another instance, a worker who helped older women obtain disability payments from a public welfare agency stated:

> We [the clients and the worker] had to learn the rules and regulations and become expert in the appeal process before we could do any good. But once we started helping other older women deal with this agency a lot of them joined the project and became helpers themselves. The big hurdle seems to be when members start to help other folks—then they become more aggressive, free about coming up with ideas and determined to win.

The welfare rights movement of the late 1960s and early 1970s did much to develop technology for securing entitlements (Pivin & Cloward, 1979). Acquiring information about income and health care resources through organizing workshops for clients, learning advocacy skills (for example, how to use appeals processes), and a wide range of related activities is critical to helping individuals and groups achieve a degree of empowerment with respect to the bureaucracies that disburse entitlements. These self-help activities, identified in the empowerment-oriented practice model as Dimension 2 and 3 activities, often lead to the obvious need for Dimension 4 (social action) activities.

The worker's functions include teaching techniques of resource investigation, encouraging involvement in a critical education process, and assisting with techniques for the organization and dissemination of information. In one project that developed a pool of senior volunteer mediators, the volunteers decided to establish a computer training seminar in order to better manage the data necessary for the project. The role of the worker in this instance was simply to suggest possible resources. Although more time-consuming than most case management approaches to linking individuals with resources, these kinds of strategies leave clients in charge of their own pursuit of entitlements and other monetary resources.

***Charitable Resources***   Pursuing income provided by private charities is often more difficult than accessing existing public resources. Securing private sector assistance is difficult in part because there are usually no rules or regulations that require the organization with resources to provide assistance. The individual or group requesting assistance is in the position of trying to present a persuasive argument to decision makers. Empowerment-oriented workers often find themselves faced with the task of demystifying the fund-raising process. Flanagan (1984) stresses the idea that all persons are capable of fund raising. She states, "People have two reasons why they prefer not asking . . . for money. The first is fear. . . . Second, people have been taught not to talk about money, and you have to unteach them" (p. 314). That is, values and attitudes about asking for help are again apparent when it comes to asking charitable sources for money. The experience of individual elders as they attempt to access private sector resources is often their most powerful teacher. The technique of role playing is useful when funding requests require face-to-face meetings, and group approaches to written funding requests have been helpful in encouraging the participation of elderly volunteers.

# Income Management

Another important income-related issue to which empowerment-oriented strategies can be directed is income management. Social workers who work with the elderly, especially elderly women, often report that the loss of a spouse has led to a situation in which economic decision making is left for the first time to the survivor. This sudden responsibility can lead to increased feelings of helplessness and open the door to various forms of financial exploitation. The empowerment-oriented worker can encourage these elders to seek information about different kinds of investments and means of resource development. It is important to stress that this financial information should be broad in nature and from diverse sources.

Discussion of the situation itself and the concerns common to many who find themselves in the situation can help alleviate feelings of shame associated with not knowing what to do. For example, materials that describe the common economic struggles of middle-income elderly to afford long-term care or the plight of many older persons regarding inadequate pensions can be supplemented with how-to sessions regarding money management. The AARP has developed a few educational modules that discuss such matters as investments and insurance options. Also, local resource persons who are familiar with current financial trends and who are willing to assist in education concerning financial management will often be available.

The key task of the empowerment-oriented worker is to assist elderly clients to seek this kind of education for themselves, rather than simply relying on "experts" to manage their financial resources. That is, the role of the empowerment-oriented worker lies not in finding or providing access to income management resources for individual clients, but in mobilizing individuals to find and access such resources for themselves and, if feasible, to share this knowledge with others. In other words, the goal is to encourage older people to seek and understand information and assume control and management of their own resources, not to simply provide them with information about a particular investment.

## Late Life Employment

Another important aspect of the issue of income adequacy is the development of late life employment opportunities. Age discrimination in employment looms threateningly over unemployed middle-aged and older persons, and older women and minority elders face double and triple jeopardy in this regard. Those who have reached age 65 are, by society's current standards, supposed to be retired and consequently encounter little sympathy in the job market. Rapid changes in technology and negative attitudes about retraining older workers result in job displacement for some workers in their forties or fifties, and rehiring often occurs at lower salaries and for less desirable positions (Markson, 1983; Shultz, 1988).

The discouragement, depression, and fear experienced by older individuals who become unemployed—often for the first time—can be devastating. Common causes of job losses include cutbacks by firms, temporary family caregiving responsibilities, and temporary disability. When older workers seek reentry into the job market, they often face severe discrimination. Many such employment seekers report feelings of depression, panic, anger, and frustration as they are repeatedly passed over in favor of younger workers for positions for which they feel well qualified. One older man reported his experiences this way: "I found myself being interviewed by younger men who knew less than I did about the job I wanted. They were usually very polite but they just never called again—I got scores of 'we regret' letters." Many report even greater frustration after seeking and failing to secure jobs with far lower status, skill level, and pay than their previous employment. A 59-year-old woman who had a long, successful work history at the middle management level described her situation:

> I finally, after literally two years of consistent failures [in the job search], started looking for secretarial and even receptionist jobs. . . . Sometimes they would say I was overqualified, but mostly I just got rejection letters. Somehow in my mind all through the years I thought I could always get a job as a secretary no matter what happened to the companies I worked for.

Older people who find themselves in these situations report experiencing helplessness, anger, loss of self-confidence, isolation, and self-blame.

The aim of Senior Aides and other senior employment programs is to assist older workers, but their minimal resources often confine their activity to job placement and limited job development. Of the approximately 25% of people over 55 who are income-eligible for senior community services programs, only about 1% participate (Gelfand, 1988). Empowerment-oriented social workers can develop outreach services to find individuals suffering from the effects of job discrimination and job displacement. This task, however, is often made difficult by the elders themselves, who view unemployment as a shameful private experience and make every effort to hide the problem. Public education approaches that provide information about the prevalence of the situation and help define the political issues relative to work in this society may be useful in reducing the self-blame factor for some individuals. OWL's newsletter, for example, frequently covers employment issues; one group of older job seekers used material from this source as a basis for discussions about their own struggles and, later, to facilitate an outreach effort directed to others suffering from job discrimination.

Few social work services exist to identify elderly persons suffering from employment loss and to provide empowerment-oriented education, mutual support, consciousness raising, and other useful interventions. Empowerment-oriented workers must provide services that link elderly employment seekers to one another so that they can share their experiences. This type of intervention lessens the sense of individual failure, blame, and isolation and encourages mutual exploration of options. Support groups can identify and share training and employment opportunities and gather knowledge about the problem in general. Active pursuit of job development targeted toward older persons can be initiated. In one Colorado county, for example, a senior tax relief program was developed that allows departments of city government to hire seniors to work 80 hours for $250, which can be used for tax payment. The program has led to several permanent part-time jobs and to many ongoing volunteer positions for participants. A social worker in a western Colorado city has organized and trained teams of elderly unemployed workers to carry out job development activities for themselves and other elders. This self-help strategy is an effective means of both job creation and political education.

Opportunities for collective action and participation in ongoing social action efforts can also be realized. The support of the empowerment-oriented worker is critical to mobilization of these efforts. The membership of groups concerned with employment issues is often characterized by rapid turnover because of employment of members. Consequently, the development of ongoing institutionalized programs that can engage in aggressive outreach is important to both the workers and the elderly clients who become engaged in action concerning this issue.

## Generating Supplemental Income

There is a wide range of self-help income-generating projects that can be of great value to those elders who are in need of supplemental income. International aging programs have done a lot to stimulate efforts in this regard. The American Association of International Aging and Help-Age in England are sources of many ideas about programs to develop income-generating projects and information on the issues involved in their development and management (Tout, 1989). Participation in such projects—whether through referral to existing programs or through the establishment of collective efforts such as communal gardens, child care programs, home repair programs, skills banks, and arts and crafts co-ops—can result in valuable income supplements for elderly clients. For example, food has been made available through inner-city communal gardens, gleaning projects, food-buying co-ops, and programs that pick up and distribute perishable leftovers from bakeries and restaurants on a daily basis. Elderly volunteers can initiate and participate in a wide range of such programs in order to provide food for themselves and others (see, for example, Moody, 1988, pp. 169–189).

The development and success of such projects depend on the interests, talents, and resources of each group, as well as each group's cultural values and historical experiences. For example, a VISTA volunteer reported the opening of a canning factory that came into existence because of the needs and interests of elderly retired fishermen in a small seacoast town. Many income-generating projects located on Native American reservations rely on artistic and other skills that have been passed from generation to generation. In a self-help project in a small northwestern town,

thirteen women, ranging in age from 72 to 91, set up a canning enterprise. They were able to use a church kitchen, and jars and other sup-
plies were donated. During the summer months this group canned fruits
and vegetables that were brought to them by community members. The
project grew over a three-year period to the point where more than four
facilities were in use and more than 40 individuals were working. In ap-
praising the program, the social worker stated, "All of the participants
made money and were also able to obtain a useful supply of food. But,
just as important, was the sense of community and pride they gained
from their efforts."

Programs that include voucher or service-credit systems allowing
seniors to provide a wide range of services that are counted as credits
toward the purchase of long-term care are being carried on at several
sites. Encouraging participation in these projects and assisting in their
organization and administration constitute an area of service for which
empowerment-oriented social workers must prepare. Many practitioners
report that skills banks and other labor exchange projects can be valuable
sources of income supplementation. However, one practitioner cautions:

> You always have to encourage constant recruitment of new skills bank
> members, because needs change, members become disabled, die, and move
> or just lose interest. In order to keep a skills bank going, a lot of participa-
> tion is required. . . . Even with all the work that goes into it, people are
> feeling more valuable and become more active in a lot of things through
> their involvement in the bank.

Acquiring information about the legal aspects of co-op establishment
and issues of management is an arena for mutual effort by worker and
clients. Retired elders can contribute knowledge about tax regulations,
rental negotiations, and advertising.

Cooperative programs represent an area of income supplement that
has great promise for the near future and that allows participants to gain
more power over problems related to limited resources.

In sum, participation in mutual support and group activities that
lead to late life employment and other sources of income helps clients
identify mutual concerns and needs. This consciousness-raising process
is a prerequisite to local action and participation in national groups.
Throughout the pursuit of solutions to income deficits among elderly
constituencies, the empowerment-oriented workers seeks to fill the roles
of mobilizer, educator, and partner. Mobilizing elderly individuals to pursue values clarification, to challenge values and attitudes that interfere
with the quality of life, to seek charitable resources and entitlements, to
participate in income-generating efforts, and to join actively in social action efforts aimed at securing employment opportunities and late life income is the basis of the empowerment-oriented approach to income issues
of the elderly.

# SECURING HEALTH CARE

Generating health care resources—whether these are hospital care, intensive physicians' services, or funds to pay for community-based long-term care services—is a task as complex as generating late life income resources. Public programs are limited in scope, and many of the elderly are not covered by these programs. Caught between red tape and the extremely high cost of health care, many elderly citizens and their families are left on their own to seek resources to meet health care needs. This process entails identifying needs and, in some instances, reassessing beliefs and expectations about health care.

## Values, Attitudes, and Beliefs about Health Care

Values, attitudes, and beliefs have as critical an impact on health care issues as they have on income issues. Fear of the use of medical care, or of confronting and dealing with medical problems, is often confused with issues of appropriateness and availability of services. Many complaints about "horrible treatment" at a specific medical facility have been traced to a fear of medical care in general; conversely, many fears of medical care result from experiences, directly or indirectly, with "horrible treatment."

Beliefs concerning who should pay for health care, what kind of health care is acceptable, and when health care is appropriate are diverse. The attitudes of different cultures and the growing interest in alternative methods of health care are strong elements of this diversity. The social worker must gain a clear understanding of client preferences and perceptions about health care before attempting educational activities concerning specific diseases, care alternatives, and how to be an informed and effective patient.

Confronting clients' values, beliefs, and fears concerning health care utilization is an essential prerequisite for helping them make health care decisions. Social workers often have elderly clients with acute health care needs who refuse to seek medical help. Comments such as "I've never seen a doctor I could trust," "I've made it 72 years without doctors or hospitals, and I don't need them now," and "If they find something bad wrong, I can't afford to pay them to fix it anyway" are common. Life patterns of medical care usage may have to be challenged. Decisions are often influenced by a mixture of values, fears, ignorance, and realistic doubts about the quality of available care. The empowerment-oriented worker must urge clients to actively confront their fears, separate the real from the imagined, and evaluate the alternatives.

Empowerment-oriented groups focused on health care issues can provide a strong source of mutual support for older people faced with these difficult tasks. However, if group support is not feasible, the worker can begin discussion of these subjects on an individual basis, an excellent context for the presentation and processing of relevant material. It may be possible to link individual elderly clients to others with similar concerns through phone networks or one-to-one. The use of educational materials is always helpful, but they may not be available in a form appropriate for the specific client or group of clients. The worker may need to modify the language to make it more understandable, to translate materials into another language, or to provide the information in a format useful to hearing- and/or sight-impaired clients.

## Mobilizing Health Care Resources

Once the decision to seek health care has been made, the issue of system responsiveness comes into play. Chapter 5 suggests the importance of collective activity with respect to accessing services. In one group of low-income elderly citizens, discussions of individual difficulties in getting help from a number of clinics led to the creation of a buddy system. Elderly group members volunteered to accompany each other to medical facilities to help assure that services were received and to reassure each other about seeking care. A variety of other approaches can be applied to assist individuals in the pursuit of health care resources.

Educating oneself and one's elderly clients concerning existing health care resources is not an easy task; investigative research skills are often required. There are many sources to tap for current information on Medicare and Medicaid coverage (starting with social security offices and state departments of social services). However, identifying respectable and high-quality supplemental insurance plans—common secondary resources—is problematic. Resources for payment of medication costs, in-home care not covered by Medicaid or Medicare, and long-term care are difficult to find.

In an effort to find trustworthy supplemental insurance, one group, consisting of seven frail elderly persons (individuals in need of help with the tasks of daily living), compiled a list of questions regarding potential supplemental insurance policies. Group members then divided up a list of insurance companies that offered supplemental plans, interviewed company representatives using the list of questions, and put together their own information booklet. This activity led to their inviting representatives of selected companies to present information at a neighborhood meeting. The group then attempted to establish a permanent source of updated information regarding these policies through a local senior center.

Another group of elders tackled the compilation of information regarding physicians who would accept Medicare and Medicaid. They also provided information about cooperative arrangements that a local senior action group had made with individual hospitals. This group had drawn up contracts with specific hospitals to provide all services for the amount of the Medicare or Medicaid consignment only and to provide uncovered services either for free or at very low cost. Membership in the organization sponsoring this option was not restricted and was available at a nominal fee. These activities raised individual elderly persons' awareness of cost concerns and of the potential that group action could increase their control over medical expenditures.

Cost and quality-of-care concerns regarding in-home, long-term care services parallel those related to hospital and physician care. Teaching clients about resources and possible means of financing services becomes the focus of many empowerment-oriented practitioners. Elderly clients need information about what to expect from specific services, how to find them, and how to control the impact of these services on their lives. Because of their isolation, many frail elderly individuals are susceptible to exploitation by underqualified individuals or unethical organizations. Interventions that encourage elderly people to take active roles in policing service programs for themselves and others are critical. Chapters 5 and 12 suggest a number of strategies useful in this effort.

Resources for the payment of fees for home-based services are affected by changes in Medicare and Medicaid. Many elderly lack the necessary income to provide for such services out of pocket. In several geographic areas, foundations have donated money to pay for long-term care services for those elderly who are not eligible for Medicaid funding and are unable to pay for the services themselves. These funds are, however, limited in scope and amount. Other resources designated for this purpose are also limited, and expanding them will require increased effort on the part of legislators, social work practitioners, seniors in need of the services, and other advocates.

A growing number of free or low-fee programs offering diagnostic and health maintenance testing are available at senior centers, senior housing sites, and other places where elderly people congregate. Free clinics and health care facilities that offer discounts to seniors may also be available. Groups of elderly individuals are often involved in such projects as initiators or outreach aides. They also provide volunteer assistance in the implementation of the services.

Empowering strategies to develop health care resources are being invented and implemented every day by elderly people, their families, and their advocates across the nation. These strategies are, however, mostly local or statewide. The mobilization of elderly individuals concerned with health care issues to active participation in national decision making remains a priority. The extreme cost and high-tech nature of health care limit the achievements of self-help and local endeavors. Elderly people engaged in these activities become acutely aware of these limitations and the need for a national effort.

# ENGAGING IN SOCIAL ACTION ACTIVITIES FOR HEALTH AND INCOME RESOURCES

Empowerment-oriented education and self-help activities based on the need for late life resources provide the context for related social action. Elderly people who engage in consciousness-raising processes having to do with income and health care issues are led to question matters of social justice, to recognize age discrimination in the job market, to identify problems in existing pension and health care systems, and to learn about possible alternative systems. Through active participation in values clarification and consciousness raising regarding their own situations and those of others, many seniors become more aware of social, political, and economic issues. This process often leads to action steps in an effort to affect policies or programs. One elderly man who participated for over a year in an empowerment-oriented community service program explained, "I thought there were a lot of problems without any possible solutions. Now I think there is a lot of work to be done and plenty of things that could change." An elderly woman who belonged to a crafts co-op that operated through the same agency said, "I thought selling some quilts through this co-op was all I would need or be interested in, but I found out I could do a lot more for others. That's why I've become so involved with the council."

The important role of social action, whatever form it takes, in stimulating interest in wider social concerns has not been well-studied. Senior volunteers in service or self-help programs come to better understand their own circumstances as well as those of the people they help, become acquainted with a variety of people, and are able to comprehend the issues that need attention more fully. The empowerment-oriented practitioner can often take advantage of these states of increased consciousness to stimulate participation in social action focused on larger issues. One worker recalled:

> I had the hardest time getting members to separate their roles in the senior council [a citywide social advocacy committee representing senior issues] from their roles as volunteers for the agency [a multipurpose senior agency for which several council members made home visits and delivered meals or served on program advisory committees]. However, over the years it became apparent that both functions were critical components of social action. Situations and problems they found as volunteers were what made them so effective as council members.

The social, political, and economic aspects of late life income and health care problems are identified by individuals and groups as they attempt to find and access entitlements or as they develop self-help projects. Social action strategies become an unavoidable part of securing access to services, creating resources where they do not exist, and solving the problems of survival. As group members collect information about existing resources, they expose the gaps in resources, the stigma attached to receiving public entitlements or private charity, and the many forms of institutional discrimination. When this process occurs within groups, it is usually a first step toward devising means of addressing the issues. The educational role of the empowerment-oriented worker is crucial at this juncture; expertise is readily available from group or network members. Also, initial links to appropriate established social action groups need to be provided.

## SUMMARY

Many elderly individuals and groups are without adequate income and health care resources. Empowerment-oriented workers assist elderly clients in addressing all dimensions of the problem of the lack of adequate survival resources. Clients' attitudes and beliefs about need must be critically assessed by them when they constitute an obstacle to quality of life. The knowledge and skills needed in order to secure resources must also be obtained by elderly clients. The use of collective efforts is often an important part of accomplishing these goals.

Empowerment-oriented workers must assist clients in identifying health care and income entitlements, as well as potential supplemental resources from private social welfare sources. Empowerment-oriented strategies that motivate individual and collective efforts to increase employment opportunities and other forms of support are also important in assisting the elderly. In addition, self-help income-generating projects and social action to address relevant legislation and agency policies are strongly encouraged.

## REFERENCES

AARP. (1991). *Aging America: Trends and perspectives* (1991 ed.) (DHHS Publication No. FCOA 91-28001). Washington, DC: U.S. Department of Health and Human Services.

Atchley, R. (1991). *Social forces and aging* (7th ed). Belmont, CA: Wadsworth.

Bass, S. A., Kutza, E. A., & Torres-Gil, F. M. (Eds.). (1990). *Diversity in aging.* Glenview, IL: Scott, Foresman.

Estes, C. L., Swan, J. H., & Girard, L. E. (1984). Dominant and competing paradigms in gerontology: Towards a political economy of aging. In M. Minkler & C. Estes (Eds.), *Readings in the political economy of aging.* Farmingdale, NY: Baywood.

Flanagan, J. (1984). How to ask for money. In F. M. Cox, J. L. Erlich, J. Rothman, & J. E. Tropman (Eds.), *Tactics and techniques of community practice* (2nd ed.). Itasca, IL: F. E. Peacock.

Gelfand, D. E. (1988). *The aging network: Programs and services* (3rd ed.). New York: Springer.

Goodin, R. E. (1990). Relative needs. In A. Ware & R. Goodin (Eds.), *Needs and welfare.* London: Sage.

Jakobi, P. L. (1990). Public policy and poverty among the oldest old: Looking to 2040. *Journal of Aging and Social Policy, 2*(3/4), pp. 85–99.

Kleyman, P. (1992). Census shows U.S. safety net fails many vulnerable elders. *Aging Today, 13*(4), p. 1.

Kutza, E. A. (1990). Responding to diversity: Is America capable? In S. A. Bass, E. A. Kutza, & F. M. Torres-Gil (Eds.), *Diversity in aging.* Glenview, IL: Scott, Foresman.

Lockery, S. A. (1988). Minority aged and income policy. *Generations, 12*(3), pp. 65–68.

Marcuse, H. (1964). *One-dimensional man.* Boston: Beacon.

Markson, E. W. (1983). *Older women.* Lexington, MA: D.C. Heath.

Minkler, M., & Estes, C. C. (1991). *Critical perspectives on aging: The political and morale economy of growing old.* Amityville, NY: Baywood.

Moody, H. R. (1988). *Abundance of life: Human development policies for an aging society.* New York: Columbia University Press.

Morris, R. (1985). *Social policy of the welfare state* (2nd ed.). New York: Longman.

Pivin, F. F., & Cloward, R. A. (1979). *Poor people's movements: Why they succeed, how they fail.* New York: Vintage.

Shultz, J. W. (1988). *The economics of aging* (4th ed.). Belmont, CA: Wadsworth.

Social Security Administration. (1991). *SSI supplemental security income* (GSA Publication No. 05-11000). Washington, DC: U.S. Government Printing Office.

Tout, K. (1989). *Aging in developing countries.* Oxford, England: Oxford University Press.

# FAMILY CAREGIVING

This chapter discusses the problems and issues associated with family caregiving, including who the caregivers are, types of care given, stresses associated with caregiving, family conflicts, care receivers' perceptions, and community-based services for caregivers. Empowerment-oriented interventions in the four dimensions of activity presented in Chapter 3 are discussed and illustrated in a case example.

Family caregiving is a critical and timely issue in the aging field. The myth that families have abandoned elder members has been adequately dispelled. The portion of the population that comprises the 85-and-older category requires the most intense caregiving. The projected increase in this age group means that caregiving issues will continue to intensify as more families find themselves involved in caregiving and caregiving decisions. Prolonged caregiving creates many strains and stresses for caregivers. Potentially, this can result in the collapse of the caregiving arrangement and the deterioration of the health and welfare of the caregiver. Empowerment-oriented interventions with caregivers include service brokerage, family education, counseling, mediation, support groups and other forms of mutual aid, networking, and political activism for policy change.

## *CAREGIVING AS A FAMILY ISSUE*

Families provide the majority of in-home services to older people. It is estimated that families furnish 80% of in-home care for those who are 75 and older and suffer chronic disabilities (Hooyman & Lustbader, 1986). The common conditions in old age that cause elders to need assistance include:

- Physical illnesses and disabilities such as hip and joint difficulties, arthritis, fractures, heart disease, cancer, stroke, and vision and hearing impairments

- Mental deterioration such as dementia, memory loss, depression, and paranoia

- Social isolation due to physical impairments or financial difficulties

Although old age and illness are not synonymous, the likelihood of chronic illness or disability increases with age. Although most non-institutionalized elders are able to care for themselves, nearly 5.1 million older persons living in the community need assistance with some aspect of personal care or home management (AARP, 1986). Only 5% of adults aged 65–74 need assistance in performing one or more of the basic activities of daily living (such as shopping, household chores, preparing meals, or handling money), but that percentage increases to more than 33% in the 75–84 age group (AARP, 1986). The aging, or "graying," of the population over the next 40 years will double the number of such persons with activity limitations, resulting in greater need for services given to families and performed by the formal service delivery system (Ory, 1985).

About 4–5% of the elderly population 65 and older suffers from Alzheimer's disease or other severe dementia, and 11–12% has mild to moderate dementia (Schneck, 1982). At least two people in each dementia victim's network are affected emotionally or financially, to some degree, by caregiving responsibilities, for an estimated total of 9 million people affected by dementia alone (Pilisuk & Parks, 1988).

## Who Is Doing the Caregiving?

Caregiving is rarely a team effort. The responsibility nearly always falls on a single individual in the family. It falls on old people who have health problems of their own (35% of caregivers to the elderly are over 65, and more than 10% are over 75), on poorer people who cannot afford to purchase help (one-third of caregivers are poor or near-poor), and on women.

The average age of caregivers is 57; however, 25% of caregivers are between 65 and 74, with another 10% 75 or older. Husbands are the oldest group, with 42% being 75 or older (Greenberg, Boyd, & Hale, 1992).

The greatest number of caregivers are women. OWL estimates that roughly three out of four, or 72%, of caregivers are women, for a total of 1.6 million female caregivers. The most common relationships of female caregivers to the care recipients are daughter (29%) and spouse (23%); another 20% are more distant relatives (Sommers & Shields, 1987). Although males assume at least 25% of all caregiving, they tend to hire

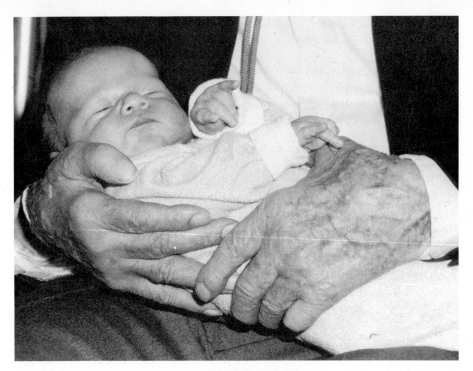

***Caregiving and care receiving: A partnership of love***
*(Photo courtesy of Senior Resource Center, Wheatridge, Colorado)*

out the daily tasks and are less likely to be involved in direct "hands-on" care (Hooyman, 1988). Of course there are some males who give devoted and traditional care to either spouse or elder parents. However, among children who are primary caregivers, daughters outnumber sons three to one.

The reasons why women are most often the primary caregivers are many and well-documented:

- Caregiving is defined as a female role in this society, whether it involves caring for small children, nursing the sick, or caring for elders and other family members.

- Women are socialized to feel guilty if they do not assume the caregiving roles society says belong to them.

- Women are covertly and implicitly rewarded when they do assume caregiver roles.

- Because of women's socialization, they often believe that they should be able to carry out caregiving responsibilities without help, and they tend to refuse to call upon others in the family for help.

- Because of the socialization experience, women do not always choose freely or rationally but are driven or forced to assume caregiver roles by society's and their families' assumptions that caring is women's work.

Caregiving roles, however, are often in conflict with the increasing demands on women to provide financial support for their families. In addition to the greater number of two-income households, the high divorce rate has resulted in more women and children living in low-income circumstances where the woman is the sole source of financial support (Hooyman & Lustbader, 1986). Although one-third of caregivers are employed, both male and female caregivers are less likely to be employed than noncaregivers (Greenberg, Boyd, & Hale, 1992). The demands of caregiving can jeopardize employment. Stone, Cafferata, and Sangle (1986) report that although only 12% of the female caregivers they studied had actually left their jobs to care for disabled relatives, the impact of caregiving on employment status was greater than this figure seems to indicate, for many reported cutting back on their work hours, changing schedules, and taking leave without pay. (See also Bunting, 1989; Pilisuk & Parks, 1988.)

Gaps continue to exist between the earnings of men and women for the same work, and women do not have full access to higher-paying jobs in the labor market. At least 12% of the gap between men and women, however, is attributed to interruptions in employment due to taking time off to care for others (Soldo & Agree, 1988). The caregiving role mitigates against women closing the economic gap between themselves and men. The double bind consisting of barriers to economic gain in the workplace and lack of public support for caregivers serves to facilitate the disparity.

Other sources of stress for females in caregiving roles include the multiple roles carried by most women. Many women are in the "sandwich" position of caring for members of more than one generation at a time (Brody, 1985). Approximately 25% of people caring for elderly parents and 33% of other caregivers (other than spouses) have children under the age of 18 living at home (Greenberg, Boyd, & Hale, 1992). Even when women work outside the home, there is no substantial relief from housework, and assumption of the caregiver role often simply adds another responsibility to a woman's life, with no relief from other roles to make time and energy for caregiving duties. An increasingly common caregiving arrangement is the older woman caring for her ill spouse. The average age of a wife who cares for her husband is 65 (Sommers & Shields, 1987). The provision of care often exacerbates the chronic conditions of aging itself for such an elderly spouse.

# What Types of Care Are Given?

The forms of assistance given by family members to those who are frail and elderly are diverse. Arling and McAuley (1984) describe five broad types of care:

1. Housekeeping/homemaking
2. Meal preparation
3. Personal care (assistance with dressing, bathing, and/or eating)
4. Continuous supervision
5. Nursing care

Many of these go beyond a social-emotional supportive relationship. Supervision and nursing care, in particular, often require the sharing of living arrangements. Three-fourths of the caregivers for the elderly live with those who require the care. On an average day, primary caregivers spend more than six hours assisting with personal hygiene, medication, household chores, shopping, and transportation (Pilisuk & Parks, 1988).

Caregiving varies from once-a-week visits to 24-hour, live-in care. Tasks frequently include either direct care or the hiring, supervision, and monitoring of caregivers and the relevant decision making. Family decisions regarding caregiving may focus on issues such as hospital discharge planning, hospice placement, nursing home placement, assisted living arrangements, and home health care arrangements, as well as what type and level of care is required, who will be involved and in what ways, who will pay, and how much. Participants in the decision-making process can be nearly anyone with an interest in the elderly person's welfare, such as the elderly person himself or herself, children and siblings of the elder, members of the designated caregiver's family, and the elder's friends and neighbors (Parsons & Cox, 1989).

# What Are the Stresses Associated with Caregiving?

Prolonged caregiving is associated with a decrease in health status for the caregiver. Ory (1985) concludes that extended caregiving (or caregiving without support and relief) is associated with serious deterioration in the health of the primary caregiver. Symptoms of depression and anxiety, feelings of helplessness, lowered morale, and emotional exhaustion are all associated with caregiving (Greenberg, Boyd, & Hale, 1992). Many caregivers find the loss of personal freedom, the lack of time for social and recreational activities, and the restriction of mobility particularly bothersome. Lowered life satisfaction as well as clinical depression can result from accumulated burdens of caregiving. Ory (1985) also reports that those caregivers who live in the household with the elder experience more stress than those who do not.

Cutler (1985) summarizes the following stresses of caregiving:

- The physical strain of meeting the elder's need for help with routine activities of daily living (dressing, eating, bathing, toileting, transportation, lifting, laundry, and/or housecleaning)

- Isolation and loneliness (caused by decreased opportunities to participate in social and community activities)

- Lack of sleep (many caregivers report that lack of sleep, resulting in physical exhaustion and mental fatigue, is one of their greatest sources of stress)

- The emotional reaction to the decline and anticipated death of a loved one, resulting in the triggering of the grief process

- Adjusting to having another person living in one's home

- Financial strain (resulting from assisting with payments for such services as health care and supervision and from reduction of the caregiver's opportunity to earn)

- Family distress (the family encompasses all of the primary caregiver's near relatives; grandchildren especially have difficulty coping with the mental and physical deterioration of grandparents and are intolerant of their conditions)

- Physical and emotional abuse from the dependent elder, particularly in cases of dementia

- Lack of relief and support for the caregiver, either from other family members or from the service sector, resulting in limited leisure activity and inability to meet personal needs*

The dichotomy of subjective and objective burden has often been studied (Montgomery, Gonyea, & Hooyman, 1985; Parsons, Cox, & Kimboko, 1989). *Subjective burden* relates to the mental outlook and feelings of the caregiver about the caregiving situation. *Objective burden* refers to the actual strain on the caregiver in such areas as health, income, and time. Ory (1985) has found that the subjective burden causes the dissolution of informal care arrangements and leads to institutionalization more frequently than does the objective burden, or the actual level of care needed. The variability among caregiving situations is great; some families have better support networks and coping skills than others. Subjective burden is not directly associated with objective burden. It is more likely to be associated with the relationship between the caregiver and the

*Adapted from "Counseling Caregivers" by L. Cutler, in *Generations, 10*(1), 1985, pp. 53–57. Copyright © 1985 by the American Society on Aging.

elderly care receiver (Cox, Parsons, & Kimboko, 1988), the extent of personality change in the elder as a result of disease, the past history of family dynamics, the coping abilities of the caregiver, the degree of social support available, other demands on the time of the caregiver, and demographics such as sex, age, income, and ethnic background (Ory, 1985).

## Conflict Arising from Caregiving

Family conflict is often a result of caregiving. Although family caregiving is common, decision making related to such arrangements is not always harmonious. Resolution of family conflict has been found to be one of the five most frequent interventions among social workers in home health care agencies (Levande, Bowden, & Mollema, 1987). More than half of caregivers report family conflict as a stress of caregiving (Rabins, Mace, & Lucas, 1982). Conflict due to caregiving may lead to elder abuse (Circirelli, 1986) and is often the object of family therapy (Montalvo & Thompson, 1988).

Sources of family conflict include:

- Guilt on the part of family members arising from their lack of participation or their negative feelings about the necessity for care
- Grief reactions connected with the loss of the elderly family member's health
- Disparate investments and interests in the caregiving arrangements for the elder
- Scarce resources for caregiving, which demands commitment and substantial sacrifices from family members
- The resurrection of old, conflictual family dynamics through the decision-making process (Parsons & Cox, 1989)
- Limited experience with joint decision making

One of the principal sources of conflict is the unequal sharing of the caregiving burden by family members. Usually one person does the hands-on caregiving, and this person is generally a female. Although women do a major portion of the caregiving, they are not often asked to provide input for decisions about the caregiving tasks and the general situation. The siblings or children who are emotionally closest to the care receiver (and males in general) tend to have the greatest influence on decision making. Family members who do not participate in decision making but are asked to contribute to the caregiving effort may resent their lack of inclusion in the decision-making process. When family members are excluded, they feel less capable of lending a hand in the caregiving situation. Dysfunctional family dynamics may be resurrected by such a situation and, if unresolved, may sabotage caregiving (Parsons & Cox, 1989). Unresolved family conflict often results in fragmentation of effort and a breakdown in the elder's support network, which is associated with increased institutionalization (Berkman, 1983) and elder abuse (Knight, 1985).

## Elders' Perceptions of Caregiving

Much attention has been given to the caregiver in the caregiving relationship, but the experience of the care receiver has not been widely considered. Elders' satisfaction and perceptions of the caregiving arrangement were assessed in a study of 34 elders receiving care (Parsons, Cox, & Kimboko, 1989). Satisfaction of elderly care receivers was related to the components of the relationship between the elder and the caregiver, not to the level of impairment suffered by the elderly person. The elders' greatest concern about the caregiving situation seemed to be the fear of being a burden to others. Almost none who were interviewed in the study reported that they had assigned tasks or perceived a feeling of mutual responsibility in the household. It is interesting to note that care receivers were very reluctant to tell their troubles to their caregivers, believing that the caregivers had "enough troubles of their own." Care receivers did not want to add to the burden they already perceived themselves to be by unloading their feelings on their caregivers. This reluctance no doubt detracted from the communication and problem-solving capacity of the pair. Elderly care receivers seemingly saw themselves and their caregivers as victims of an unhappy situation that should be minimized and not talked about so that it would not become worse.

## Community-Based Aid to Caregiving Families

A great deal of time, energy, and money has been expended in the name of community-based care for elderly people. Competition for scarce dollars, however, has created a less than effective or efficient system of services to aid families in their caregiving roles. Traditionally, the government has not supported families' caregiving efforts or functions (Biegel & Blum, 1990). Less than 10% of caregiving families receive supportive services from community-based agencies. A study of 54 caregiving families provided the following information regarding utilization of services, which suggests that caregivers often do not utilize services, even when they are available (Cox, Parsons, & Kimboko, 1988, p. 432):

*Services Utilized (from most to least utilized)*

1. Social and recreational
2. Personal care

3. Nursing care
4. Transportation
5. Continuous supervision assistance
6. Meal preparation
7. Telephone reassurance
8. Physical therapy
9. Day care

*Services Not Utilized (from most to least needed)*

1. Physical and mental assessment
2. Social and recreational
3. Meal preparation
4. Information and referral
5. Personal care
6. Continuous supervision assistance
7. Homemaker services
8. Nursing care
9. Transportation
10. Telephone reassurance
11. Physical therapy
12. Day care

Service programs are fragmented and fill only a part of the needs of caregivers, and the gap between community-based services and the needs of caregivers is widening. Restrictive eligibility policies limit access to community-based care, and augmentation of Medicare coverage has been left primarily to the states (Pilisuk & Parks, 1988). Entitlement to Medicaid is available only to the poor, and funds designated in the Older Americans Act for such services have been cut, leaving even more gaps in an already fragmented service delivery system. Although clear evidence exists that there is ample public support for government responsibility for caregiving for the elderly (Gilliland & Havir, 1990), assistance to caregiving families is not forthcoming.

The political problem is that no one wants to pay for something that is currently being done for free. The crux of the matter, however, is that this service is *not* free—the costs to the families giving the care have not been calculated. Such costs to families are hidden in the health decline of family members and premature placement of elderly care receivers in nursing homes because of lack of support for the caregivers.

Family members should not be forced to make sacrifices without adequate support.

# EMPOWERMENT-ORIENTED INTERVENTIONS FOR FAMILY CAREGIVING

The initial goal of empowerment-oriented interventions is not only to achieve results related to clients' immediate or presenting problems, but also to transmit to clients the knowledge and skills necessary to take action for themselves and others. The overall goal is to mobilize elderly consumers of services, their families, and their communities toward self-care and active involvement in the creation of a better environment. To achieve such a goal, empowerment-oriented workers must try to leave clients with better skills and knowledge to cope with their environment than they had before they received professional help.

Activities designed to reach empowerment goals were conceptualized in Chapter 3 along four dimensions of focus, representing a range of consciousness and problem assessment extending from private troubles (internal) to public issues (external). The four dimensions of intervention activities range from personal to sociopolitical. (Table 9.1 shows the four dimensions of activity with respect to the caregiving situation.)

## Initial Contact and Assessment

As with most problems affecting the elderly population, the stresses and needs of caregivers are usually brought to the attention of the service delivery system through individual referrals. These referrals may come from doctors, ministers, hospitals, or the families themselves. If the initial contact with the family is through individual referral, then the intervention begins in Dimension 1 with a thorough assessment (see Figure 9.1). The assessment begins with evaluation of the elder's functional and need-of-care levels. It also includes assessing the stresses of the caregiving situation, the support coming from the family members and from informal and formal support systems, and the health status of and burden on the caregiver. The assessment must also gauge the family's perception of the problem—from private trouble to public issue.

Most families tend to believe that the problems associated with caregiving are private troubles, that caregiving is their job. If they are experiencing stress and strain, they see those problems as unique to them and theirs to work out. They often do not know about basic resources in the community that might bring them at least partial relief. The family may often resist support and assistance from outside sources. The assessment must include gauging the degree of guilt, martyrdom, denial,

**Table 9.1** *Levels of Problem Understanding, Assessment, and Intervention with Caregivers and Care Receivers*

| Four Dimensions of Intervention | Specific Examples of Activities |
| --- | --- |
| Individual and/or family* | Assessing, educating, and counseling elders and their families |
| | Linking clients with basic services |
| | Developing relationships |
| | Sharing information with clients about the problem situation and possible solutions |
| | Teaching clients how to find and use available resources |
| Individual, family, and small groups | Learning skills and knowledge to cope with the problem |
| | Developing support networks |
| | Forming telephone reassurance networks |
| | Engaging in continuing education regarding the issues |
| Individual, family, groups, organizations, and networks | Engaging in self-help and in helping others |
| | Forming and joining support networks |
| | Participating in mutual problem solving |
| | Forming and joining mutual aid groups |
| | Arranging shared caregiving |
| Individual, family, groups, networks, organizations, communities, and larger sociopolitical systems | Creating new programs |
| | Taking political action |
| | Lobbying |
| | Organizing groups and networks for political action |
| | Endeavoring to change social policy |

*Activities in this dimension are performed or led by the social worker; all other activities may be led by the worker or by the clients themselves.

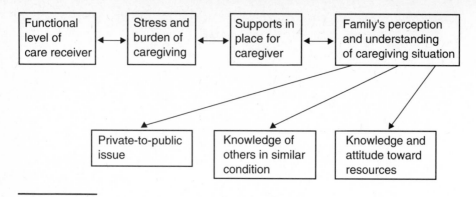

**Figure 9.1  Dimension 1 Assessment**

and unrealistic expectation that has been incorporated by the family, particularly by the primary caregiver. In order for the caregiver and the professional helper to reach a mutual understanding of the problem, the cause, and the possible solutions, the caregiver's perceptions about the larger issue of caregiving, about others in the same situation, and about solutions that others have found helpful must be expanded.

Interventions with caregiving families include all dimensions of the model presented in Chapter 3. These dimensions are discussed below.

## Dimension 1 Interventions

A primary activity in Dimension 1 is *social casework* with caregivers, to help them cope better with the caregiving situation. Social casework includes exploring feelings, tensions, burden, needs, and services; clarifying stresses and needs; evaluating service options and feasibility of access; formalizing an agreement for work; and ongoing problem solving and education regarding caregiving issues (Getzel, 1981). Caregivers are often overwhelmed, so setting realistic goals can bring them a measure of hope (Cutler, 1985). A major part of social casework with a caregiver includes education and consciousness raising, to enable the caregiver to make appropriate decisions. Issues prevalent in caregiving situations are those of guilt (because caregivers cannot accomplish their tasks well on their own), lack of self-care, and denial of the caregiver's own needs.

Comprehensive social casework in this situation can be broken down into six components: education, support, involvement of family members, teaching of coping techniques, facilitation of resources, and mediation of family disputes.

**Education**  The primary educational need of caregivers is for medical information that provides a basic understanding of the care receiver's condition, the treatment prognosis, and disease management. Caregivers also need to know about common behaviors associated with the disease, the aging process, common family responses to the stresses of caregiving, and community resources available to the family.

**Support** Caregivers have usually exhausted their coping abilities before a referral is made to a professional helper. They need to vent their emotions, tell their stories, be heard, learn that their feelings are similar to those of others in their situation. Professional helpers need to bring the family to an understanding of the broader context of caregiving.

**Involvement of Family Members** An important aspect of Dimension 1 interventions is assessing the degree of involvement by other family members and attempting to get them to assist in the care. Often older spouses who are primary caregivers see the caregiving role as theirs alone and are very reluctant to bother their children or other relatives. Workers must explore with the caregiver the feasibility of involving other family members. If there are conflicts with family members that prevent the family from working together, workers can offer mediation or other conflict resolution strategies.

**Teaching of Coping Techniques** There are many sources of information on how to cope with caregiving. These include books written for caregivers and pamphlets put out by support agencies (such as the Alzheimer's Disease and Related Disorders Association), which contain suggestions from caregivers themselves. Social workers need to be familiar with these written materials, and if the caregiver cannot become involved in an education and support group outside the home, the worker should bring this information to the family.

**Facilitation of Available Resources** No part of service to caregivers is more critical than providing information about, links to, and brokering and advocacy for community-based direct services to the family. The following is a partial list of relevant community-based services that can be found in most communities (Eldercare Management Group, 1988):

- *Adult day care.* Social day care centers focus on adults who suffer from memory loss, loneliness, depression, or other social or psychological difficulties. Health day care centers work with people who need rehabilitation after a hospital stay or who have chronic medical conditions that require routine nursing care. . . .
- *Attendant care.* Severely disabled persons may need full-time aides to help with feeding, bathing, and other essential activities.
- *Home health care.* Nursing services (such as injections of medicine and changing of bandages) are provided in the home. These services are often required after hospitalization.

- *Hospice.* A range of medical, social, and psychological services are offered for persons who are terminally ill. Hospice patients may be served at home, in a hospital, or in a facility such as a nursing home.

- *In-home support services.* A program of personal care is offered, providing help such as assistance with bathing and dressing and chore services such as shopping or housecleaning.

- *Meals.* Nutritious meals are provided for a small donation in congregate settings such as churches, schools, or senior citizens' centers. Home-delivered meals are available for those unable to get to meal sites.

- *Respite care.* Designed to aid families who are caring for a frail or disabled person, respite care offers short-term relief from caregiving duties. Adult day care and weekend or vacation residential care are examples.

- *Social services.* Social services are provided by staff and volunteers working for profit, nonprofit, voluntary, and government entities and include the following kinds of assistance: transportation and escort, personal care and home chore services, friendly visits and telephone reassurance, case management (care coordination), counseling, information and referral, and money management.*

***Mediation of Family Disputes***   Social workers can make a significant contribution to empowerment-oriented practice by facilitating the resolution of family conflict so that family members can work together in support of the elder member, rather than against one another. Mediation is the application of the problem-solving process to conflict in an attempt to find a behaviorally oriented solution. Conflict may arise from substantive issues, from the emotional dynamics around an issue, or from value differences. Conflict is often defined as substantive even though it may result directly from emotional dynamics; in other words, families may find substantive issues to symbolize or rationalize their emotional differences. The mediator must therefore find a way to vent the feelings or emotions before directing the participants' attention to the substantive issues and initiating negotiation and bargaining (Parsons & Cox, 1989). The mediator's goals include:

*From "A Listing of Community-Based Services" by Eldercare Management Group, in *Personnel Journal,* September 1988. Copyright © 1988 by *Personnel Journal.* Reprinted by permission.

- Eliciting the family members' perceptions of the problem
- Isolating the issues within the conflict
- Assisting family members to separate their interests and needs from their wants and wishes
- Listening to, supporting, and validating the often painful experiences of family members
- Helping family members find alternative solutions and resources
- Facilitating decision making with respect to the alternatives
- Assisting the family to make plans for carrying out their agreements

Although not all family conflicts are easily mediated, many misunderstandings or poorly communicated situations that might have been amenable to mediation escalate and create serious conflict if unattended. Social workers need to know how to facilitate conflict resolution in addition to other family intervention skills. The overall role of the social worker as mediator is to engage with the caregiving family in conflict resolution and problem solving in many arenas.

## Dimension 2 Interventions

In Dimension 2 interventions, the activities may be similar to those described for Dimension 1. One difference, though, is that more of the interventions are carried out in a group format than in an individual format; another is that the emphasis shifts more to education. Caregivers may attend meetings—with or without the worker—where support and education are given. From an empowerment-oriented perspective, there are many advantages to this type of activity. The group provides the collective experience thought to be necessary in the empowerment process. The all-in-the-same-boat feeling helps caregivers realize that they are not alone and that others in similar situations have similar problems, that the effects of caregiver stress are normal. From the standpoint of understanding or acknowledging the problem, this level of intervention provides the opportunity for caregivers to see that the feelings they have (and may have been ashamed of) are not only normal but prevalent and that others have worked out solutions that may be useful for them.

Learning about communicating with elders, conflict resolution in the family, the aging process, and support and telephone reassurance networks can help the caregiver give and receive support and connect with others in the same situation. Caregiver support groups have been found to be an effective intervention that provides a network of supportive persons and helps caregivers increase their knowledge of community resources, handle anxiety, find time for self-care, work with other family members to share responsibilities, increase interpersonal competence in dealing with problems and issues, and improve relationships with care receivers (Toseland, Rossiter, & Labrecque, 1989). There are many good educational programs available for caregivers. For those who are home-bound and cannot get out to meet with others, there are videotapes, news-letters, books, and other materials to bring these types of interventions into the home (Aronson, 1988; Jacobsen, 1988; Springer & Brubaker, 1984).

## *Dimension 3 Interventions*

Caregivers are ready for Dimension 3 interventions once they begin to understand the problems they are experiencing from a broader perspec-tive and start to seek out contact and support from others in similar situa-tions. This type of intervention is not significantly different from those in Dimension 2, except that the direction and control of the assistance being provided to the caregivers are in the hands of other clients like themselves, instead of under the direction of helping professionals. The major activity at this level is participation in self-help groups.

Enabling members to cope is the goal of self-help and mutual aid groups. These groups focus on the actual exchange of services among members as well as conjoint problem solving, making suggestions to one another, and sharing of resources. Members may teach one another new skills in areas such as family mediation and conflict resolution, behavioral management, and other coping techniques. The research literature on self-help groups suggests that these groups have a positive impact on members' self-esteem, life satisfaction, and levels of depression (Toseland & Rossiter, 1989).

Self-help groups are typically led by members, not by professionals; such a group may decide to involve professionals in a variety of ways, but the control of the group remains with the membership. Agency spon-sorship is usually necessary, however, in order to provide the structure and context for the group. Caregivers' self-help groups are sponsored by hospitals, community centers, chapters of the Alzheimer's Disease and Related Disorders Association, and other community agencies. *The Doll-maker* (Schmall & Stiehl, 1987) is a packaged program—including video-tapes for caregivers—designed for self-help groups.

An informal support network is critical to elders and their caregiving families. Caregivers often find it easier to discuss emotional problems with someone such as a member of the clergy or a family physician than with a professional social worker. Informal help does not have the stigma at-tached to it that more formalized professional help can have. It may con-sist of a variety of helpful services, from peer counseling, training and education, or support to companionship, trips to the supermarket, or just good advice. Peer counseling groups, where caregivers become in-dividual and family counselors for one another, may grow out of such activities. One innovation in this area is the creation of cooperative respite care arrangements between caregivers. Built on the idea of child care cooperatives, these arrangements allow a family to "bank" hours of care for other families' elder members in exchange for care for their own elder member. This arrangement is economically affordable, and it helps some families feel more comfortable about care arrangements than if they utilized respite care services from formal agencies.

Dimension 3 activities are critical to the empowerment process because the caregiver and family become not only the receivers of services but also the deliverers of services to others. Such activities form the basis for clients' belief that they can effect change in their own lives and in the lives of others. These activities are self-esteem builders and enable caregivers not only to be better caregivers, but also to feel less like victims and more like active participants in the resolution of their problems. Such activities are not meant in any way to substitute for basic services needed by families doing caregiving but rather to supplement those services and allow the empowerment process to occur.

## Dimension 4 Interventions

Dimension 4 interventions are useful when caregivers define problems in a context of public issues and understand that the situation they are facing is partially the result of a lack of adequate and affordable community-based services for elders. Interventions focus on the political arena rather than on the private arena. The goal of the interventions is to create programs and change policies regarding caregiving. Participation in such activities by caregivers may occur after or during active caregiving. Such activities are often led by caregivers, who have a firsthand knowledge of the issues. They may become involved with national organizations with similar agendas, such as the AARP and OWL.

Although there is no integrated public policy in this country supporting the family's role in caregiving, a few scattered policies address some of the relevant issues. Some states have introduced tax deductions or tax credits for family caregivers; some states pay family members who provide in-home care; the 1984 reauthorization of the Older Americans Act mandated training and support of caregivers of persons with Alzheimer's disease (Kane, 1985). In general, however, this country has no strong policy regarding caregiving. Society has preferred family care or mutual support groups to institutional care when these can be justified as cheaper alternatives (Pilisuk & Parks, 1988). Some public agencies, such as the Public Health Association, have taken positions on the need for a national policy on caregiving, but an organization of elders' family members is needed to lobby legislators to address the issue at the state and national levels.

The following case example will show how the four dimensions of interventions are relevant to a specific case.

## CASE EXAMPLE: A Family Caregiving Situation

Jim is a retired insurance salesman, age 78, who was active immediately after his retirement but over the past eight years has become less and less functional. Jim suffers from a dementia that appears to be due to Alzheimer's disease. About two years ago he began to require close supervision from his wife. Mary is 74 and, except for a heart condition and moderate arthritis, is in reasonably good health. Mary works in ceramics and enjoys showing her creations at local arts and crafts shows. She has had an active and busy retirement after years of work as a secretary in the insurance business.

As Jim's condition has deteriorated, Mary has become unable to pursue her interests in crafts as much as she would like. In fact, Mary's life has changed drastically in the last six months. She used to take orders for ceramic pieces from private customers, but has had to stop because of the increase in Jim's need for supervision. She can no longer trust Jim to be safe in the house alone. She feels protective of Jim and tries to hide from her daughter and her sister, as well as the general community, the rapid deterioration of his condition. She worries about the future but tries to hide her concerns.

Mary's daughter, Sue, and Sue's family live nearby. Sue has two teenaged sons, and she and her husband are both employed full-time. Although they are concerned about Jim and Mary, they lead very busy lives and are not available to lend much hands-on support. Sue talks to her mother often and empathizes and gives verbal support, but she is not really aware of the degree of care her father now requires. Sometimes she even thinks her mother is exaggerating about her father's condition, for it is painful to her to view her father as someone with severe dementia. When she is around, his condition does not seem to be as bad as her mother describes. Her father has been respected by many in their relatively small community, and she wants his reputation and position protected. So, in some ways, Sue denies his condition.

Mary's sister, Jane, who is 65 and recently retired, also lives nearby. She has begun to notice changes in her sister as well as in Jim's condition. She has offered to help, but Mary has refused. She tries to talk to Mary about her concerns for Mary and for Jim, but Mary always changes the subject.

As winter approaches, Mary and Jim find excuses for not attending church and other community activities and for turning down invitations to meals with friends and to family gatherings. Jim's dementia is becoming more and more apparent, but Mary holds firm in her determination to protect him from embarrassment and withdraws from all her support systems. By early November, Mary's heart condition worsens; she suffers a mild heart attack and must have constant bed rest. A social worker at the senior health clinic learns in the discharge planning session of Mary and Jim's plight.

In beginning the assessment of the case, the social worker asks Sue to come in and discuss Mary and Jim's situation. Sue is very worried about both of her parents but believes that she and her husband can help by hiring someone to come into her parents' home to provide partial care, meal preparation, and household help. She plans to visit often and check up on them, and she proceeds to work with the social worker on finding the help her parents need.

   Within a few hours, the social worker receives a call from Mary's sister. Jane wants to talk to the social worker about Mary and Jim's situation and asks for an appointment. She comes in to discuss her concerns about the plan to have part-time help in the home, with Mary still serving as the primary caregiver. She is angry at Sue, her niece, and says that Sue is making a plan that will kill Mary. In Jane's view, Mary cannot be Jim's primary caregiver, even with part-time help.

After having a discussion with Mary herself, in which Mary voiced concern about receiving help from outsiders but also acknowledged her sister's adamant position and her own strength limitations, the social worker decides to hold a family mediation conference. The purpose is to air everyone's perception of the problem and generate alternative solutions. The social worker also assembles information about relevant resources that may be useful for the family. Because the social worker knows that family caregiving must be the responsibility of the whole family and not of a single individual, she attempts to gather together as many family members as possible for the mediation conference. Sue and her husband and teenaged children agree to participate, as do Jane and her husband. Mary and the social worker decide to include Jim in the discussion.

First, the social worker gives everyone information regarding the progressive nature of Alzheimer's disease and the issues in caregiving. She supports Mary's past efforts to perform this task alone but seeks commitment from other family members to share in the responsibilities. During the meeting, the developing conflict between Sue and Jane is pinpointed: Can Mary and Jim continue as they are with some additional help, or must Jim be temporarily placed in a care facility in order to give Mary an opportunity for the rest she needs? The social worker asks that all perceptions and the feelings attached to those perceptions be voiced. She validates the feelings and clarifies positions and perceptions. She works toward a common definition of the goal and a common understanding of resources and alternatives. Throughout the session, she is educating everyone regarding the nature of the situation they are facing.

After the initial meeting and one follow-up meeting with Mary, Sue, and Jane, some decisions are made about Jim's care. He will go to a day care center for at least six months; Sue and Jane volunteer to drive him there and back. A neighbor will come in and spend the night in order to help Mary with any needs Jim may have in the night.

As Mary's condition improves and she regains her strength, the social worker helps her join a support group for caregivers, within which she can deal with her own guilt for not being able to give Jim the care she would like to give him. She meets others in the same situation and discovers that there are many unmet needs among people like herself. She learns the importance of not giving up her health and relationships or even her interests so that she can remain a support to Jim. Sue is encouraged by the worker to learn the facts about her father's disease and the issues and dangers inherent in providing full-time caregiving for an older person suffering dementia. She is given videotapes and other materials that will assist her to comprehend what her parents are going through. Both mother and daughter are encouraged not to hide Jim's condition, but to share their experience with others. In this way, they not only receive help from a broader support system, but also educate others about a common situation.

Mary and Jane begin to speak at meetings of a group at their church and to tell others about caring for family members with dementia. Their church group becomes interested in starting a respite service for church members in need. Jane and Mary ask the social worker to provide some training for the group so that it can get started. When the social worker speaks, she includes information on employer benefits for elder care and other policy issues that bear on this problem.

Sue raises the issue of elder caregiving benefits with her employer. She asks the social worker to help her find information on companies that have adopted such policies. She also begins to explore respite care programs and talk to her friends about the need for such services.

Even though Mary is not able to be as active in the community as she would like to be, she finds she can do many things from home. She organizes telephone networks for caregivers and helps with a newsletter that highlights caregiving activities. Meeting other people dealing with the same issues helps her cope better with her own situation as well as understand the breadth of the problem and its solutions. She learns that OWL does legislative lobbying for public support for family caregiving and becomes a member and supporter of that organization out of her home, going to meetings when possible. Because she and members of her support system have gained knowledge regarding the disease, the problems associated with caregiving, the dangers of doing it alone, and the resources available, they are able to face the issues with relevant skills and a willingness to act in their own behalf and on behalf of others like them.

Mary becomes less stressed and less reluctant to ask for and accept help. Not only does she perceive the problem differently, she perceives herself differently. She learns that her own health, relationships, and support systems are primary to her well-being and her ability to care for Jim.

Mary continues to keep and care for Jim in their home, with help from formal service agencies and from informal support networks such as her church and family. She is not ashamed of receiving help, and she assists others like herself to accept the help they need. When the time comes when she is no longer able to care for Jim in their home, she will know what her options are and will be able to act.

# SUMMARY

Family caregiving is very prevalent, but too often at a sacrifice of quality of life for its participants. Caregiving is being performed at the expense of family members' financial, emotional, and physical health. Common stresses are isolation and loneliness, lack of sleep, emotional and physical drain, and family conflict. Most primary caregivers are women who are already in a precarious position economically, and caregiving only exacerbates that circumstance.

Caregiving presents many problems and issues that can be addressed through empowerment-oriented interventions. Such interventions with caregivers must address the problems identified with the act of caregiving as well as the lack of available services and the social policies that create that shortage. Specific activities for empowerment-oriented interventions with caregivers are focused along four dimensions.

Dimension 1 interventions include social casework, which involves problem identification; assessment of needs, resources, burden, and stresses; service options and feasibility of access; formulating an agreement for work; and planning for problem solving. Comprehensive casework also includes education, support, involvement of all family members, teaching coping skills and resource access, and mediation of conflicts. Dimension 2 interventions shift to education regarding caregiving issues and other late life issues. Learning about communication with the care receiver, conflict and its resolution, and mutual aid activities helps empower caregivers. Dimension 3 interventions include self-help groups and education of self and others regarding problems and solutions, resources, and service provisions. Dimension 4 interventions encompass the public and political aspects of caregiving issues. Policy and program changes are the goals of such activities.

## REFERENCES

AARP. (1986). *A profile of older persons: 1986.* Washington, DC: AARP.

Arling, G., & McAuley, W. J. (1984). The family, public policy and long-term care. In W. H. Quinn & G. A. Hughston (Eds.), *Independent aging: Family and social systems perspectives.* Rockville, MD: Aspen.

Aronson, M. D. (1988). *Understanding Alzheimer's disease.* New York: Scribner's.

Berkman, L. F. (1983). The assessment of social service networks and social support in the elderly. *Journal of American Geriatrics, 31,* p. 745.

Biegel, D. E., & Blum, A. (Eds.). (1990). *Theory, research, and policy.* Newbury Park, CA: Sage.

Brody, E. (1985). Parent care as a normative family stress. *The Gerontologist, 25*(1), pp. 19–30.

Bunting, S. M. (1989). Stress on caregivers of the elderly. *Advanced Nursing Science, 11*(2), pp. 63–73.

Circirelli, V. G. (1986). The helping relationship and family neglect in later life. In K. Pillemer & R. Wolf (Eds.), *Elder abuse: Conflict in the family.* Dover, MS: Auburn House.

Cox, E. O., Parsons, R. J., & Kimboko, P. J. (1988). Social services and intergenerational caregivers: Issues for social work. *Social Work, 33*(5), pp. 430–434.

Cutler, L. (1985). Counseling caregivers. *Generations, 10*(1), pp. 53–57.

Eldercare Management Group. (1988). A listing of community-based services. *Personnel Journal,* September, pp. 65–67.

Getzel, G. S. (1981). Social work with family caregivers of the aged. *Social Casework, 62,* pp. 201–209.

Gilliland, N., & Havir, L. (1990). Public opinion and long-term care policy. In D. E. Biegel & A. Blum (Eds.), *Aging and caregiving.* Newbury Park, CA: Sage.

Greenberg, J. S., Boyd, M. D., & Hale, J. F. (1992). *The caregiver's guide.* Chicago: Nelson-Hall.

Hooyman, N. (1988). Gender, caregiving, and equity: A feminist perspective. Invitational paper presented at the annual program meeting of the Council on Social Work Education, Chicago.

Hooyman, N. R., & Lustbader, W. (1986). *Taking care*. New York: Free Press.

Jacobsen, J. (1988). *Help! I'm parenting my parents*. Indianapolis, IN: Benchmark Press.

Kane, R. (1985). A family caregiving policy. *Generations, 10*(1), pp. 33–36.

Knight, B. C. (1985). The decision to institutionalize. *Generations, 10*(45), p. 45.

Levande, D. I., Bowden, S. W., & Mollema, J. (1987). Home health services for dependent elders: The social work dimension. *Journal of Gerontological Social Work, 11*(3/4), pp. 15–17.

Montalvo, B., & Thompson, R. F. (1988). Conflicts in the caregiving family. *Networker,* July/August, pp. 31–35.

Montgomery, R. J., Gonyea, J. G., & Hooyman, N. R. (1985). Caregiving and the experience of subjective and objective burden. *Family Relations, 34,* p. 19–26.

Ory, M. G. (1985). The burden of care: A familial perspective. *Generations, 10*(1), pp. 14–18.

Parsons, R. J., & Cox, E. O. (1989). Family mediation in elder caregiving decisions. *Social Work, 34*(2), pp. 122–127.

Parsons, R. J., Cox, E. O., & Kimboko, P. (1989). Satisfaction, communication and affection in caregiving: A view from the elder's perspective. *Journal of Gerontological Social Work, 13*(3/4), pp. 9–20.

Pilisuk, M., & Parks, S. H. (1988). Caregiving: Where families need help. *Social Work, 33*(5), pp. 436–440.

Rabins, P. V., Mace, N. L., & Lucas, M. J. (1982). The impact of dementia on the family. *Journal of the American Medical Association, 248,* pp. 333–335.

Schmall, V., & Stiehl, R. (1987). *The dollmaker.* Corvallis, OR: Department of Gerontology, Oregon State University.

Schneck, M. K. (1982). An overview of current concepts of Alzheimer's disease. *American Journal of Psychiatry, 139,* pp. 165–173.

Soldo, B. J. & Agree, E. M. (1988). America's elderly. *Population Bulletin, 43*(3), p. 31.

Sommers, T., & Shields, L. (1987). *Women take care.* Gainsville, FL: Triad.

Springer, D., & Brubaker, T. (1984). *Family caregivers and dependent elderly.* Beverly Hills, CA: Sage.

Stone, R., Cafferata, G., & Sangle, J. (1986). *Caregivers of the frail elderly: A national profile.* Washington, DC: National Center for Health Services Research.

Toseland, R. W., & Rossiter, C. M. (1989). Group interventions to support family caregivers: A review and analysis. *The Gerontologist, 29*(4), pp. 438–488.

Toseland, R. W., Rossiter, C. M., & Labrecque, M. S. (1989). The effectiveness of three group intervention strategies to support family caregivers. *American Journal of Orthopsychiatry, 59*(3), pp. 420–429.

# CARE RECEIVERS

This chapter addresses issues of empowerment that emerge with dependency, as individuals become unable to take care of their own physical needs and the social and emotional needs that emerge with declining physical capacity. Interventions useful to those elders who are required to accept assistance from others are suggested. Issues related to accepting help from personal caregivers (family members and friends) and professional providers are addressed. (Chapter 12 will discuss additional issues related to in-home services provided by paid caregivers.)

## LATE LIFE DISABILITIES

Most individuals need care from personal or professional caregivers from time to time throughout their lives, but the degree of dependency and the duration of the dependent status increase greatly with the onset of physical incapacity, which typically results from a chronic condition. Physical losses that necessitate the long-term assistance of friends and family members are perhaps the most feared form of dependency. Over 15% of people aged 65–69 and 49% of those 85 or older require help with one or more activities of daily living (AARP, 1991). Increasingly greater numbers of people are living into their late eighties. An individual's highly prized independence is strongly challenged when direct assistance from others is required because of declining physical capacity. This is especially true when one requires help with personal activities for daily functioning such as eating, bathing, and dressing. One's sense of privacy and control over daily living is severely threatened. Rzetelny (1985) explains the potential losses that elderly persons may suffer as a result of declining health:

The loss of health . . . can occur suddenly as with a stroke, or gradually as with a chronic condition such as emphysema. Illness, especially where the resulting incapacity lasts a long time or is permanent, can be devastating to an older person, in part because of the potential it has for triggering other losses such as loss of independence, loss of mobility and loss of opportunities for social, vocational and avocational activities. (p. 142)

# COPING WITH RECEIVING CARE

One of the most difficult problems faced by caregivers to the elderly is the attitude of the care receivers about accepting assistance. However, few interventions are targeted specifically toward assisting care receivers to cope with the issues of dependency and declining physical abilities. The empowerment-oriented worker can play a crucial role in an elderly person's struggle with the onset of illness that causes disability.

## The Role of Values

Once again, value issues, as well as other personal and political aspects of the problem, must be confronted. In American society the predominant experience is a *lifelong, culturally sanctioned struggle for independence,* which is linked to achieving financial security and social status. Americans from all social and financial backgrounds subscribe to a value system that emphasizes individual achievement and competition and expects outcomes of material wealth, physical and emotional strength, and rising social status. These values leave little room for mutual support and the acceptance of any form of assistance.

Today's older Americans have spent a lifetime interacting with this individualistic, achievement-oriented environment. Lowy (1989) notes:

> As people grow older the socioeconomic aspects of the independence/ dependence continuum are particularly significant. To allow for oneself to rely upon the support of others is frequently difficult to achieve, particularly in our culture which extols independence, mastery, activity, doing as strengths and perceives reliance upon others (people, services, institutions, bureaucracies) as weaknesses. The present elderly population has also been socialized into this culture and its values system and regards "being dependent" frequently as a personal deficit. The case of physical illness exemplifies this well. The wish to be independent is often in conflict with the wish to be taken care of. (p. 139)

A focus on the care receivers requires empowerment-oriented workers to assist these clients not only to deal with the many aspects of facing illness, but also to focus on values and attitudes about who should give needed care and under what circumstances. Beliefs about who should take care of elderly persons in the event they need physical care have not been widely explored from the perspective of the elders themselves. General assumptions are made that elderly members of American society expect family members (especially spouses and children) to provide this care. Studies confirm that 80–90% of all care is provided by families (Taeuber, 1990). Little documented research exists, however, on how elderly people really feel about this situation.

Case records on work with the elderly and their caregiving families reflect great diversity in the feelings of older care receivers about their situations. Most people never anticipate that they will need care from a family member. In a study of 33 elders who were receiving care from their families, Parsons, Cox, and Kimboko (1989) found that most were satisfied with the caregiving arrangements but that the level of satisfaction was related to the nature of the relationship between the elder and the caregiver. Nearly 20% were unhappy with their arrangements. Few saw themselves as able to contribute to the caregiving situation. The most common perception expressed by the elders was that they were a burden to their caregivers. Moreover, many were reluctant to voice concern or dissatisfaction to the caregiver because they wanted to avoid adding to what they felt was an already heavy burden of caregiving tasks.

Feelings of some seniors that children or spouses are supposed to provide care and that they are entitled to this care are offset by feelings of other seniors that they have somehow failed their children if they are in need of any assistance. Seniors experience different degrees of concern and/or guilt regarding the sacrifice required of family members in order to care for them. Such sacrifice may include the stress and physical exhaustion caused by the workload, a change in employment status, or an inability to meet the needs of other family members as a result of the time necessary to assist the elderly person. There is also a great difference among elderly care receivers in the perception of their obligation to reciprocate for the caregiving they receive from family members and the nature of that reciprocation. Some elders try to respond with financial rewards, and some with emotional and social rewards; others believe they have no such obligation and make very heavy demands upon their caregivers.

The elderly, like most Americans, have mixed views on the appropriate source for late life care. A number of elders believe that they should be able to purchase from the marketplace any assistance they may need. Others believe that their past employers should have provided benefits to take care of their needs or that adequate services should be provided by governments, churches, or private charities.

## Developmental Tasks

From the perspective of developmental theorists, universal late life tasks include "adapting to losses and decrements of various kinds, reorganizing aspirations, self-image and time perspective and engaging in a reassessment and acceptance of the existential meaning of one's own life" (Malick, 1982, p. 116). Peck (1956) describes three major late life developmental tasks: "(1) ego differentiation versus work-role preoccupation: 'what-ness versus who-ness,' (2) body transcendence versus body preoccupation, (3) ego transcendence versus ego preoccupation, i.e., coping with the prospect of death by leaving a legacy that holds less dread of the 'night of the ego'" (p. 193).

Living through the end stages of one's life—whether viewed from the psychological, economic, or social perspective—is at best a challenge even without the onset of serious illness. This is especially true in light of the high value placed on independence in this society. "Illness brings with it a feeling of anxiety, helplessness, and vulnerability and can activate denial, projection, and other primitive defenses developed in earlier life" (Malick, 1982, p. 116).

## The Importance of Appropriate Response

The conflict between the value of independence and the need for care, if not resolved, can lead to increased dependence. Inadequate intervention and care can make way for physical decline that otherwise might be averted. Lowy (1989) states, "Allowing people to be dependent and to help them to learn that this is perfectly 'normal' has been found to give older persons a good deal of strength; in fact, it has been successfully used in psychotherapy" (p. 139). The crux of the problem of care-related dependency is the need to confront the reality that personal care will be required to enable the elderly person suffering from illness to regain previous strengths or to limit further losses. Meeting the challenge of *accepting appropriate care* is often the most powerful step that an elder can take toward maintaining the highest possible degree of personal integrity and independence.

The phenomenon of learned helplessness is also a very significant factor in coping with severe physical illness and disability. As suggested above, illness often brings an initial feeling of overwhelming helplessness that can be incorporated into one's ongoing style of dealing with the illness. Elderly clients will have very different propensities to adopt this pattern of response, as well as various patterns of belief regarding appropriate sources of assistance.

Seltzer and Charpentier (1982) describe the role of social workers in dealing with elderly people who are facing disability:

> Issues such as altered self-image, changed lifestyle, decreased generativity, reduced energy level, increased dependency, role reversal, and negative outlook on life must be openly discussed and examined. . . . Traditional casework techniques such as facilitating emotive expression, legitimizing emotive expression, legitimizing grief reactions associated with loss of bodily functions, and utilizing subjective elements within the helping

relationship must be combined with an objectively planned approach to teaching the client/family new coping strategies and/or patterns of communication. (p. 71)

It is clear that such interventions require values clarification and change if the individual experiencing the disabling illness is to cope successfully.

In sum, empowerment-oriented workers must join with their elderly clients in assessing their values and perceptions regarding the receipt of assistance and their values and beliefs concerning who should provide this assistance. These internalized aspects of care receiving may be either serious obstacles or definite assets in coping with the care receiving role, and finding appropriate ways to address them may require change-oriented interventions. Interventions that help elderly care receivers to see the need for assistance as an acceptable fact of life and to receive assistance without assuming a position of helplessness or engaging in other negative reactions will facilitate the empowerment process.

## INTERVENTIONS FOCUSED ON THE PROBLEMS OF THE CARE RECEIVER

Empowerment-oriented interventions focused on the problems of elderly care receivers must assist them to gain a clear understanding of their own beliefs and feelings regarding care receiving, to accept physical losses that are irreversible, to seek new activities or dimensions of life to replace those that are lost, and to be effective in enabling their caregivers to help them achieve these goals, as well as provide survival care. Coping patterns that involve denial of need, anger at caregivers, assumed helplessness, and other negative reactions must be replaced by positive, self-enhancing behaviors.

As discussed in Chapter 3, the empowerment-oriented practice model focuses on four dimensions of problem definition and consciousness. In working with elderly care receivers who are facing physical disabilities and/or death, empowerment-oriented workers will often find specific problems that confront their clients. Interventions along the four dimensions of the empowerment-oriented model of practice can be applied to solving such problems.

### Facing the Reality of Physical Disability

Perhaps the most difficult task facing an older person who experiences a disabling illness is getting through the process of accepting the irreversibility of the condition. The primary challenges related to this task include:

- Getting past the initial denial, fear, anger, and feelings of help-lessness brought about by the illness

- Learning about the disease or physical incapacity

- Engaging in the struggle to resist overdependence, while at the same time accepting insurmountable obstacles to recovery or return to prior health status

- Learning the best possible means of coping with the illness at hand through *medical* and *emotional/social means* of self-care

- Finding a means to replace important components of a specific loss

## The Grief Process

The social worker may be called upon to help an elderly client deal with the *grief process* associated with chronic disease or sudden or unexpected physical loss. This work is often facilitated by groups for elderly persons who share common problems and by one-to-one interactions focused on the feelings generated by illness, disability, and death.

The lack of opportunity for elders with a disability to process grief reactions is a common barrier to successful caregiving activity. Misplaced feelings of anger and/or continued denial of disability are frequent ongoing problems that make the relationship between caregiver and care receiver difficult. Empowerment-oriented workers must initiate the grieving process in these instances, in order to help their clients free their energy for positive aspects of coping with illness. Kübler-Ross (1975) identified five stages of grief involved in any loss: denial, anger, bargaining, depression, and acceptance. She suggested that it is necessary to progress through these stages in order to adjust to the loss and restore normal functioning. The worker will have to assess whether or not these phases are appropriate with each elderly client and, if so, facilitate a progression through them. It is often said that elderly people experience such excessive loss that each loss triggers another loss, and they get stuck in one of the phases, often depression.

Understanding the grief process using a stage model, however, must include an openness to individual differences. There is wide variation among individuals with respect to the sequence and length of these stages as well as whether they are experienced at all. Levine (1982) is among several authors who caution that the concept of stages can be very misleading if it is believed to be the necessary and only normal way by which all people deal with grief, rather than being simply a useful way to understand common feelings. Levine also warns workers not to rely on predetermined ideas about process to the point that they allow these ideas to get in the way of their total response to the needs of each individual.

Retsenas (1989) discusses the impact of the aging process itself on reactions to dying. She and others studying the dying mores of the elderly suggest that elders may have completed much of the psychological work of dying before being faced with an immediate concern with death. Nonetheless, familiarity with the common reactions to grief is helpful in working with individuals and families, either on a one-to-one basis or in groups.

Groups can provide a medium for education of elderly people and their families about the grief process and about ways to help oneself and others deal with grief. Groups also provide a medium for exploring the manner in which this society—*including its social service agencies*—copes with disability and death, that is, the tendency of society at large to provide minimal resources to address the special needs of disabled persons and to deny death and, in some instances, to isolate and blame the dying person.

Elderly people and their families can become valuable resources in opening discussion regarding death as a part of life. With respect to Dimension 3 and 4 interventions, some advocates believe that the high expense of burial and other costs inherent in the death process can be more clearly examined only when the denial of death as a life process is acknowledged and discussed openly.

## Overcoming Feelings of Helplessness

Workers must often assist the critically ill or disabled client to deal with *feelings of helplessness*. These feelings are frequently present during early phases of a disability or illness, but they may recede after some adjustment has been made. They may recur, however, if the disability or illness is progressive and the individual's condition worsens. Although talking about these feelings and legitimizing their existence through interaction with the worker is helpful, linking with individuals who are experiencing the same problems is well-documented as an effective tool. Sharing common feelings and reaffirming these feelings as normal or acceptable for the circumstances are important aspects of the empowerment process. When the worker cannot engage an individual client in these aspects of group process, the use of videotapes of a group may be helpful. In addition, a telephone support network can be initiated. Even without these helpful interventions, the worker/client dialogue can serve as a medium for brainstorming regarding what to do next after legitimizing feelings.

*Life Review Process*    Another useful strategy for helping clients to gain consciousness of their strengths and then bring them to bear on current challenges is the use of the life review process. Life review and reminiscence, common interventions with the elderly population, focus on the goals of increasing morale, life satisfaction, and emotional well-being. These strategies are useful in empowerment-oriented practice because of their adaptability to topical areas. In the life review process the empowerment-oriented social worker, working with either an individual or a group, can pose questions regarding:

- Attitudes and beliefs about being in the dependent role
- Perceptions of historical approaches to dealing with dependence and independence
- Attitudes about receiving help from others and about collective problem solving
- Significant political and economic events in one's life and their impact on current functioning and attitudes
- Feelings about growing old and emotional responses to it.

Discussion of these topics can serve to heighten awareness of the life cycle, including needs for dependence and nurturing. Workers can help elders reframe their perceptions of dependence and can promote consciousness raising about the status of health care in this society.

### Education and Mutual Support

Education and mutual support also must play an important role in overcoming the care receiver's sense of helplessness in dealing with disease and disability. Health education leads to identification of aspects of the elder's life-style that may be contributors to negative health conditions, as well as enhancing his or her effectiveness as a consumer of health care. Knowing about the nature of a disease can further the elder's sense of empowerment by lessening the surprise element of symptoms or reactions to medications. Such understanding can also enable the elderly person coping with illness to assume a much more active role in care decisions. In one Administration on Aging project, Lidoff and Beaver (1983) analyzed peer groups throughout the United States for health education functioning. They found that peer group experiences increased older people's knowledge about health, developed their self-advocacy skills as health consumers, and promoted behavioral practices that fostered good health.

Specifically, mutual support groups that are focused on common problems *provide information on how to cope with these problems, mutual help (if necessary), and a feeling of being cared about and supported.* Roberto's (1988) study of the social dimension of osteoporosis documents individual victims' feelings of extreme isolation because of the inability of others to understand the nature of their specific illness. For example, one interviewee described the anger her husband and children seemed to feel when she declined to attend various functions with them. To them she appeared well and able. She could manage movement around the house and most household tasks, but she lived in constant fear of breaking bones. Support from others with symptoms similar to hers could have been very helpful in overcoming her feeling of aloneness and perhaps effective in improving her communication with her family.

Empowerment-oriented workers will often participate in activities such as finding appropriate health care information, facilitating the initial linking of individuals suffering from a common illness or medical problem, organizing groups, encouraging individuals who have never participated in a mutual support group to attend, and facilitating the groups, at least initially. Groups will vary in their need for a worker's assistance. Potential group members may have levels of disability (hearing impairment, pain, difficulty getting to meetings, etc.) that require special attention from the worker. The nature of the setting (for example, a pre-release group in a hospital) may also affect the social worker's role.

Finding appropriate educational materials will require collaboration with the best-informed local health professionals. Specialized agencies, such as the cancer society, stroke association, and others, often have current educational materials. (Suggestions for assisting group members and individuals to identify and acquire such resources were made in Chapter 5.) More important than acquiring specific information about a condition or illness is engaging the clients in an ongoing search for such information.

In an atmosphere of mutual support, educational groups often lead to offers of mutual assistance (self-help activities are often the outcome). Individuals begin to share their successful strategies for dealing with disabilities. For example, a group may develop a list of alternative ways to accomplish daily activities that have become difficult because of physical changes.

The political dimensions of a problem are often brought to the surface very rapidly in group discussions of health care. In one small group, the discourse moved rapidly from discussion about recurring headaches experienced by one participant to a heated discussion about the red tape and "runaround" experienced when services were sought from a senior clinic they had all used and then to a plan for going in teams to the center in order to better articulate their care needs and service demands. This process is not uncommon in senior groups, as described in the literature and reported by practitioners. For example, Nahemow (1981) found that "participants in health education and support groups seemed committed to taking their own responsibility for remaining active and independent. However, they felt that society needed to meet them halfway. . . . These older persons were most interested in dialogue with the health care system" (p. 14).

Activities that relate to all dimensions of the empowerment-oriented practice model may be carried on during the brief space of one meeting. For some elderly people the activities of mutual support and social action (with respect to the health care system), which frequently emerge from health education groups, may become primary replacements for important activities or other valued aspects of life that have been taken away by disability or illness.

## Loss of Opportunities for Giving, Socializing, and Participating

The important task of finding ways of giving, socializing, and participating in life that do not require the use of lost abilities is a difficult challenge for many elderly people and social workers who serve them. The focus must be on what older people *can* do. Values, beliefs, and attitudes must often be analyzed in order to develop new and meaningful ways of living. For example, volunteering as a reader for a blind child in lieu of taking grandchildren on excursions may sound simple, but it can require significant adjustment by an elder who has always believed that such exchanges should be restricted to family members. Life review is often useful in assisting elderly individuals to find alternative forms of activity that are harmonious with their life experiences. Old talents and interests may be revived, and strength found in previous adverse conditions may provide encouragement.

## COPING WITH RECEIVING HELP FROM CAREGIVERS

In addition to the various problems encountered in dealing with the onset of a serious chronic illness or disability, there is the challenge of coping with receiving help from a personal or professional caregiver. It is necessary to develop positive attitudes about accepting help and learn appropriate ways to avoid learned helplessness or excessive dependency.

### Effective Use of Personal Caregivers

Empowerment-oriented workers must become aware of the knowledge and skills that facilitate effective use of assistance from personal caregivers and must find ways to ensure that this crucial information is passed on to elderly care receivers. The following skills or behaviors of care receivers will help make it easier for them to accept and function in relationships with caregivers:

- Learning to state care needs or ask for help
- Learning to state independence needs or set limits on assistance from others
- Learning to express appreciation for care
- Learning not to displace anger about the illness or disability onto caregivers
- Learning specific skills for self-care (use of mechanical assistance, self-injecting medication, special exercises, or alternative ways of performing tasks of daily living)

- Remaining open to suggestions about rehabilitation therapy or other interventions suggested by caregivers, while accepting responsibility for decisions
- Learning to accept responsibility for one's own state of mind, whether happy or depressed, rather than suggesting that the caregiver is responsible
- Avoiding, where possible, behaviors that might provoke guilt in caregivers and helping caregivers overcome their feelings of guilt
- Thinking about caregivers' needs and generating ways to help them (for example, listen to their troubles and maintain an interest in their challenges and successes), thus avoiding becoming totally preoccupied with one's own illness and needs
- Being willing to consider participation in new programs that can relieve the caregiver's burden, such as adult day-care programs and caregiver cooperatives
- Being willing to accept assistance from paid in-home service providers or other relatives and friends when personal caregivers need time for themselves or their work
- Performing tasks, within one's abilities, to assist the caregiver (such as helping with child care, answering the phone, paying bills, and supervising a service person when someone must be home to allow repairs)
- Trying to allow the caregiver as much private time as possible, as well as time with other family members
- Taking an active role in learning about the programs and policies that affect care receivers' and caregivers' resources and lives (for example, writing legislators regarding legislation to allow caregivers paid leave for elder care responsibilities or to support adult day care)

These areas of behavior are often excellent topics of discussion for groups of care receivers or for one-to-one sessions with care receivers. Focusing on his or her own role in the caregiving relationship allows the care receiver to assume responsibility and to remain a contributing family member or friend as the process occurs.

## Relating to Professional Caregivers

Accepting help from and having effective relationships with professionals are other tasks that must be mastered by elders who suffer from illness and disability. Most people have very limited experience with professional caregivers. Elderly people who have serious late life illnesses, however, find themselves subject to frequent contacts with physicians, social workers, nurses, and other helping professionals. These professionals do not always communicate effectively with their elderly clients.

Coe (1987) reviewed the research with regard to physician/patient communication. Although Coe found little work specific to elderly clients, several important conclusions emerge from the general literature: the physician's ability to communicate affects the degree to which he or she has a "placebo" effect on patients; lack of communication skills can be related to iatrogenic (caused by medical treatment) effects; communication patterns such as use of jargon are sometimes used to mask lack of knowledge or physician uncertainty; and the relationship between compliance and good communication is expected to be high. Mishler (1984) notes that "the physician's effort to impose technocratic consciousness, to dominate the voice of life by the voice of medicine, seriously impedes and distorts essential requirements for mutual dialogue and humane interaction" (p. 104). These insights and others serve to illustrate the complexity of concerns about communication between elderly patients and their medical providers.

The following are only a few of the barriers faced by social workers and their elderly constituents in their efforts to improve the communication process:

- Use of jargon
- Exploitation of superior status as a rationale for avoiding communication responsibilities
- Unexplored cultural stereotypes, ageist bias, and gender bias
- Use of closed-ended questions and other communication styles that tend to cut off communication from patients or clients

Although there are a number of programs and initiatives attempting to improve the attitudes and level of knowledge of professionals regarding their provision of care to disabled elderly people, many professionals fall far short of possessing the qualities necessary for effective communication. Consequently, the elderly care receiver is often the one who must initiate the process of improving communication.

The following measures are often important in assuring effective use of professional providers:

- Gain knowledge about available civil rights protections and remedies
- Learn how to check qualifications of providers, especially home health care providers who are not otherwise screened
- Learn about patients' rights with respect to changing professional providers if care is not adequate
- Learn how to seek second opinions and where to find out about alternative approaches, including ones not often encouraged in the current system (such as acupuncture, chiropractic, massage, and podiatry)

- Learn about health care insurance coverage and limitations, reimbursement procedures, who to contact when there are problems, and eligibility requirements for programs that may assist one or one's friends
- Find out about and participate in social action that addresses the financing or quality of health care services

Overall, these means of achieving effective access to professional assistance often require assessing old patterns of relating to professionals and developing new attitudes and communication skills. These are examples of skills that empowerment-oriented workers and peers can help a client develop. The support of peers can often help to change those perceptions of the professional/client relationship that preclude effective use of care and can encourage personal or collective demands for appropriate behaviors on the part of professionals. Larger systems issues—such as adequate and sensitive training of professionals, availability of funds to pay for needed care, focus on medical concerns of the elderly, and legislative action to support the needs of personal caregivers—are often generated by collective or worker-to-client discussions.

## Gaps between Professional Caregivers and Elders

Learning to deal effectively with professional caregivers requires, in most cases, bridging several areas of difference: the knowledge gap, the vocabulary gap, the status gap, and often the ethnicity, gender, and age gaps. Empowerment-oriented workers must assist elderly clients in spanning these gaps.

***The Knowledge Gap***  The knowledge gap is often effectively addressed in peer group situations, such as those discussed above, that focus on a particular illness. Members become familiar with what is known about their condition, alternative treatments, and the effects of commonly prescribed drugs. These groups are often able to access current research and become well versed in medical information related to their condition. Other strategies workers can employ include making written or taped information available, helping clients set up or access phone information lines, and encouraging clients to learn about their conditions. It is not uncommon, however, to find clients who do not want to learn about their conditions. "I just leave those things to my doctor" and "That kind of thing is way above my head" are common statements made by elders discussing their illnesses. Prior socialization and belief systems may strongly reinforce such behaviors and must be confronted if the knowledge gap between client and professional is to be shrunk. Fortunately for those who do seek information, many sources are being developed to allow laypeople to enhance their health care knowledge. Elderly people who have prepared themselves with information about their conditions find that interaction with professionals on an egalitarian basis is more feasible.

***The Vocabulary Gap*** The vocabulary gap is closely associated with the knowledge gap. For most consumers of medical care, the medical terminology used by care providers seems complex and often unintelligible. This situation is, of course, exacerbated when the patient has a hearing impairment or is not fluent in English, or when provider and patient have different communication styles (possibly class-based).

Many strategies have been tried to improve communication between physicians and patients (of all ages). The following are examples of behaviors that elderly individuals can use to assure that they receive appropriate information:

- Learn to ask questions in an assertive manner
- Ask physicians to slowly repeat what they have said and, if necessary, to write down the information so that it can be shared with others
- Ask for an explanation of the use and expected outcomes of each drug, including possible interactions with any other drugs being taken
- Take a companion to doctor visits for support and reassurance

In summary, the war against jargon and the struggle to assert one's right to understand what professional caregivers are trying to communicate can be won by elderly patients with assistance from peers and/or practitioners. Key to this process is cultivating the belief that it is the responsibility of professional caregivers to explain their practice and that asking for information does not constitute being a nagging patient. Efforts to make communication problems entirely the problem of the consumer must be countered with firm resistance and the expectancy of clear communication.

***The Status Gap*** The status gap, which is created by the socialization of both professionals and members of lower-status groups, is often a problem for patients with regard to communication styles. It may require a considerable effort to seek communication on an equal footing with individuals one considers to be of a much higher status. The time of high-status professionals is considered to be very valuable, and the right of individuals of lesser status to take up the time of these professionals may be questioned by both the professional and the consumer. Professional bias, as suggested earlier, may preclude both the ability and the willingness to communicate. For example, the primary goal of the professional may be to gain the patient's compliance with medical orders without regard to the cultural or personal significance of a specific care plan.

In some cases professional providers may perceive their client as being incapable of understanding the complexities of the condition or treatment. The care receiver, on the other hand, may feel unworthy or too much of a bother. Elderly individuals who are ill may not have the energy to confront what appears to be an unreachable caregiver. Empowerment-oriented workers can assist elderly persons who are in the role of patient or client to reassess their relationships to professionals and can strongly reinforce the patients' rights aspects of professional caregiving. Challenging beliefs of one's own inferiority or professionals' superiority often requires not only changing one's perspective on the professional/client relationship, but also practicing more assertive behaviors.

***The Ethnic, Gender, and Age Gaps***   Ethnic, gender, and age gaps often pose barriers between professional caregivers and their clients. Racist, sexist, or ageist attitudes and beliefs of providers can be not only the sources of serious miscommunication, but also the causes of inadequate provision of care. For example, the commonly held belief that many older women are hypochondriacs may lead to failure to provide accurate diagnoses. These kinds of barriers must be identified and dealt with. Peer groups or one-to-one interactions are useful in exploring these issues and in finding corrective strategies that are appropriate.

## SPECIAL CHALLENGES IN EMPOWERMENT-ORIENTED WORK WITH CARE RECEIVERS

The issue of outreach to and identification of care receivers in need of assistance looms over social work practitioners as a primary challenge, as does the problem of finding reimbursement for services of this nature. Many elderly people who are receiving care from personal caregivers are living in their own homes or the homes of family members. These individuals are often isolated and removed from contact with service agencies. Multifaceted approaches are thus required to identify care receivers. In addition to using the service network, workers can contact elderly care receivers and their caregivers through churches, popular media, local civic groups, and informal settings such as beauty shops and clubs.

Even when elderly care receivers are located and the problems of reimbursement are solved, facilitating empowerment remains a challenge. Workers are called upon to assist those who must rely on professional and/or personal caregivers to make many changes and take on many new tasks. Important aspects of the elders' self-image are often threatened, both by the physical disabilities they are forced to deal with and by having to accept assistance. Workers find themselves helping clients reassess the parameters of what they value about themselves and seek new avenues by which they can satisfy their changing definitions of a meaningful life. At the same time workers must address both the personal and the political dimensions of this problem situation.

It is often difficult to find a medium by which the collective consciousness-raising process can occur for care receivers. Many elderly individuals who need assistance with physical care are in isolated situations, and the problems of transportation, lack of physical stamina, and other physical restrictions may prevent care receivers from attending meetings. The group process, although proven to be a very effective strategy with respect to health conditions, may not be possible. Creative strategies are also required to assist both care receivers and their often exhausted caregivers to focus on the collective issues related to the personal and political dimensions of their particular situation. Self-help and collective strategies require considerable effort, as do political and social actions. However, the empowerment-oriented worker is often able to assist clients to find ways of addressing issues related to personal life changes and to articulate the collective nature of their dilemma.

## SUMMARY

Many elderly people are forced to accept some degree of assistance from personal and/or professional caregivers. It is important for empowerment-oriented workers to initiate interventions that encourage elderly persons receiving care and in need of care to engage effectively in this process as partners with their caregivers. Often values and attitudes about dependency must be addressed before active participation in self-care can begin. Empowerment-oriented workers encourage clients who are care receivers to participate in problem solving along all four dimensions of the empowerment-oriented model. Knowledge about a wide array of supportive services, professional jargon, and specific illnesses, skills in communication, and specific self-care skills can be developed. Knowledge of policy issues that affect caregiving resources is also important for clients concerned about late life care. A focus on the needs of care receivers is an important accompaniment to work being done regarding caregivers. Elderly people with the necessary knowledge and skills will be helpful partners in their own care.

## REFERENCES

AARP. (1991). *Aging America: Trends and projections.* Washington, DC: U.S. Senate Special Committee on Aging.

Coe, R. M. (1987). Communication and medical care outcomes: Analysis of conversation between doctors and elderly patients. In R. A. Ward & S. S. Tobin (Eds.), *Health in aging.* New York: Springer.

Kübler-Ross, E. (1975). *Death: The final stage of growth.* Englewood Cliffs, NJ: Prentice-Hall.

Levine, S. (1982). *Who dies?: An investigation of conscious living and conscious dying.* Garden City, NY: Anchor.

Lidoff, L., & Beaver, L. (1983). *Peer groups for health education,* Vol. III. Washington, DC: National Council on Aging.

Lowy, L. (1989). Independence and dependence in aging: A new balance. *Journal of Gerontological Social Work, 13*(3/4), pp. 133–146.

Malick, M. D. (1982). Understanding illness and aging. In G. S. Getzel & M. J. Mellor (Eds.), *Gerontological social work practice in long-term care.* New York: Haworth Press.

Mishler, E. G. (1984). *The discourse of medicine: Dialectics of medical interviews.* Norwood, NJ: Ablex.

Nahemow, L. (1981). *People care for people.* Final report submitted to the Administration on Aging, Washington, DC.

Parsons, R. J., Cox, E. O., & Kimboko, P. J. (1989). Satisfaction, communication and affection in caregiving: A view from the elders' perspective. *Journal of Gerontological Social Work, 13*(3/4), pp. 9–20.

Peck, R. (1956). Psychological development in the second half of life. In J. Anderson (Ed.), *Psychological aspects of aging.* Washington, DC: APA.

Retsenas, J. (1989). A theoretical reassessment of the applicability of Kübler-Ross's stages of dying. In H. Cox (Ed.), *Aging* (6th ed.). Guilford, CT: Dieshkin.

Roberto, K. (1988). *Women with osteoporosis: Physical, psychological, and social adjustment.* Final report submitted to AARP/Andrus Foundation, Washington, DC.

Rzetelny, H. (1985). Emotional stresses in late life. In G. Getzel & J. Mellor (Eds.), *Gerontological social work practice in the community.* New York: Hawthorne.

Seltzer, G. B., & Charpentier, M. O. (1982). Maximizing independence for the elderly: The social worker in the rehabilitation center. In G. S. Getzel & M. J. Mellor (Eds.), *Gerontological social work practice in long-term care.* New York: Haworth Press.

Taeuber, C. (1990). Diversity: The dramatic reality. In S. A. Bass, E. A. Kutza, & F. M. Torres-Gil (Eds.), *Diversity in aging.* Glenview, IL: Scott, Foresman.

# EMPOWERMENT-ORIENTED SOCIAL WORK IN NURSING HOMES

Social work practitioners are finding the quality of social services in nursing homes throughout the country to be very uneven. Professionals in this field are challenged to define their potential contribution in that setting clearly and to find ways of implementing this contribution. This chapter describes the issues that affect the quality of life in nursing homes and the challenges facing professional social workers in that environment and then suggests appropriate empowerment-oriented strategies based on the four dimensions of the empowerment-oriented model (identified in Chapter 3).

## *BACKGROUND AND CURRENT ISSUES*

Regardless of occasional research or written or verbal pronouncements to the contrary, most elderly people and their families have strong negative feelings about the possibility of nursing home care (Smith & Bengston, 1989). Elders' fear is based on a number of concerns, including:

- Being isolated from one's family, friends, and familiar home setting and relegated to living with "strangers"
- Having one's life "taken over" or "run" by the nursing home staff
- Losing privacy and dignity—for example, by being put in a room with someone unknown
- The extreme financial cost of nursing home care
- The fear of dying in an alien setting

Their family members, on the other hand, often experience feelings of guilt based on:

- Perceptions of being considered a bad spouse or child for allowing institutionalization of an elderly relative

- Perceived inability to be an effective advocate for the elderly relative following institutionalization

Research reporting the actual living conditions in nursing homes in many instances confirms the validity of these concerns. Three decades ago, Goffman (1961) described the negative effects of the "total" institution on human integrity. In 1974, Mendelson published her famous exposé of the nursing home industry, *Tender Loving Greed,* which was one of a number of nationally known reports of abuse of nursing home residents. Gutheil (1990) notes that:

> Frailty and infirmity make it difficult for residents to monitor or protest infringement of their rights. In addition, feelings of powerlessness and the fear of retaliation engendered by being dependent on institutional caregivers frequently prevent residents from speaking up on their own behalf. These factors, together with the alarming history of abuse in some nursing homes, underscore the need for someone to advocate for and protect the rights of residents in long term care facilities. (p. 532)

Her review of current conditions demonstrates the persistence of problems facing elderly individuals when they are institutionalized.

## Autonomy and Well-Being

Important work has been done in exploring the concepts of locus of control and learned helplessness and their relationship to depression (see, for example, Abramson, Seligman, & Teasdale, 1978; Benson & Kennally, 1976; Cohen, Rothbart, & Phillips, 1976; and Seligman, 1975). The impact of institutionalization on locus of control and learned helplessness has also been explored. Keddy (1987) states that learned helplessness is fostered by a system that emphasizes efficiency rather than promotion of competency in institutionalized elders. The implication of these findings for survival in routinized nursing home settings is clear. Institutionalized elderly individuals are deprived of the right to make decisions about even the most rudimentary aspects of daily life, such as when to get up and, in many homes, what to wear. The loss of the ability to effect outcomes has strong potential to produce learned helplessness. Overall, helplessness as a result of institutionalization appears to correlate with increased cognitive impairment, withdrawal or decreased activity, increased depression, and increased mortality (Kart, Metress, & Metress, 1988; Weinstein & Khanna, 1986).

Additional support for these conclusions has come from recent exploration of life in nursing homes with respect to the concept of late life autonomy. Hofland (1988) summarizes the findings as follows:

> A considerable body of psychological research exists which focuses on aspects of autonomy among institutionalized older adults, but usually

under the rubrics of "control," "iatrogenic dependency," and "learned helplessness." Despite a variety of measures and conditions, the research shows impressive convergence of findings. Lack of control has negative effects on the emotional, physical, and behavioral well-being of nursing home residents. (p. 5)

Jameton (1988) has added an important dimension to thinking about autonomy in affirming the view of many practitioners that the opportunity for residents to assume responsibilities for their own care and for assistance to others is a critical aspect of their ability to express autonomy or counter feelings of helplessness. Jameton also cites the significant difference between being assigned tasks or manipulated into performing activities and the willing assumption of responsibilities that residents believe to be their own. Wetle, Levkoff, Cwikel, and Rosen (1988) raise the critical issue of the role of elderly individuals in nursing homes in making decisions about their medical care. Overall findings of their study indicate that although there were great individual differences among residents in the level of their desire to have information about medical conditions, approximately 20% of them wished for more information and wanted a stronger say in their medical care.

Social workers must often engage with nursing home residents in decisions about their care and their wishes to be involved in that care. When residents are cognitively unable to participate, their relatives are faced with the dilemma. There are few studies that specifically describe the situation of nursing home residents and their families. Research by Steen, Linn, and Steen (1986) has confirmed the ability of nursing home residents to report the quality of care they receive and the importance of their having this opportunity.

## Residents' Perspectives

In a study conducted by the University of Denver Institute of Gerontology (1988) in 20 randomly chosen nursing homes in the state of Colorado, residents expressed an overwhelming sense of hopelessness and powerlessness with respect to taking an active role in controlling their environments and in making decisions about their daily lives. The following comments from residents, taken from the study, are a representative sample of concerns expressed in response to specific questions:

*Why Concerns Were Not Expressed in Resident Council Meetings*
"No one is interested in what I need—I'm just a bother."
"They listen but don't do anything—so I don't talk anymore."
"No one pays any attention."
"There are no solutions—it's a waste of time."

"It wouldn't do any good—just makes someone mad."

"It's run by the staff, who hear what they want to hear."

"Once they are mad at you it's over."

"We pay them to run the place."

"I don't care what they do anymore, I just survive."

"I'm too tired to fight anymore."

"You're all alone anyway—there is no use pretending someone is going to listen to you."

### Things Residents Found Disturbing

"When other people take my place at the dinner table."

"I don't get disturbed about anything anymore."

"Everything . . . but who cares?"

"Shortages of aides; it makes it hard for everyone."

"The food is awful, but then everyone likes something different so we can't do anything about it."

"Complaints don't pay."

"Rooms are too small for two people."

"Lots of time staff are unavailable and people have to wait even to go to the bathroom."

"I need someone to help me walk . . . no one has the time."

"People always make me wait and they never come back."

"I hate being stuck here—I want to get out more."

### The Opportunity to Make Suggestions

"Yes, I can suggest, but they would be disregarded."

"We're not considered to be important here."

"No use; life is just ending here."

"I'm just surviving until it ends—I don't need them mad at me."

"Sure, but nothing happens."

"Yes, but I don't. It's none of my affair—those things are the boss's affair."

Overall, these comments support the findings of social science research about nursing homes, which strongly suggests that the physical as well as mental health of the residents is threatened by the sense of powerlessness and helplessness created by institutional environments (Cohen, 1990; Coons, 1991; Hofland, 1990; and Kane, Freeman, Caplan, Aroskar, & Uru-Wong, 1990). The critical need for empowerment-oriented interventions is firmly established by these findings.

# THE ROLE OF SOCIAL WORK IN NURSING HOMES

The history of social work in nursing homes, though it extends over four decades, is sketchy. Hooker (1976), in an initial attempt to relate the findings of learned helplessness theorists to social work practice, noted the importance of learned helplessness to the inducement of depression and withdrawal responses and the need for social workers to assist in countering such effects. Beaver and Miller (1985) summarize the need for social work services in nursing homes as follows:

> According to Linstrom (1975) and Brody and Brody (1974), the greatest and most common area of neglect in our nation's nursing homes is the psycho-social aspect of care. Kosberg (1973) also points out that the patient's social needs are usually ignored, with the result that social and psychological capabilities deteriorate.
>
> A study by Halbfinger (1976) concludes that frustration, helplessness, hopelessness, and powerlessness prevail among nursing home patients because they are not provided with social supports. Mercer and Kane (1979) report that helpless and hopeless feelings can be minimized when patients are given the opportunity to make some choices and exercise some control over their daily lives. This is the area in which the social worker can make a valuable contribution to the patient's quality of life. (p. 198)

Silverstone and Burack-Weiss (1982) state:

> Although social work services in the nursing home are customarily considered secondary at best to nursing and medical care, their importance is paramount both in terms of helping clients adapt to a very different way of life, and for the frail in terms of ensuring the implementation of the auxiliary function. (p. 27)

Despite the wisdom of social work practitioners regarding the importance of the *psychosocial aspects* of nursing home residents' lives and the lives of their families, very little attention and status are given to the role of social work in nursing homes. The nursing home industry as a whole allocates only limited resources to social work services in its facilities, and the medically based funding sources from which the industry receives reimbursement for its services provide little encouragement to allocate more.

## Access to and Status within Homes

The first and often most frustrating challenge facing empowerment-oriented social workers is securing employment in any capacity that will allow them access to nursing home residents and their families. The most obvious alternative is to be hired by a particular facility, but this is sometimes not possible. Employment as an ombudsman or in other community-based services that follow their clients into the institutional setting is another alternative. States as well as individual nursing homes differ in their requirements regarding the delivery of social work services to residents. Social work *designees* (individuals assigned to perform social services in nursing homes) may be trained in any of a number of other disciplines and have varying levels of education. In most states these designees are supervised on a limited basis or provided with occasional consultations with master's-level social workers.

A study conducted by graduate social work students for the University of Denver Institute of Gerontology (1990) regarding professional social work activities in nursing homes in Colorado found that fewer than twenty professional social workers were employed in that state's nursing homes. Most of the social workers who were surveyed reported severe difficulties arising from the conflict between their attempts to focus on residents' rights and quality of life and the nursing homes' priorities of keeping beds full and maintaining cost efficiency. Efforts to enhance residents' decision-making opportunities were directly contradictory to the precise routines and other techniques used by the nursing homes to assure compliance and smooth operation. Limited staff, use of pool personnel, and rapid turnover severely limited social workers' ability to provide the personal attention needed by residents to reinforce their efforts toward self-care, adaptation, and personal growth in the nursing home setting. Other obstacles to social workers' performance included low status and salaries, assignments unrelated to the workers' training and ability, and the common problem of bureaucratic red tape and excessive reporting requirements.

In order to bring about a significant increase in social workers' abilities to aid elders requiring nursing home care (especially as staff members in nursing homes), a great deal of legislative and organizational change will be required. To improve conditions, social workers must be actively involved in the efforts of the National Association of Social Workers (NASW), National Coalition of Nursing Home Reform (NCNHR), and local and statewide nursing home advocacy groups (including residents' and family members' groups).

## Goals and Sanction Base
## for Nursing Home Practice

In spite of the difficult hurdles social workers face, many of them are able to make significant contributions in nursing home settings. The goal of social work in nursing homes has been suggested by a number of long-term care professionals. Brody (1977), for example, has stated that professional social workers are needed to identify social-emotional needs

*Original art by Keith Tillery*

and modes of treatment for residents and should provide and direct social services. Beaver and Miller (1985) state that the primary goal of intervention with this population is to promote the best possible level of personal functioning, while preventing further decline.

According to Abrahamson (1988), social work in nursing homes tends to focus on the following:

- Psychosocial aspects of care and individualization of care
- The family and its resources as a system

- The community and its resources as a system
- The interaction of the resident with his or her family, peers, staff, and community
- The transition of the resident through the continuum of care

Many other authors who have given special attention to nursing home issues agree that these are areas of focus (see, for example, Beaver & Miller, 1985; Freeman, 1989; Hancock, 1990; and Silverstone & Burack-Weiss, 1982).

Empowerment-oriented practice is concerned with the same overall goal and areas of concern. However, *empowerment-oriented practice maintains a strong emphasis on the development of a partnership with elderly residents that will encourage their fullest possible participation in problem-solving activity on all dimensions of the problems they encounter, including the political dimension.* One practitioner with more than ten years of experience in nursing home work put it this way: "Perhaps the most difficult dilemma in care in institutions is the challenge of ongoing assessment with the elder regarding the fine line between meeting needs which individuals cannot meet for themselves and encouraging and allowing the individual to do what he or she can do for himself or herself." In fact, much of the struggle related to empowerment in nursing homes is rooted in this dilemma.

Social workers often use the regulations regarding residents' rights as their *main source of sanction for empowerment-oriented activity.* The current focus on residents' rights is highlighted in the Omnibus Reconciliation Act of 1987. The act emphasizes appropriate care for residents who suffer from mental incapacity and addresses other important aspects of residents' rights as well. This legislation increases the importance of residents' autonomy and thus can provide a strong supportive policy framework for empowerment-oriented interventions.

A commitment to upholding residents' rights in daily living in nursing homes, coupled with the struggle for organizational and societal change that will back up this commitment, is the essence of empowerment-oriented social work with nursing home residents and their families. Interventions on all dimensions of the problems faced by residents can be incorporated into this focus. Residents' rights include, at a minimum, the following:

- To be fully informed
- To participate in one's own care
- To make independent choices
- To have privacy and confidentiality
- To enjoy dignity, respect, and freedom
- To have security of possessions

- To remain in the facility
- To register complaints

The realization of these rights requires an ongoing struggle by residents, their families, and social workers. The following section suggests a limited number of strategies that have been initiated by social workers toward that end.

## EMPOWERMENT-ORIENTED INTERVENTIONS IN THE NURSING HOME SETTING

A social worker's first contact with an elderly client who requires nursing home care often finds the resident, or potential resident, feeling extremely helpless and/or isolated. The contact most often occurs when the client or the family or both are in the process of deciding about admission. Even if the contact is made later, however, institutionalized elders often feel powerless, as evidenced by the comments of residents cited earlier. Many nursing home residents believe that their actions and expressed wishes will have very little impact on their environment and lives (Kautzer, 1988).

Few nursing home residents are active participants in their environment. Empowerment-oriented workers are faced with the challenge of initiating empowerment-oriented groups in the nursing home setting and implementing individual interventions that will mobilize residents to take more control of their daily lives. This process often runs counter to the existing, highly routinized activities in the nursing home. Residents and their relatives frequently express fears that retaliation may follow self-expression and requests for more autonomy.

### Dimensions 1 and 2 Activities: Awareness of Common Concerns

Group discussion can be a crucial first step in helping residents deal with the cognitive or internalized aspects of feelings of powerlessness. Clarification of feelings, mutual exploration of the reasons for these feelings, discussion of what their consumer status means, and consideration of various approaches to solving common problems can be key to engaging elderly residents in the empowerment process. This type of group discourse often leads to a reaffirmation of personal rights and of a sense of value and purpose with respect to life in the nursing home. Feil (1983) provides examples that demonstrate that group work can help residents, even those with severe mental impairments, to gain a sense of orientation and purpose. Lee (1983) notes that "a sense of self is restored through community, and through providing opportunities for recall through doing, talking, and sharing common feelings" (p. 43).

Empowerment-oriented approaches use group activities, as suggested by Lee (1983), in order to enable residents to see the potential for gaining more autonomy through the experiential exercise of rights. Asking staff, either individually or in a group, to knock before entering residents' rooms is an example of an action step that might be taken as the result of a group's efforts in problem identification. The following topics may be useful as areas of focus for initial meetings of empowerment-oriented groups in nursing home settings:

- What can we expect from life in a nursing home?
- What is quality of care, and what is quality of life?
- What are residents' rights and how are they defined?
- How can we incorporate these rights into our daily lives?
- How do we cope with the necessity of receiving physical care, and how do we help the staff help us?
- How do we feel about family visits, and how can we make visits a good experience for our visitors?

These and similar topics often lead to the expression and identification of residents' feelings about their current life situation, as well as to thoughtful explorations of alternatives.

One effective tool for sensitizing elderly residents to their rights is "Residents' Rights Bingo." This game was created by Virginia Fraser, the Colorado state ombudsman, and is being used nationwide. It identifies more than 75 rights that elders have in nursing home settings and provides discussion questions that can be used by social workers or volunteers to elaborate on those rights. Figure 11.1, which shows one of the game cards, illustrates how different rights are highlighted as the facilitator calls out numbers. This game is an effective supplement to small group discussions and is often used as a recreational activity.

Regulations require the establishment of a resident council in all nursing homes; such a group can also be the focus of empowerment-oriented interventions. In some homes the social worker is given the opportunity to staff the council. A resident council can play a big role in communicating with the administration and with other residents. It can also set the tone with respect to how residents' rights are implemented in the home.

Many residents adopt the role of either the "good (submissive) patient" or the "bad (angry or demanding) patient" (Taylor, 1979). This behavior is perhaps the institutional equivalent of the fight-or-flight reaction that is common to all high-stress situations. Living in an institutional environment is a challenge to individual autonomy and integrity at any age. Elders who are forced to move into nursing homes are also coping

**Figure 11.1**  **Residents' Rights Bingo Card Showing Some of the 75 Rights Illustrated on Such Cards** (From the Colorado Ombudsman Program by Virginia Fraser. Copyright © 1990 by the Legal Center Serving Persons with Disabilities. All rights reserved. Reprinted by permission.)

***Playing is learning.***

with dependency-creating illnesses. Even though increasing numbers of elderly individuals are living to an age when nursing home life becomes a definite possibility, few give much forethought to what this experience will be like. Few prepare themselves in advance either emotionally or intellectually to achieve high levels of autonomy within a nursing home setting. Knowledge about assertiveness with regard to care, the nature of residents' rights, and working collectively with other residents to realize these rights is not usually acquired prior to nursing home placement. All residents have had life experiences that can prove valuable to them in their new circumstances, providing these experiences can be translated to the new setting. Such experiences might have taught them, for example, how bureaucracies function, self-care skills, and relationship skills.

In one-to-one contacts, workers are able to demonstrate the essence of residents' rights through respectful treatment of residents. Workers might also facilitate one-to-one discussions with residents on the topics suggested earlier for group discussion. In these cases, the worker attempts to assist the resident to understand the commonalities that he or she has with others in the same situation. The worker also attempts to share with more socially isolated residents the experiential wisdom and insights of other elderly regarding these common situations. Audio tapes of group discussions among elderly residents can be used to provide such sharing with isolated clients. One worker who was interviewed concerning the challenges of empowerment-oriented work in a nursing home setting observed:

> One of the most difficult obstacles to empowerment is the tendency of many residents to remain isolated in the home. Often it takes a long period of one-to-one work to bring a resident to the point that he or she is interested in people around them. Residents are often so preoccupied with their own fears that concern for other residents is limited. Once I get them to establish small support networks, the road to mutual concerns is not so hard to travel. For example, in one home there were six residents from rural farming backgrounds. I was able to plan some initial activities that got them talking to each other, and eventually they became very involved with each other.

Both group and individual interventions are used to facilitate self-help and educational strategies (Lee, 1983). Residents are helped to find information about their rights and ways in which these rights have been realized in different nursing homes. Workers' roles are similar to their roles in other settings: assisting individuals to locate educational materials and suggesting ways in which group members might help each other and other residents to make autonomous decisions and participate in mutually rewarding activities. Self-help strategies emerge from these activities. Residents often come up with ways of providing appropriate degrees of self-care, as well as ways of communicating to the staff their need to be responsible for as much self-care as possible and ways of gaining the staff's respect and cooperation.

Self-help activities that nursing home residents participate in include, but are not limited to, the following:

- Assisting one another with daily activities
- Respecting one another's need for privacy
- Helping one another to communicate clearly with and resolve disputes with staff
- Helping one another to acquire useful information about the nursing home's informal organizational system, programs and services available in the home and the community, ways to be a good family member while residing in a nursing home, ways to be a valuable community member while residing in a nursing home, and ways to make the nursing home more like a personal home for the residents
- Facilitating active participation in resident council activities and other activities of benefit to all residents

- Providing emotional support to one another
- Helping one another to respect and deal with "difficult" fellow residents
- Dealing with ethnic needs and ethnic issues
- Doing small tasks that help to improve the quality of care for everyone (delivering mail, combing hair for other residents, etc.)
- Helping to increase all residents' respect for the personal property of others and finding ways to secure personal property
- Providing information and support for one another with respect to coping with pain, disability, and reactions to medications
- Facilitating the work of the staff in order to improve the quality of care for everyone
- Learning about community resources (including funding sources such as Medicaid and Medicare and sources for glasses, dentures, clothing, etc.) and how to secure these resources for oneself and others
- Finding ways to reach out to fellow residents who do not participate and who appear to be lonely and isolated
- Learning advocacy and mediation skills in order to help self-care efforts and to improve one's environment
- Learning how to become fully involved in decision making about medical care
- Learning about and expressing feelings about living wills and other decisions that relate to death and the dying process
- Participating in peer counseling training for nursing home residents

Many of these are tasks that the social worker may perform for residents in the absence of ways to engage residents in them.

## Dimensions 3 and 4 Activities

McDermott (1989) describes an approach that fosters resident empowerment and encourages problem-solving activity with respect to nursing home life. In her example, a residents' rights campaign was organized in one home. The campaign incorporated education, mutual support, specific implementation activities (mutual action), and ongoing support groups.

A group of Colorado-based nursing home social workers offered the following insights into attempts to assist residents with the realization of autonomy in their decision-making behavior (University of Denver Institute of Gerontology, 1990):

1. In order for residents to achieve the goal of more control over their environment, work with the staff is essential. If key staff members in the home value resident independence and reinforce these activities, numerous tasks can be accomplished. If other staff members are not committed to empowerment-oriented activities supported by social workers, such activities are often seen as "subversive." (The following section deals with this issue in greater detail.)

2. Educational programs and organizing strategies will be short-lived unless the social worker can find a way to integrate these efforts into an ongoing structure.

3. Resident councils can be helpful, but small support groups that reinforce the council's activities are crucial if a number of residents are to be full participants in the council.

4. New residents need to be incorporated into empowerment-oriented activities as quickly as possible. (pp. 28–30)

These four observations reinforce the contention that the presence of empowerment-oriented social workers in nursing homes is essential for the mobilization of activity necessary to the physical and mental health of the residents. They highlight the fact that workers must be very clear about the goal to transfer decision-making power to residents and engage them in the process of assuring the home's responsiveness to their autonomous behavior.

Perhaps the arena in which it is most difficult to motivate nursing home residents to participate is the political one. Examples of Dimensions 3 and 4 activities in which nursing home residents can engage include:

- Promoting residents' rights to the administration through small groups or through the resident council
- Making phone calls or writing letters to inform the state ombudsman or other advocates of nursing home issues
- Making phone calls or writing letters to legislators about the lack of funds for adequate care or about other conditions affecting their lives
- Preparing and delivering testimony to appropriate audiences
- Participating in media presentations

Social workers in the nursing home are usually the primary staff members concerned with organizational change, generation of outside (private and public sector) resources, legislative issues, integration of nursing home residents into the larger community, and collaboration with residents in these larger efforts. Silverstone and Burack-Weiss (1982) note that "change is sought in the nursing home for a variety of reasons: to change rules and regulations . . . which are too restrictive;

to enhance opportunities for staff enrichment and training; and to increase communications among staff and between staff and patients" (p. 29).

Many *organizational barriers* to the achievement of empowerment-oriented goals were identified by social workers in Colorado (University of Denver Institute of Gerontology, 1990). The following represent a sample of these barriers:

- Minimal emphasis placed on the social-emotional aspects of care
- Burdensome paperwork and reporting requirements that impinge on time for services and client interventions
- Apparent conflict between the needs of residents to be autonomous and participate in their own care and in decisions affecting all aspects of their life and the operational efficiency gained from routines and mass interventions
- Little emphasis on linkages between the nursing home and the larger community
- Little focus on the role of family members in the resident's life
- Conflicts between the needs of residents and the occupancy needs of the home
- Private-pay versus public-pay issues, especially with regard to status shifts (circumstances where private-pay residents become impoverished and must seek Medicaid funds)
- Low pay for nursing home aides, social workers, and other staff members, which often leads to poor service and rapid turnover
- Overall concerns about the lack of sufficient resources to operate homes in a manner conducive to a high quality of life for the residents

These issues obviously concern not only residents and social workers, but residents' families, gerontologists, and social advocates in general. Residents can, however, play an important role in advocacy and social action with respect to such issues. *Nursing home residents' input is key to identification and documentation of these problems, and residents have the potential to be strong participants as advocates for change.*

An example of the strong potential for social action within nursing homes is given by Kautzer (1988). He provides a review of Living In For the Elderly (LIFE), an organization that was founded by social workers at the Veterans' Administration Hospital in Bedford, Massachusetts in 19█ LIFE has expanded to include 100 nursing homes in five geographic regions in the greater Boston area. LIFE has over 1,000 resident members and seeks to form coalitions to lobby Massachusetts state representatives regarding residents' rights and living conditions in nursing homes. LIFE members mobilize support for LIFE-sponsored legislation by participating in demonstrations at the state house, conducting phone-calling and letter-writing campaigns targeted at legislators, and testifying at legislative hearings. This program provides an excellent model for empowerment-oriented workers who seek examples of the potential of residents to engage in Dimension 4 activities in order to remedy their mutual problems.

Two key resources available to social workers in nursing homes are especially useful with respect to Dimension 4 activities: state ombudsman programs and the National Citizens' Coalition for Nursing Home Reform (NCCNHR). State ombudsman programs can supply a wealth of educational materials regarding federal and state policy, nursing home programs across the country, residents' rights, and information for families. Most ombudsman programs sponsor special educational programs, and all have staff to assist residents and their families with complaints and special concerns. Ombudsman staff and volunteers will often provide a special program in a nursing home at the request of its residents or staff.

NCCNHR also has a variety of educational materials and current information on legislation related to nursing homes. The goals of this organization are to achieve the following:

- Quality medical care
- Residents' rights and self-determination
- Access for residents and families to community services, community advocates, and ombudsman programs
- Training and improved working conditions and wages for nurses' aides and other caregivers
- Reintegration of residents into community life
- Services to meet residents' social needs
- Accountability of providers of long-term care for tax dollars received
- Policies and treatment that do not discriminate on the basis of race or ethnicity, medical condition, or ability to pay
- Reimbursement systems that focus on the delivery of quality care
- Effective regulation and enforcement of standards for nursing homes and board-and-care homes
- Cooperation and understanding from citizens and health care providers

NCCNHR is involved in special projects to educate consumers and to create certification programs with respect to quality of life and quality of care in nursing homes. These projects provide support for the struggle for empowerment in institutional settings.

# Empowerment-Oriented Strategies for Working with Other Staff Members

The culture of nursing homes is, for the most part, antithetical to the goals of empowerment. Common descriptive parameters of that culture include:

- A *bottom-line concern with profit* or, in the case of not-for-profit homes, with adequate operating resources
- The *strong influence of the medical model* and a *focus on the physical aspects of care*
- A tendency toward *a high degree of routine* as opposed to flexibility and individualized service
- Frequent *use of chemical therapy and physical restraints* to deal with behavioral problems
- *Burdensome workloads* for staff
- High *staff turnover*
- Copious organizational *red tape* and constraining *liability issues*
- Existence as a fairly *closed system* with respect to the geographical community

Social workers focused on empowerment must work to minimize the effects of these factors on the daily lives of residents and to gain the support of other members of the nursing home staff in this endeavor.

Staff members are in most cases struggling to keep up with their daily workload. Introducing a philosophy to them that supports residents' rights, autonomy, self-help, and overall empowerment with respect to the home and larger policy issues affecting it is not an easy task. It is, however, an essential challenge that must be met to whatever extent possible by the empowerment-oriented social worker. Many social workers who have tried to change the attitudes of staff members and gain their support report *cultivating their respect over a long period of time* before attempting to directly introduce training in the importance of autonomy, self-determination, and other social-emotional supports to the mental and physical health of the residents. Social workers who assist staff with residents presenting behavioral problems, who intervene in difficult situations involving residents and their families, and who find badly needed community resources that aid the work of other staff members are able to establish the relationship necessary to begin communication about empowerment. A common interest in the welfare of residents provides many opportunities on a case-by-case basis to emphasize the importance of empowerment-oriented work.

It is sometimes possible to demonstrate the critical role that mental health plays in the physical aspects of survival. Challenging overly strict routines, providing social and emotional supports, and demonstrating alternative care approaches to physical restraints and chemical therapy will often be effective after rapport has been firmly established. A strong barrier to gaining staff support for an empowerment-oriented philosophy lies in a negative perception of the cost-effectiveness of such an approach. Cost-effectiveness is, unfortunately, often correlated with the *time spent* in allowing residents individual choices about when to sleep or eat and so on, rather than being evaluated on the basis of the *positive effects on the mental and physical status of the residents.*

In order to sustain support for empowerment-oriented strategies, social workers must continuously assure other staff members of their common interest in residents' welfare and *illustrate how these approaches meet that commitment.* Success in gaining the support of nursing home staff is most often achieved when the support of the home's administrators and owners can be enlisted. Their support is often contingent on reinforcement from legislation and regulations. Consequently, successful intervention with staff requires the social worker to be engaged in all four dimensions of problem solving.

## Empowerment-Oriented Interventions with Family Members

Family members of nursing home residents are usually given very little social work intervention to assist in their struggles. Solomon (1983) identifies four events in the lives of institutionalized elders that often stimulate the need for social work intervention with the families: "(1) the decision to enter, (2) entry into the institution, (3) the move to a more intensive level of care and (4) death of the elderly resident" (p. 85).

**The Placement Process**    The University of Denver Institute of Gerontology (1989) conducted a study in the metropolitan Denver area based on in-depth interviews of 55 family members of nursing home residents. Their findings strongly supported findings of other studies (Hancock, 1987; Ory, 1985) that identified feelings of helplessness, guilt, depression, and loss experienced by family members without social work intervention. Feelings of guilt about the decision to institutionalize an elderly relative, feelings of inadequacy with respect to advocacy skills that could be used to protect and support the needs of an elderly relative after institutionalization, feelings of having inadequate information, and family conflicts are a few examples of common problems enumerated by these interviewees. The following comments are typical:

> "We'd tried everything we could by the time we gave up and decided on a nursing home. . . . We had no energy left."

> "Everything was too rushed. They took Mother straight from the doctor's office to the nursing home."

"It was terrible . . . I had a real hard time leaving her there."

"It was one of the worst experiences of my life; a hard, unsatisfactory process. Corporate nursing homes are cold and insensitive. They're just salespeople."

"Brought up a lot of past losses . . . a physically draining, emotional process."

"Difficult. Mom didn't want to stay there. She was very angry."

"I'm still overwhelmed with guilt feelings. I should have found a way to do something else."

The study by the University of Denver Institute of Gerontology (1989) also concluded that the needs of family members were severely neglected during the process of institutionalization. Only 23% of the family members reported that they had received support with their emotional concerns. Only 50% of the respondents recalled receiving any information about the ombudsman program, only 20% were involved in the nursing home care plan for their relative, and only 36% reported that the nursing home staff assisted them in their efforts to maintain a sense of family after placing the resident. A number of families had serious concerns about oversedation, restraints, or other possible abuse. Social workers often report these kinds of concerns among the family members of their nursing home clients (Hancock, 1990).

*Time constraints frequently limit empowerment-oriented social workers' ability to carry out adequate interventions with families. It is necessary to work closely with social workers in other settings who can supplement efforts from the nursing home base.* Well-informed hospital-based social workers, especially those in charge of discharge planning, can provide valuable assistance, as can case managers who work with home health care agencies or in other settings where they are likely to have contact with family members of nursing home residents. It is important to work closely with such resource persons to assure that they have adequate information to help future residents and their families make informed choices. The concepts of residents' rights and autonomy can be introduced at this juncture and be made a part of the placement decision and of residents' expectations.

***Family Needs after Institutionalization***   Family concerns and needs continue to require the attention of the social worker throughout the residency of an elderly member in a nursing home facility. Social workers can facilitate a number of things families of nursing home residents need:

- Information about nursing home procedures and community resources (including Medicare and Medicaid)
- Assistance in dealing with emotional issues

- Mediation with respect to family conflicts or communication deficits
- Help with successful visits
- Help in coping with the elderly relative's decreasing physical and mental capacities
- Help in becoming effective advocates for nursing home residents
- Assistance in dealing with the death of the elderly relative

Many family members do not know how to express these needs or that they can find assistance in coping with them. There are many ways workers can incorporate empowerment-oriented strategies into their efforts to meet families' needs. A focus on interventions that help family members to increase their repertoire of knowledge and skills must be maintained. Empowerment-oriented groups for family members can be one effective means of intervention. Family members have many common concerns but, like residents, frequently feel themselves isolated in their problem situation. Family-member groups allow them the opportunity to share feelings and concerns, as well as acquire critical information. Residents' rights, nursing home administration, effective advocacy, and legislative issues are examples of educational topics appropriate to family-member groups.

Empowerment-oriented social workers, family members, and other advocates have found that establishing statewide self-help and support organizations for family members can be an effective tool for working on the political aspects of problems. This type of organization holds the potential for effectiveness in problem solving on all dimensions but can be especially effective for Dimensions 3 and 4 (nursing home organizational changes and state and federal legislative changes), because such a group is not laboring under the restrictive climate that may be present for family-member groups connected with specific homes. The following case example describes a statewide organization that illustrates the interrelatedness of the dimensions of problem solving that such groups can address.

## CASE EXAMPLE: Project Kinship

Project Kinship, an organization of family members of nursing home residents in Colorado, has the following goals: (1) the development of mutual education concerning nursing home issues, (2) the development of self-help and mutual support mechanisms (such as a telephone support line), and (3) the development of a common effort to improve the quality of life for nursing home residents in Colorado.

During the first year of Kinship, the general membership grew to over 130. Attendance at monthly meetings, however, averaged between 10 and 20. Larger meetings were held several times a year. These larger meetings were community education meetings that focused on special issues or concerns such as implementation of new regulations, use of restraints, and so forth. The smaller monthly meetings focused primarily on educational topics and interpersonal support.

Over the years an interest in social action was generated by three or four members and the social worker. However, because Kinship was initiated through a small two-year grant from a foundation that restricted the use of its funds with respect to social action, issues identified by the group were not officially addressed by Kinship. At the end of the second year a separate social action committee was formed. The committee was composed of more than a dozen Kinship members and combined the functions of education, support, and social action. The focus of this group shifted back and forth, even within the time period of one meeting. The social worker's role included bringing in resources, providing support to individual members in crisis, and linking members to each other to develop mutual support systems.

Overall, practitioners find a wide range of needs and possible empowerment-oriented interventions directed toward members of nursing home residents' families. The circumscribed job descriptions and heavy workloads of social workers in nursing home settings often restrict the amount of time that can be spent with family members and/or the nature of services that can be provided to them. Consequently, empowerment-oriented workers are challenged to find a base for provision of badly needed social work services to family members concerned about placement of or ongoing interaction with an elderly relative in a nursing home.

## SUMMARY

Living in a nursing home is an experience often feared and accepted only as a last resort by elders. Institutionalization as a process tends to foster a sense of helplessness and powerlessness. Staff members, family members, and elderly residents often require empowerment-oriented interventions. Knowledge of residents' rights and of strategies to assure that they are respected is critical. Knowledge of the impact of social policies on the quality of life and the quality of care in nursing homes, as well as of strategies for affecting those policies, is also important. Empowerment-oriented social workers who work in nursing homes and in related settings strive to engage elderly residents, their families, and staff members in activities on all dimensions of problems related to nursing home life. Interventions that forward this goal can be carried out in a one-to-one or group format or through involvement in statewide self-help and support organizations.

# REFERENCES

Abrahamson, J. (1988). Social services in long-term care. In G. K. Gordon & R. Stryker (Eds.), *Creative long-term care administration.* Springfield, IL: Charles C Thomas.

Abramson, L. Y., Seligman, M., & Teasdale, J. D. (1978). Learned helplessness: Critique and reformation. *Journal of Abnormal Psychology, 87*(1), pp. 49–74.

Beaver, M. L., & Miller, D. (1985). *Clinical social work practice with the elderly.* Homewood, IL: Dorsey Press.

Benson, J. S., & Kennally, K. J. (1976). Learned helplessness: The result of uncontrollable reinforcements of uncontrollable aversive stimuli? *Journal of Personality and Social Psychology, 34,* pp. 138–145.

Brody, E. M. (1977). *Long-term care of older people: A practical guide.* New York: Human Sciences Press.

Cohen, E. S. (1990). The elderly mystique: Impediment to advocacy and empowerment. *Generations, 14* (supplement), pp. 13–16.

Cohen, S., Rothbart, M., & Phillips, S. (1976). Locus of control and the generality of learned helplessness in humans. *Journal of Personality and Social Psychology, 34,* pp. 1049–1050.

Coons, D. H. (1991). Improving the quality of care: The process of change. In D. H. Coons (Ed.), *Specialized dementia care unit.* Baltimore: Johns Hopkins University Press.

Feil, N. (1983). Group work with disoriented nursing home residents. In S. Saul (Ed.), *Group work with the frail elderly.* New York: Hawthorne.

Freeman, I. C. (1989). The consumer's role. *Generations, 13*(1), pp. 31–34.

Goffman, E. (1961). *Asylums.* New York: Doubleday.

Gutheil, I. A. (1990). Long-term care institutions. In A. Monk (Ed.), *Handbook of gerontological services* (2nd ed.). New York: Columbia University Press.

Hancock, B. (1990). *Social work with older people.* Englewood Cliffs, NJ: Prentice-Hall.

Hofland, B. F. (1990). Why a special focus on autonomy? *Generations, 14* (supplement), pp. 5–9.

Hooker, C. E. (1976). Learned helplessness: Reading 2-1. In B. Compton & B. Galaway (Eds.), *Social work processes.* Homewood, IL: Dorsey Press.

Jameton, A. (1988). In the borderlands of autonomy: Responsibility in long-term care facilities. *The Gerontologist, 28* (supplement), pp. 18–23.

Kane, R. A., et al. (1990). Everyday autonomy in nursing homes. *Generations, 14* (supplement), pp. 69–71.

Kart, C. S., Metress, E. K., & Metress, S. P. (1988). *Aging, health and society.* Boston: Jones and Bartlett.

Kautzer, K. (1988). Empowering nursing home residents: A case study of Living In For the Elderly (LIFE), an activist nursing home organization. In S. Reiharz & G. D. Rowles (Eds.), *Qualitative gerontology.* New York: Springer.

Keddy, B. A. (1987). The institutionalized elderly: Custodial versus rehabilitative care. *Activities, Adaptation and Aging, 9,* pp. 85–93.

Lee, J. (1983). The group: Chance at human connection for the mentally impaired older person. In S. Saul (Ed.), *Group work with the frail elderly.* New York: Hawthorne.

McDermott, C. J. (1989). Empowering the elderly nursing home resident: The resident rights campaign. *Social Work, 34*(2), pp. 155–157.

Mendelson, M. A. (1974). *Tender loving greed.* New York: Alfred A. Knopf.

Ory, M. G. (1985). The burden of care: A familial perspective. *Generations, 10*(1), pp. 14–17.

Seligman, M. (1975). *Helplessness: On depression, development, and death.* San Francisco: Freeman.

Silverstone, B., & Burack-Weiss, A. (1982). The social work function in nursing homes and home care. In G. S. Getzel & J. M. Mellor (Eds.), *Gerontological social work practice in long-term care.* New York: Haworth Press.

Smith, K. F., & Bengston, V. L. (1989). Positive consequences of institutionalization: Solidarity between elderly parents and their middle-aged children. In H. Cox (Ed.), *Aging* (6th ed.). Guilford, CT: Durkheim Publishing Group.

Solomon, R. (1983). Serving families of the institutionalized aged: The four crises. In G. S. Getzel & J. M. Mellor (Eds.), *Gerontological social work practice in long-term care.* New York: Haworth Press.

Steen, S., Linn, M. W., & Steen, E. M. (1986). Patients' perceptions of nursing home stress related to quality of care. *The Gerontologist, 26*(4), pp. 424–431.

Taylor, S. E. (1979). Hospital patient behavior: Resistance, helplessness or control? *Journal of Social Issues, 35,* pp. 156–184.

University of Denver Institute of Gerontology. (1988). *The state ombudsman program: A formative study.* Unpublished manuscript.

University of Denver Institute of Gerontology. (1989). *Family members of nursing home residents: Family member perceptions.* Unpublished manuscript.

University of Denver Institute of Gerontology. (1990). *Social work in Colorado nursing homes: Social workers' perspectives.* Unpublished report.

Weinstein, W. S., & Khanna, P. (1986). *Depression in the elderly.* New York: Philosophical Library.

Wetle, T., Levkoff, S., Cwikel, J., & Rosen, A. (1988). Nursing home residents' participation in medical decisions: Perceptions and preferences. *The Gerontologist, 28* (supplement), pp. 32–38.

# LATE LIFE HOUSING AND IN-HOME SERVICES

This chapter provides some historical background on the issues related to late life housing and in-home services. Interventions that assist older people in selecting appropriate housing and accessing resources for housing and in-home services are suggested. The interrelatedness of appropriate housing and in-home services to survival and quality of life for the elderly is elaborated on as being a key factor in empowerment.

## *HISTORICAL BACKGROUND*

Gerontologists in the early 1960s seldom addressed housing issues. Even though poor elderly people required help in locating adequate housing, a choice of living units was usually available to them. The units were often in poor repair, and slum landlords were a concern among old age assistance workers in departments of social service (public welfare departments) across the country. Older homeowners, especially older women living alone in inadequately maintained housing, also came to the attention of social workers. However, the general issue of housing was perceived as a secondary concern by the providers of social casework services and health care and by those who identified priorities at the 1961 White House Conference on Aging. Nutrition, transportation, health care, social work services, and even recreation were given more attention in those earlier efforts at identifying a national agenda for the aging.

In-home services were also just being recognized as an increasingly important resource for older Americans in the 1960s. Caseworkers from public welfare agencies nationwide visited their clients who were receiving an old age pension at least once or twice a year to (1) redetermine eligibility for financial assistance, (2) conduct assessments with regard to psychosocial and economic needs, and (3) make appropriate referrals to needed resources. In addition, on the basis of need, social casework services were provided in an ongoing fashion. Departments of public assistance offered a wide range of social work services through their casework system, including work with elderly clients and their families or other significant persons to establish social support and to enhance self-care skills. Most in-home care was provided by relatives and other members of an elder's support network or was secured directly by the elder from informal providers. In the late 1960s, many departments of welfare had developed homemaker services to assist those who were elderly or disabled, as well as families with dependent children that were unable to maintain their own households. In the event that clients exhibited health problems, referrals were made to a home health care provider (the primary providers in the 1960s were the publicly sponsored visiting nurse services).

This system was much like the system still in operation in Great Britain. Caseloads were heavy, sometimes consisting of more than 200 cases per worker, but outreach was built into the system, and it was possible to maintain at least some focus on the psychosocial needs of the elderly population that was receiving old age pensions. That population was quite similar to the currently defined "population most in need." After the 1967 amendments to the Social Security Act, a number of these services were made available to elderly persons of all income levels; however, this effort was short-lived. Another important aspect of services in the 1960s was the prevalence of the nursing home as the primary long-term care option for those elderly and disabled individuals who became very frail and required nursing supervision.

Two shifts in social policy radically changed this system of in-home services in the late 1960s and the early 1970s. First was the passage of Medicare and Medicaid legislation in 1965, which led to the progressive medicalization of services to the elderly. Second was the separation of services and eligibility within the public welfare system and the consequent shift to Title XX funding for social services within departments of welfare. Under the new system, which became effective in the early 1970s, elderly people who had been receiving social work services on the basis of their eligibility for an old age pension were no longer seen by social workers unless they were somehow found to be specifically in need of social work service. The only mandatory contact with old age pensioners became the annual reinvestigation review to determine their continuing economic eligibility. These annual reviews were made by eligibility technicians, often paraprofessionals trained only to assess financial eligibility for a pension, who were not always cognizant of social-emotional needs or signs of need for health care in their elderly clients. Mechanisms for cost control—such as the mailing out of eligibility forms—were also used. Consequently, outreach was to a large extent lost, as was social work assessment of clients' needs.

During the mid-1970s, concern about future housing for elderly people became the focus of several gerontologists' studies (see, for example, Green, 1975; Smith, 1977; Struyk, 1977). Concern also arose regarding the impact of relocation on older Americans (Bell, 1976). Furthermore, in the mid to late 1970s, there was increasing interest in the role of single room occupancy hotels (SROs) in housing older Americans (see, for example, Eckert, 1979; Stephens, 1976; and Tally, Black, Thorncock, & Hawkins, 1978).

The need for social work and health care services in public housing units serving the elderly became an issue for some advocates, as noted in hearings held by the United States Senate Special Committee on Aging (1975a, 1975b). The dismantling of public social work services left large, federally subsidized high-rise apartment complexes, as well as the private sector housing that served an elderly and aging population, without services. Lowy (1979) found that 30,000 homemakers and home health aides were available throughout the United States—and 300,000 were needed. Lowy also clearly described the growth of medical services and the curtailing and loss of social services from 1965 through the late 1970s.

Discussion of housing options in the late 1970s and early 1980s increasingly emphasized the need to link housing with appropriate in-home services. Unfortunately, the emphasis has been almost entirely on health care services, and only erratic and inadequate social work services are provided in most settings.

In the 1980s and 1990s, social workers' interest and knowledge have expanded in several areas having to do with housing for elders. Social workers have begun to study and articulate: (1) the need for appropriate linkage of housing, health care, and social services among diverse populations of elderly constituents, (2) the status of appropriate housing for low-income elderly, both now and in the future, and (3) life-styles of elderly citizens within the parameters of a variety of housing options. As gerontologists have discovered the critical role that housing and in-home services play in late life survival for their elderly clients, the need for empowerment-oriented interventions, especially those that emphasize education, has become evident.

## CURRENT POLICY ISSUES AND TRENDS

Policy issues currently of interest to professional gerontologists focused on the subject of housing include:

- Is there adequate housing now, or will there be in the future, for elderly people living on low or moderate incomes?
- How can the elderly find and maintain appropriate social work, health, and homemaking services necessary to support them in their housing and neighborhood choices?

- How do late life housing choices affect personal independence and quality of life?
- What is the impact of age segregation on the elderly and their families?
- What role does zoning play in the creation or existence of adequate housing options?
- What can older citizens do about crime and the deterioration of their neighborhoods?
- How can elderly consumers find out about the increasing range of options for housing and in-home services and be involved in the creation of more such options for themselves and others?
- What are the interpersonal skills necessary to live in shared housing, board-and-care homes, and other communal options?
- How can elderly persons who become frail or who suffer from dementia retain the greatest possible control over their late life choices about housing and in-home services?
- What about the affordability of housing and service options?
- What role can family members, friends, and communities assume in making the best options possible and workable?

This book cannot address this whole range of concerns but does emphasize their importance to daily work with elderly clients and their families as they come to understand the political dimensions of their problems. Many of these questions are the presenting problems that first engage social workers with elderly clients and their families. Practitioners and their clients usually find that successful resolution of one or more of these issues, at least on a limited scale, is the key to avoiding or postponing institutional housing, which is often more costly and almost always less acceptable to elderly consumers.

The 1980s saw the beginning of the conceptual—if not the physical— development of a wide variety of late life housing options. These options have been developed with a conscious concern for their relationship to potential long-term care needs. Some of them have been structured specifically to meet the social and health care needs of frail elderly in lieu of more intensive health care options such as nursing homes. A corollary development in in-home services is also in evidence.

## Social and Political Aspects of the Housing Problem

The current and future status of housing relative to the needs of the elderly is as complex a subject as that of housing for all Americans. The following factors are some of the many that influence this situation:

- The number of older Americans is increasing relative to the rest of the population.
- The poorest, oldest, frailest, female, and minority members of the elderly population require special consideration.
- The government's role in housing these special segments of the elderly population greatly decreased during the Reagan years and continues to be restricted during the early 1990s.
- The design and rate of development of private sector housing have been strongly influenced by investment and profit concerns rather than by need and use concerns.
- A large proportion of elderly individuals are homeowners.

The need for and use of housing by older Americans require ongoing research and analysis with special attention to those populations most at risk (Atchley, 1991; Callahan, 1992; Lacayo, 1991). The great diversity among seniors with respect to income and wealth, ethnicity and race, physical and mental health, family support, and home ownership requires an array of options, as well as careful determination of need. Overall, needs assessments of the elderly indicate that by 2000 older Americans will need 7 million more units of housing (Hancock, 1987). This estimate is based on the assumption that existing housing is maintained.

Many researchers interested in housing prospects are concerned about threats to existing housing stock. Although more than 73% of today's elders own their own homes, many of these structures are over 40 years old and in need of repair (Sherman, 1990). A nationwide telephone survey conducted by the AARP (1990a) found that most older Americans were generally satisfied with their housing. However, those with serious health limitations, those who live alone, women and members of ethnic minority groups, and owners of mobile homes expressed some concerns and dissatisfactions with their housing situations. In its 1987 Housing Policy Statement, the AARP reported that housing had virtually disappeared from the national agenda of priorities. Extreme concern was expressed over the lack of housing for future generations of elderly Americans (AARP, 1987).

Other problems on the horizon include the dilemma facing elderly persons living in rent-subsidized units. Current economic incentives have encouraged many private holders of Housing and Urban Development (HUD) mortgages to exercise their prepayment option, a move that could displace thousands of low-income elderly from their public housing units. Rising rents have displaced many older residents, and rents continue to increase, swelling the ranks of elders who need subsidies. Gentrification continues to destroy thousands of units of low-income housing. The growing need for board-and-care units, often improvised from low-rent housing units, has also become a problem because of difficulties finding or identifying such units (McCoy & Conley, 1990). Finally, the growing number

***Homelessness in a country of great wealth***

of elderly people who are homeless (Aging Health Policy Center, 1985) speaks to both the seriousness of and lack of control over the overall housing situation for the elderly as the 1990s begin.

Only a few of the realities affecting the projected housing needs of elderly citizens have been mentioned. As many of the elderly who reside in threatened units become older and more frail—"aging in place"—the situation will become even more frightening. The drastic cuts in funding to replace existing federally subsidized units and to build additional units leave the provision of future housing for this population in private hands. In reaction to the escalating urgency of the problem, many are calling for the resurgence of government responsibility (National Council on Aging, 1989) and for a movement for social ownership of low-income housing (AARP, 1990b). Private enterprise, motivated by profit, will provide only limited solutions to the problems outlined here. Many poor elderly people are currently faced with the task of finding and sustaining *any* form of shelter, much less a choice of shelter alternatives appropriately matched to their health and social needs. Middle- and upper-middle-income elderly are more likely to be faced with choosing "appropriate" housing.

## Appropriate Late Life Housing

*Appropriateness of housing* refers to the match between one's housing and one's overall needs. A key factor in this match for elderly people is the availability of necessary health and social services. The services of social workers, health care personnel, and homemakers are often required. Assistance with food preparation or transportation and many other individualized services are also important components (Golant, 1992).

In addition, consultation regarding barrier-free construction or modification to remove physical barriers to self-care is an important component of appropriateness. Housing situations that impose barriers to the receipt of long-term care services are numerous. Examples of such barriers are the location of housing (for example, in relatively isolated suburban areas or high-crime areas), regulations requiring all residents of housing units to be independent of supportive services, lack of accessibility for the disabled within and outside of housing units, a justified fear of crime that decreases mobility, and inability of elderly homeowners to provide adequate upkeep and repairs.

In summary, there are many warning signs that the future of housing for elderly citizens (particularly for those who are also disabled, frail, or poor) must be given increased attention by gerontologists and all Americans concerned with the welfare of elderly citizens. While this crisis in housing has been escalating, however, a movement has been launched for the creation of multiple housing options allowing for appropriateness of housing and availability of services. The following section discusses the development of such housing options in response to the housing needs of the elderly population.

## Housing Options

In the past fifteen to twenty years there has arisen an international movement toward the invention and development of a wide variety of housing forms suited primarily to the needs of frail and elderly persons. Homes and apartments, mobile manufactured units (including "granny mobiles"), condominiums, cooperatives, accessory apartments, and retirement communities are among these forms. During recent years programs have been developed that specifically stress the utilization of existing housing stock; these include home equity conversion programs, sale-leaseback programs, home matching programs (shared housing), programs that provide rent subsidies, and programs that provide funds for home maintenance and utility costs (*Aging Network News,* 1989; Hancock, 1990; Mutschler, 1992; and Newcomer, Lawton, & Byerts, 1986).

In addition to these efforts, housing alternatives more clearly associated with long-term care needs have been created and expanded. Congregate housing, assisted-living units, board-and-care facilities, foster care homes, and nursing homes are among these options. Some practitioners refer to these facilities as domiciliary care homes or life care complexes. The primary variable distinguishing this array of options is the nature and number of supportive services available to individual elderly persons to help them maintain their independence. Most of the housing options providing personal care must be licensed and require some degree of state supervision; however, board-and-care facilities, at this point, have very limited supervision.

Tables 12.1 and 12.2 suggest the wide range of housing options that are possible for the elderly. The creativity and usefulness of these living situations cannot be denied. Issues of accessibility that would make these alternatives truly housing options are far from resolved, however. Issues of critical significance are number of available units, their locations, consumer knowledge of these alternatives, and internalized barriers to utilizing them.

## Home Care Services

As noted earlier, the growth of home care services in the 1980s and early 1990s in the United States has been *dominated by the medical model,* and funds for these services come primarily from medical funding sources such as Medicare and Medicaid waiver programs. A cutback of public funding for social work services to elderly clients in their homes has occurred simultaneously with the rise in the provision of health care services.

The growth of in-home services has been driven by the increasing needs of users (frail, elderly people attempting to remain in their own homes as long as possible), the profit motivation of a privatized social welfare system, and, to a very limited extent, governmental responses to needs not met by the private sector. This haphazard development of primarily for-profit services has led to numerous documented problems. The following outcomes of the expansion of in-home services have been documented nationwide and brought to society's attention through public hearings and the popular press:

- A primary focus on health care needs has meant that little attention is given to social, emotional, and economic needs of clients (Estes, 1989; Kane, 1989). Elderly clients in need of home care often lack eligibility under the medical model, and the opportunity to obtain services that could maintain a degree of independence or serve to prevent disability or crisis is lost.

## Table 12.1 Housing Options Encouraging Residential Relocation by Older Persons

| Options | Levels of Independence | | |
| --- | --- | --- | --- |
| | Independent | Semi-independent | Dependent |
| Age-segregated conventional shelter strategies | | | |
| Active adult planned retirement communities | X | | |
| Manufactured-home parks | X | | |
| Financial strategies | | | |
| Low-rent government-subsidized rental accommodations | X | | |
| One-time capital gains tax exclusion on home sale | X | | |
| State supplements to recipients of SSI (Supplemental Security Income) living in board and care homes | | X | |
| Household strategies | | | |
| Availability of child's or sibling's residence | X | X | |
| In spare bedroom | X | X | |
| In accessory apartment or in-law suite | X | X | |
| In ECHO (elder cottage housing opportunity) or granny flat | X | X | |
| Residence shared with unrelated housemate | X | X | |
| Group shelter strategies | | | |
| Emergency shelter | X | | |
| Congregate housing | X | X | |
| Shared housing or small group communal living (agency assisted or managed) | X | X | |
| Board and care or foster care | | X | |
| Assisted living or assisted care facilities | | X | |
| Continuing care retirement community (CCRC) | X | X | X |
| Nursing home care | | | X |

From *Housing America's Elderly: Many Possibilities/Few Choices* by S. M. Golant, p. 6. Copyright © 1992 by Sage Publications. Reprinted by permission.

### Table 12.2 Housing Options Allowing Older Persons to Stay Put in Their Current Dwelling (age in place)

| Options | Levels of Independence | | |
| --- | --- | --- | --- |
| | Independent | Semi-independent | Dependent |
| Financial strategies | | | |
| Reverse mortgages (some plans are FHA insured) | X | | |
| Sales leaseback plans | X | | |
| Home equity loans | X | | |
| Mortgage interest and property tax deductions | X | | |
| Property tax relief programs | X | | |
| Rent subsidies linked to current residence | X | | |
| Home energy and weatherization assistance programs | X | X | |
| Household strategies | | | |
| Family caregiving assistance | X | X | X |
| Residence of elderly person shared with housemate | X | X | |
| Elderly-initiated shared arrangements | X | X | |
| Agency-assisted shared matches | X | X | |
| Accessory apartment conversions to accommodate housemate | X | X | |
| Home-based service strategies | | | |
| Home nursing care | X | X | X |
| Home personal or custodial (nonmedical) care | X | X | X |

| Service | | | |
|---|---|---|---|
| Home modification and repair programs | X | X | |
| Home-delivered meals | X | X | X |
| Special transportation and escort services | X | X | X |
| Home monitoring and alert services | X | X | X |
| Telephone reassurance and friendly visiting programs | X | X | X |
| Personal emergency response systems | X | X | X |
| Information and referral | X | X | X |
| Case management | | X | X |
| Community-based service strategies | X | | |
| Congregate meals in community sites | X | X | |
| Respite care | X | X | X |
| Adult day care | X | X | X |
| Senior centers | X | X | |
| Group shelter strategies | | | |
| Congregate and personal care for existing residents of government-subsidized rental housing | | X | |
| Assisted living facility in congregate housing facility | | X | |
| Assisted living facility on continuing care retirement community (CCRC) campus | X | X | |

- The privatization of human services has dismantled public provision of in-home services (including social work services) and fostered the growth of a plethora of private for-profit and not-for-profit agencies.

- Problems related to access (including location of services, ethnic or cultural relevance, and costs of service) have escalated.

- The quality of home care services, including inadequate service and incidences of elder abuse, has become cause for concern.

- Concern has been expressed about the qualifications of home care providers, as well as their salaries, benefits, training, and supervision.

- There has been an increasing loss of control by clients over the in-home care they receive.

- The cost of insurance coverage for liability has inflated; consequently, there has been a cutback in overall productivity of volunteer services and amount of volunteer effort.

- Confusion has arisen about the roles, rights, and responsibilities of family, friends, hired helpers, and formal providers (Berger & Anderson, 1984).

The following summary statement is from a report of the United States Senate Special Committee on Aging (1988), which describes the findings of three hearings on issues of quality in home care services:

> The present regulatory system contains little in the way of protection or recognition of clients' rights. If quality of care is addressed, it usually is by regulation rather than through the quality of the care actually delivered. There is virtually no client input or client feedback in the determination of what constitutes quality care.
>
> In addition, if home care clients have complaints of problems with the quality of care—or with any aspect of the care they receive—they essentially have no place to turn. Those receiving home care services by definition are ill and dependent upon their care givers, and therefore are often reluctant to complain, regardless of the situation. It also is difficult for an advocate, if one exists, to visit the client because of where the services are delivered—in the home. (p. 19)

In a recent personal assistance bill drafted for congressional action, the World Institute on Disability (1989) also stresses quality concerns:

> The present "system" for delivering personal assistance services is fragmented among different funding sources and different sets of administering and regulatory agencies, with the result that the services vary widely in quality and are distributed inequitably among the states, and only a small proportion of the total need for personal assistance services is being met. (p. 1)

Kapp (1990a, 1990b) is one articulate leader of a growing number of gerontologists concerned about the possible abuse of elderly consumers as a result of the "out of control" provision of in-home services in this country. Kapp analyzes the relative risks to older people and finds very little opportunity to control quality of services, as program auspices shift from government to private, for-profit administration. A growing number of advocates urge careful attention to the rights of in-home service clients. Additional complexities arise from the mental disabilities of large numbers of consumers of in-home services.

## THE ROLE OF VALUES AND BELIEFS

The issues related to both housing and in-home services for the elderly clearly demand the attention of empowerment-oriented social workers. To begin with, they must address the internalized beliefs and values that can stand in the way of finding resolutions to problems involving late life housing and in-home services.

A number of values and beliefs have a strong effect on the late life choices of elderly persons who are in need of appropriate housing as a result of increasing disability or changing financial status (Fogel, 1992). These values and beliefs are often deeply felt and go a long way toward determining elders' satisfaction with housing choices. In this country one of the most important values concerning housing is the concept of *choice*. Individual citizens are assumed to have the right to choose the location and type of housing they prefer. *Privacy* is also highly valued. For example, Howell (1985) notes the recurring attempts by elderly tenants to modify efficiency units by putting up makeshift walls to create a private sleeping space. In Denver there is a high vacancy rate among efficiency apartments even though they are relatively inexpensive and some are located in "good" neighborhoods.

Research efforts have been made to identify some of the other prevalent values that affect elders' housing decisions. An AARP (1990) study found that fear of losing one's own home ranks high among older people's concerns. Seventy-eight percent of the respondents wanted to remain in their current residence. Another AARP (1990c) study found that 84% of the respondents preferred to remain in their own homes until death.

The high value placed on home ownership has been identified by many gerontologists working with elderly homeowners. Owning one's own home has been a significant and integral part of American culture. Home ownership both serves as a solution to shelter needs and represents a major investment for most middle-class Americans. Many elderly people view their home not only as the main manifestation of their life savings and the fruit of their lifelong labor, but as their primary legacy to their

***Home is the essence of independence.***
*(Photo © W. Hill, Jr./The Image Works)*

children. Home ownership is also a measure of one's status relative to others less fortunate. Longtime residence in one's own home further encompasses the value placed on familiar surroundings, neighborhood, friends, and commercial centers. Many elders refuse to leave their homes even when the neighborhood has badly deteriorated.

The subject of home sharing as a housing alternative quickly leads social workers and their clients to issues of value-based preferences. An AARP (1990c) study notes that 82% of elderly respondents stated that they would not consider shared housing, defined as *"sharing your home with one or more persons who are not relatives."* Shared housing programs report that more individuals are willing to share their own homes than are willing to move into someone else's home. These preferences can greatly affect the quality of life of older individuals whose financial situation does not allow them to comfortably maintain their current residence. Property tax and home repair costs rank high among late life concerns of elderly homeowners. The reasons for hesitancy with respect to home sharing have not been fully explored. Knowledge derived from social work practice, however, suggests that fear of the unknown and a strong belief that family is the only appropriate source of support or resources are key barriers to home sharing.

Other concepts of importance to understanding internal barriers to making appropriate late life housing choices include psychological attachment to current housing situations. Howell (1985), in an exploration of attachment and housing, notes that the perception of control is central to the decision to stay in or move from a longstanding housing arrangement. O'Bryant (1982) identifies the following as the four most significant factors in determining an elder homeowner's wish to remain in her or his own home: (1) competence in a familiar environment, (2) traditional family orientation and memories, (3) status value of home ownership, and (4) a cost-versus-comfort tradeoff.

A number of other researchers interested in late life housing have approached their subject by studying the situations of elders who have elected to move. Golant (1984) found that attachment to place does not need to remain constant over time. Lawton (1986) and Longino (1986) summarized the findings of several studies and added their own perceptions to the phenomenon of migration of elderly people to different housing settings. Longino noted that older individuals moving to service-enriched settings frequently feel "pushed" into these environments by health conditions, while many younger elderly who move to retirement communities (perhaps even across the country) feel "pulled." Regardless of research efforts to date, much is yet to be learned about the internalized aspects of housing preferences in late life. Practical social work experience reveals that *many elderly citizens are resistant to moving even when personal care requirements demand change, that many are unaware of options, and that options are unavailable to some.*

The use of in-home services poses another set of issues, and again values and beliefs can have great impact on an elderly person's ability to effectively use such services. (Chapter 10 discusses a number of these issues.) Perceptions of privacy, fears of providers who are not relatives, and racial and ethnic prejudice are among the common internalized barriers to full use of in-home services.

# EMPOWERMENT-ORIENTED INTERVENTIONS FOR PROBLEMS WITH HOUSING AND IN-HOME SERVICES

Social workers' interventions can once again be focused on all four dimensions of the practice model presented in Chapter 3.

## Dimensions 1 and 2 Interventions

Challenges to the empowerment-oriented worker who wishes to assist elderly individuals to gain an increased sense of control over their housing and/or use of in-home services are complex and varied. The first tasks of empowerment-oriented workers are often assisting with immediate shelter needs and engaging clients in a consciousness-raising process regarding their values and beliefs. Those that frequently require discussion and analysis (either with individuals or in small groups) include:

- Fear of losing status as a result of a housing change
- Fear of losing the love of children or other relatives if they will not inherit the elder's home
- Fear of loss and termination of memories and familiar surroundings
- Resistance to leaving friends and neighborhoods and relocating to unknown geographical areas
- Fear of economic loss from selling one's home
- Fear of losing independence as a result of a move to a facility providing supportive services
- Fear of living either with nonfamily or with family members (see discussion of fears of dependency in Chapter 10)
- Fear of dealing with authorities and regulations (landlords or managers, zoning regulations, regulations affecting mobile homes, etc.)
- Extreme fear of nursing home placement

Confronting one's preferences and then either changing them or clearly identifying and accepting their consequences for one's quality of life are prerequisites to freely considering a wider range of late life housing alternatives. Dimension 1 and Dimension 2 interventions, such as education and consciousness-raising activities that relate to internalized aspects of housing problems, are critical in addressing issues of housing choice. When feasible, having clients participate in groups can be especially effective in helping them see their problems without crippling amounts of self-blame for "being in this predicament" and in helping them gain a sense that others in similar circumstances have dealt with such problems successfully or that broader social change is necessary to alleviate their difficulties. Confronting and clarifying their fears, coupled with gaining a better knowledge of alternatives, is often necessary before elders can assume more control over their environment.

Table 12.3 lists areas of knowledge that elders and social workers have found to be relevant to specific late life housing options.

## Timeliness as a Critical Factor

Educational interventions that offer information regarding housing options should include the opportunity to visit different facilities, observe the programs, and talk with program participants. Empowerment-oriented workers must stress *early* consideration of late life housing options. Learning about and comparing these options and participating in values clarification *prior to* the onset of a situation that may necessitate a sudden housing change will allow maximum participation of the elder involved. Learning about ways to cope with the financial demands of different options is also critical.

Home-share programs require significant lead time with respect to the decision to participate. A number of comprehensive training programs have been developed by home-share programs across the country and by the national Gray Panthers Home Share Center (see, for example, Horne & Baldwin, 1988). These training programs focus on specific issues that arise from living with others in a residential setting. Some also touch on issues involved in moving in with family members. Success of the home-share option, however, is strongly tied to the elder's having adequate time and resources for these educational experiences.

Many elderly people lose the opportunity for effective involvement in decisions about late life housing because they put off such decisions until a time of crisis—for example, when a temporarily disabling illness strikes. When an elderly person is deemed ready for discharge from a hospital but has no place to go where personal care can be provided and does not feel well enough to aggressively plan or advocate for himself or herself, professionals and/or family members must make a decision with little or no involvement of the elder (Congdon, 1989; Huckstadt, 1990). Knowledge about the range of alternatives *acquired before a crisis arises* can be an important factor in the formulating of decisions that are compatible with the elder's personal preferences.

## Dimensions 3 and 4 Interventions

Real external barriers to elders' acquiring appropriate housing and in-home services exist and often foster a sense of powerlessness.

## Table 12.3 Areas of Knowledge Relevant to Various Housing Options for Elders

| Housing Options | Relevant Areas of Knowledge |
| --- | --- |
| Own home | Taxes<br>Repair opportunities and programs<br>Zoning issues<br>Weatherization programs<br>Reverse mortgage potential<br>Neighborhood changes<br>Accessibility of transportation and health care and social services<br>Changes in property values<br>Applicable federal, state, and local laws and regulations |
| Rental housing | Landlord/tenant laws or regulations<br>Tenants' rights<br>Safety rules or regulations<br>Quality control of maintenance<br>Landlord/tenant communication skills<br>Moving services<br>Rent subsidy services<br>Age segregation and intergenerational issues<br>Neighborhood changes<br>Alternative means of cost control (such as rent control legislation)<br>Barrier-free options<br>Cooperatives and laws regulating them<br>Financial issues, including taxes, ownership rights, and so forth<br>Participatory management models<br>Accessibility of transportation and health care and social services<br>Zoning issues |
| Assisted living unit | Cost<br>Nature of services provided<br>Short-term and long-term benefits and risks<br>Qualifications of staff<br>Tenants' rights<br>Tenants' participation in decisions affecting their lives<br>Mechanisms for quality control<br>Rules or regulations governing tenancy (such as level of competency required for continued residence)<br>Home sharing and potential home-share facilities<br>Zoning issues<br>Interpersonal skills necessary for shared living arrangements |

*Table 12.3* *(continued)*

| Housing Options | Relevant Areas of Knowledge |
|---|---|
| Assisted living unit | Availability of low-cost loans for remodeling<br>Accessibility of health care and social services |
| Mobile home | Applicable state and local laws<br>Trailer court restrictions<br>Mobile home owners' rights<br>Repair programs<br>Safety issues<br>Zoning regulations (with respect to placement near a relative's home, for example) |
| Other options | Home-sharing issues (successful models, participants' training needs, and so on)<br>Issues related to living with children or other relatives<br>Rules or regulations concerning granny mobiles, ECHO housing, and other temporary structures |

Overcoming this sense of powerlessness calls for organized efforts that have at least five goals. These goals are

1. Supporting the production of more units of appropriate housing
2. Supporting improvements in habitability of existing units
3. Demanding the implementation of options such as the use of "granny mobiles" (often a zoning issue)
4. Demanding an increase in quality control of in-home services
5. Addressing the almost unlimited other problems with respect to appropriate late life housing and in-home services

Participation in organized efforts to address issues of housing and in-home services is critical to elders' gaining a sense of belonging and of control over their environment and to their developing a more critical understanding of the political dimensions of the problems at hand. Furthermore, the situational struggle of one elderly person is often representative of the struggle of many. Examples of such sociopolitical commonalities are the needs for increased income to sustain housing costs, the waiver of restrictive zoning regulations, protection from neighborhood crime, more voice in the management of senior high-rise residences, increased in-home services at affordable costs, and involvement of elderly consumers in monitoring and assuring their rights with regard to housing and in-home services.

The effort of a group united by a common cause is likely to be a crucial strategy for addressing these needs. Referring elders who have gained an increased sense of the political aspects of their problems to national or state organizations that engage in advocacy or lobbying on these issues, as suggested in Chapter 4, is important. For example, an older woman who needs safe, comfortable, low-rent housing may find membership in OWL very reaffirming. The functions of the empowerment-oriented worker are to help the client access and analyze information necessary to address the issues, engage the client in skill-building activities, and encourage the client to participate in social action, as suggested in Chapters 4 and 5. (A wide range of activities that can be effective in the political dimension of the late life housing dilemmas faced by many elderly citizens are suggested in Chapter 4.) Finding and sharing information about tax issues, zoning regulations, rent subsidies, and so on (see Table 12.1) is often the substantive focus of empowerment-oriented groups when housing issues are a central concern.

## Consumer Choice and In-Home Care

Consumer choice with respect to in-home care is an area of concern. Kapp (1990b) suggests several areas of consumer responsibility that are important to maintaining control over one's in-home environment:

Consumers must thoroughly demand, collect, and study information from public and private health and social service agencies about available alternative home care delivery models in their own jurisdiction, how those models operate in practice, and the process of assignment of an individual to a particular model.

Where insufficient alternative home care delivery models exist in one's state, the consumer should lobby public officials for development of a wider range of alternatives to enhance opportunities for consumer choice and control.

Consumers must vigorously demand, and then be willing to participate in, adequate training for the difficult role of selector and director of one's own home care program. Few consumers enter the world of home care prepared to competently recruit, hire, supervise, and possibly fire one or more home care workers, and the need for such preparation must be pressed effectively upon relevant public and private agencies.

Consumers must be willing to explicitly assume a certain amount of legal risk in return for the right to exercise choice and control over their home care services. While consumers should not be expected to waive or give up their legitimate legal right to seek redress for injuries caused as a direct result of provider wrongdoing, neither is it reasonable to impose on home care providers legal accountability for risks created or exacerbated by consumer choices. Improved provider support of, and respect for, consumer choice in this sphere will depend in large part on the willingness of consumers to explicitly, at the beginning of the consumer/provider relationship, accept a fair apportionment of legal responsibility commensurate with the exercise of choice and control over the inevitable risks of home care. (pp. 15–16)

The role of empowerment-oriented workers in engaging and enabling elders to understand and assume these challenges is critical. Skill-building training, which develops recruitment, management, and supervisory skills, is essential to late life competency for many elderly people. Only appropriate knowledge and skills will allow elderly clients to play a key role in monitoring their own in-home services. Because most in-home service consumers are isolated from one another, innovative strategies must be developed—such as telephone support networks and consumer feedback systems—that do not put the consumer at risk of loss of services or other forms of retaliation. Empowerment of elders with respect to in-home service delivery provides a growing challenge to workers and clients in the 1990s. (See, for example, Sabationo, 1989.)

## Neighborhoods

Another area that requires attention is the development of interventions that help elderly people empower themselves with respect to their neighborhoods. Neighborhood deterioration often involves an increase in crime, the loss of friends through demolition of housing units, the loss of shopping areas, and many other negative impacts. Most of these effects can be countered to some extent through the organization of self-help efforts such as crime watches, neighbor-to-neighbor telephone networks, and shopping escort services, as well as of neighborhood improvement projects such as communal gardens or alleviation of traffic hazards. Programs like these allow neighbors to become better acquainted with one another. In some neighborhoods, workers have found that intergenerational programs, in which young and old work on projects together, have greatly decreased harassment of the elderly by youths. The establishment of neighborhood-based skills banks can strongly reinforce other neighborhood improvement strategies. Overall, Dimension 2 and 3 strategies, including self-help and service delivery modification, can greatly enhance neighborhood support.

The political (Dimension 4) aspect of neighborhood development and change is another arena in which elderly residents can participate. For example, the introduction of new housing options into an area may require neighborhood-based political work. Gaining approval of a neighborhood for developing a board-and-care home, building a senior high-rise, or installing or constructing a "granny mobile" may be very difficult. Elderly clients and workers must join together in educational and persuasive strategies in order to gain residents' support for these options.

The introduction of empowerment-oriented approaches within residences (nursing homes, high-rises, board-and-care units) often leads to actions that also affect neighborhoods. Self-help efforts among residents to provide social-emotional support and to assist each other in daily tasks are an important move toward self-empowerment. Joint actions to increase safety, control rents, assure prompt and appropriate repairs, assure delivery of promised services, and monitor the quality of services are also common functions of empowerment-oriented groups in these facilities. Skills in advocacy, mediation, and negotiation learned by residents in these settings are quickly transferred to neighborhood efforts. Often a number of facilities can be encouraged to cooperate in, for instance, crime watch programs.

## SUMMARY

Appropriate housing and in-home services are interrelated concerns for many elders, especially those who are disabled. Often, changes in circumstances—such as having to live alone when this was not expected or a change in income that precipitates a change in residence—bring the issue of housing to the fore. Knowledge about the availability, appropriateness, affordability, and variety of housing options is key to making late life housing choices. Empowerment-oriented workers must often help elderly clients to reassess the values and beliefs they hold about what constitutes appropriate housing. The effects of the political-economic system on housing and housing options are also key to understanding problems and should be used to guide Dimension 4 activities.

Provision of in-home services has escalated during recent decades. Empowerment-oriented practice encourages clients to assess the nature of in-home services in the United States, explore the influence of the medical model, and investigate other factors of the political economy that affect these services. Knowledge and skills related to consumer choice are very important to elders who must supervise helpers in their homes. There are a number of strategies empowerment-oriented workers can use to assist their clients who must deal with these issues.

## REFERENCES

AARP. (1987). 1987 housing policy statement. Unpublished policy manual.
AARP. (1990a). Understanding senior housing for the 1990s. Washington, DC: AARP.

AARP. (1990b). Social ownership would reduce cost of housing, says report. *Housing Report,* Winter, pp. 1–3.

AARP. (1990c). AARP's 1990 housing survey shows more older people want to age in place. *Housing Report,* Spring, pp. 1–3.

Aging Health Policy Center. (1985). *The homeless mentally ill elderly: Working paper.* San Francisco: University of California Press.

*Aging Network News,* 6(2), June 1989 (entire issue).

Atchley, R. C. (1991). *Social forces and aging* (6th ed.) Belmont, CA: Wadsworth.

Bell, B. D. (1976). The impact of housing relocation on the elderly: An alternative methodological approach. *International Journal of Aging and Human Development,* 7(1), pp. 27–28.

Berger, R. M., & Anderson, S. (1984). The in-home worker: Serving the frail elderly. *Social Work,* 29(5), pp. 456–460.

Callahan, J. I. (1992). Aging in place. *Generations,* 16(2), pp. 5–6.

Congdon, J. (1989). Analysis of discharge readiness and the use of nursing diagnosis in the hospitalized elderly. Unpublished doctoral dissertation, University of Denver, Denver, CO.

Eckert, K. I. (1979). The unseen community: Understanding the older hotel dweller. *Aging,* Jan./Feb., pp. 28–35.

Estes, C. L. (1989). The biomedicalization of aging dangers and dilemmas. *The Gerontologist,* 29(5), pp. 587–596.

Fogel, B. S. (1992). Psychological aspects of staying at home. *Generations,* 16(2), pp. 15–19.

Golant, S. M. (1992). *Housing America's elderly: Many possibilities/few choices.* Newbury Park, CA: Sage.

Golant, S. M. (1984). The effects of residential action behaviors on people's environmental experience. In M. P. Altman & I. Laughton, (Eds.), *Elderly people and the environment.* New York: Plenum Press.

Green, I. (1975). *Housing for the elderly: The development and design process.* New York: Van Nostrand Reinhold.

Hancock, B. L. (1987). *Social work with older people.* Englewood Cliffs, NJ: Prentice-Hall.

Hancock, B. L. (1990). *Social work with older people.* Englewood Cliffs, NJ: Prentice-Hall.

Horne, J., & Baldwin, L. (1988). *Home-sharing and other lifestyle options.* Washington, DC: AARP.

Howell, S. C. (1985). Home: A source of meaning in elders' lives. *Generations,* Spring, p. 58.

Huckstadt, A. A. (1990). *Enduring: The experience of hospitalized elderly patients.* Unpublished doctoral dissertation, University of Colorado School of Nursing, Denver, CO.

Kane, R. A. (1989). The biomedical blues. *The Gerontologist,* 29(5), pp. 583–586.

Kapp, M. B. (1990a). *Home care client-centered systems: Consumer choices vs. protection.* Unpublished manuscript.

Kapp, M. B. (1990b). *Consumer choice regarding home care services: Some legal issues.* Unpublished paper, based on research funded by Commonwealth Fund Grant 11177.

Lacayo, C. (1991). Living arrangements and social environments among ethnic minority elders. *Generations, 15*(4), pp. 43–46.

Lawton, M. P. (1986). Housing preferences and choices: Implications. In R. J. Newcomer, M. P. Newton, & T. Byerts (Eds.), *Housing in an aging society.* New York: Van Nostrand Reinhold.

Longino, C. F. (1986). Personal determinants and consequences of independent housing choices. In R. J. Newcomer, M. P. Newton, & T. Byerts (Eds.), *Housing in an aging society.* New York: Van Nostrand Reinhold.

Lowy, L. (1979). *Social work with the aging: The challenge and promise of the later years.* New York: Harper & Row.

McCoy, J. L., & Conley, R. W. (1990). Surveying board and care homes: Issues and data collection problems. *The Gerontologist, 30*(2), pp. 147–153.

Mutschler, P. (1992). Where elders live. *Generations, 16*(2), pp. 7–14.

National Council on Aging. (1989). Thursz asks partnership on housing. *Networks, 1*(1), p. 9.

Newcomer, R. J., Lawton, M. P., & Byerts, T. (Eds.). (1986). *Housing in an aging society.* New York: Van Nostrand Reinhold.

O'Bryant, S. L. (1982). The value of home to older persons. *Research on Aging, 4,* pp. 349–363.

Sabationo, C. (1989). Homecare quality. *Generations, 18*(1), pp. 12–16.

Sherman, S. R. (1990). Housing. In A. Monk, *Handbook of Gerontological Services* (2nd ed.). New York: Columbia University Press.

Smith, B. K. (1977). *The pursuit of dignity: New living alternatives for the elderly.* Boston: Beacon Press.

Stephens, J. (1976). *Loners, losers, and lovers: Elderly tenants in a slum hotel.* Washington, DC: University of Washington Press.

Struyk, R. J. (1977). The housing situation of elderly Americans. *Gerontologist, 17*(2), pp. 130–139.

Tally, M., Black, E., Thorncock, M., & Hawkins, I. (1978). Older women single-room-occupant (SRO) hotels: A Seattle profile. *Gerontology, 19,* pp. 67–73.

United States Senate Special Committee on Aging, Subcommittee on Housing for the Elderly. (1975a). *Adequacy of federal response to housing needs of older Americans.* (Response to the severe needs of the elderly residents in public housing.) Hearing, part 13, October 7 (94th Congress, 1st Session).

United States Senate Special Committee on Aging, Subcommittee on Housing for the Elderly. (1975b). *Adequacy of federal response to housing needs of older Americans.* (Concerning delivery of supportive services to elderly residents of public housing projects.) Hearing, part 14, October 8 (94th Congress, 1st Session).

United States Senate Special Committee on Aging. (1988). *Home care at the crossroads: An information paper.* Washington, DC: U.S. Government Printing Office.

World Institute on Disability. (1989). The Personal Assistance for Independent Living Act of 1989: A draft. Berkeley, CA.

# EPILOGUE

This book has described a model of social work practice with the elderly and their families that emphasizes the *fullest possible involvement of elders* in their own life choices and care and in contributions to society. The empowerment-oriented approach is sympathetic with Moody's (1988) observation that increasing numbers of elderly persons must be mobilized as a "growing national resource rather than be seen as a burgeoning problem" (p. 10). The empowerment orientation strongly values prevention (with respect to physical and mental decline) as well as clients' engagement in the struggle for quality of life.

In line with the current practice situations of most gerontological social workers, this book has focused on problem areas that reflect long-term care and survival issues. Only minimal attention has been directed toward the many critical problems and issues affecting elders' quality of life or integration of the growing elderly population into society now and in the future. The common struggle of many older people to reassess the meaning and purpose of life constitutes an ongoing challenge for empowerment-oriented social workers. Involvement in the related issue of creating and maintaining meaningful late life roles will take many forms in future decades.

Empowerment-oriented workers need to form partnerships with elders and other concerned persons in order to ensure that elders will have full opportunity to:

- Reassume valued former roles and forge valued new roles
- Continue *by choice* in the paid work force or as valued volunteers
- Gain the knowledge and skills required to meet the challenges of new roles and of the developmental tasks of aging
- Explore spirituality to the fullest possible extent
- Explore issues related to the "right to death with dignity," including society's position on euthanasia and related ideas
- Engage in a wide variety of late life educational experiences, of both practical utility and artistic/philosophical value
- Express themselves creatively through the fine arts (creative expression through drama, painting, writing, and other media has proven to be invaluable to the quality of life of many elders)

- Participate to the fullest possible extent in meaningful relationships with relatives and others
- Participate in a wide range of intergenerational programs, which reduce alienation between age groups and dispel derogatory myths about the elderly
- Struggle for social justice and the creation of a better environment for humankind

A consciousness-raising process that challenges preconceived notions about "appropriate" late life roles may be a prerequisite to achieving such goals. An openness to changing an earlier life-style will often be a pivotal factor in successfully engaging an elderly person in activities that will enhance the quality and meaningfulness of life.

As has been evidenced in this book's discussion of long-term care and other survival matters, there is no clear separation of many of the issues affecting elders. Issues of quality of life and meaningfulness of roles are at the heart of many concerns of frail and disabled elders and are an integral part of empowerment-oriented practice. However, *most elders,* their families, and others interested in gerontological issues are concerned about the quality of life and the opportunity for meaningful roles during their own old age, regardless of their need for long-term care or their level of disability.

The focus of the empowerment-oriented practice model on the *political dimension* of personal problems provides a vehicle for elders' meaningful involvement in the creation of an environment more responsive to their needs. The ways in which empowerment-oriented social workers and elderly clients become engaged in solving problems are largely dependent on the availability of social workers in strategic settings. The response of the social work profession to the challenge of meeting the needs of older Americans is closely related to the roles that social workers will be able to create for themselves in the human services during the 1990s and thereafter.

An extremely critical issue is *empowerment within the social work profession itself,* especially as it relates to work with the elderly. Finding and/or creating practice positions that will enable social workers to promote empowerment-oriented practice is a high priority for the profession as a whole.

The social work profession suffered loss of status and of support from the public sector during the conservative-dominated 1980s. It faces challenges in all areas of practice in the 1990s. The commitment of American society to social justice and to quality of life for all citizens, including poor or oppressed populations, must be held up to question and reaffirmed in order to allow for adequate expansion of social work practice (Hefferman, Shuttlesworth, & Ambrosino, 1988). Issues that must be addressed are (1) cuts in public sector support for social services, (2) the increasing needs of the older population, (3) the need for better integration

***The generations are one.*** *(Photo © James Schaffer/PhotoEdit)*

of that population into core societal activities, and (4) clarification of the current and potential role of professional social workers. The special contribution of empowerment-oriented practice must also be emphasized. The 1990s will open up many possibilities for the introduction of social work services into new settings and arenas, as well as for the improvement of the status of and opportunities for practice in existing settings.

The ability to articulate clearly what empowerment-oriented workers have to offer in all settings will be critical. This articulation must include enumeration of the ways in which the contributions of empowerment-oriented workers will improve the *quality of life* of elders, their families, and society as a whole and the pragmatic effect, or *cost-effectiveness,* of these services. Morales and Shaefor (1989), in addition, suggest that the social work profession must demonstrate and make known the importance of preventive services with respect to mental health in future decades. The expected outcomes of empowerment-oriented interventions include stronger social support networks and the increased capacity of elderly people and their families for self-care, contributions to society, and participation in social change to make society as a whole more compatible with human needs. These outcomes will meet both pragmatic cost-effectiveness and quality of life criteria.

Empowerment-oriented social workers will, however, be faced with the task of finding auspices under which their contributions may be made.

To effectively develop empowerment-oriented strategies and integrate them into existing service structures, empowerment-oriented social workers must develop strong professional networks. Empowerment-oriented workers in a variety of key positions in a community can enhance their own work through collaboration.

The privatization of social services has led to the necessity of "selling" these services to a wide variety of potential supporters. First, empowerment-oriented workers must continue to lobby and actively participate in work to regenerate public support for meeting human needs and to reaffirm the values of social justice and quality of life for all citizens. Second, workers must identify the decison makers in private for-profit and not-for-profit organizations who can be persuaded to support social work services that relate to their primary interests. Finally, *gerontological social workers must educate the elderly and their families about the value of social work services.* The client population is often called upon to pay for these services out of pocket and may therefore become an increasingly active lobby on behalf of their availability.

Empowerment-oriented social workers face two critical professional challenges: (1) to increase the positions and settings in which they can contribute their knowledge and skills to the field of gerontology, and (2) to continue to enhance the appropriateness and effectiveness of professional knowledge and skills—in particular, by incorporating the empowerment-oriented approach into all aspects of their work.

# *REFERENCES*

Hefferman, J., Shuttlesworth, G., & Ambrosino, R. (1988). *Social work and social welfare: An introduction.* St. Paul, MN: West Publishing.
Moody, H. (1988). *Abundance of life: Human development policies for an aging society.* New York: Columbia University Press.
Morales, A., & Shaefor, B. (1986). *Social work: A profession of many faces.* Boston: Allyn and Bacon.

# LIST OF ACRONYMS

| | |
|---|---|
| AAA | Area Agencies on Aging |
| AARP | American Association of Retired Persons |
| ADA | Age Discrimination Act |
| ADC | Aid to Dependent Children |
| ADR | Alternative dispute resolution |
| AOA | Administration on Aging |
| EOA | Economic Opportunity Act |
| HUD | Department of Housing and Urban Development |
| LIFE | Living In for the Elderly |
| NARFE | National Association of Retired Federal Employees |
| NCCNHR | National Citizens' Coalition for Nursing Home Reform |
| NCOA | National Council on Aging |
| NCSC | National Council of Senior Citizens |
| OAA | Older Americans Act |
| OWL | Older Women's League |
| RSVP | Retired Senior Volunteer Program |
| SRO | Single Room Occupancy |
| SSA | Social Security Act |
| SSI | Supplemental Security Income |
| VISTA | Volunteers in Service to America |

# NAME INDEX

AARP, 21, 145, 166, 189, 237, 238, 245, 246
Abrahamson, J., 213
Abramovitz, M., 26, 27
Abramson, L. Y., 208
Aging Health Policy Center, 238
*Aging Network News,* 240
Agree, E. M., 168
Akins, R. E., 19
Akins, T. E., 110
Akiyama, H., 10
Anderson, B., 26
Anderson, S., 244
Antonucci, T., 10
Arling, G., 169
Aronson, M., 180
Astreen, B., 77
Atchley, R. C., 3–7, 21–23, 25, 145, 237
Axinn, J., 7, 85

Bailey, R., 87
Baldwin, L., 249
Bass, S. A., 3, 7, 145
Beaver, L., 196
Beaver, M. L., 10, 211, 212, 213
Bell, B. D., 235
Bengston, V. I., 207
Benson, J. S., 208
Berger, P. L., 50
Berger, R. M., 244
Berkman, L. F., 172
Binney, E. A., 85, 89
Binstock, R., 6
Binstock, R. H., 82, 90
Black, B. L., 89
Black, E., 235
Borson, S., 23

Boyd, M. D., 166, 168, 169
Brake, M., 87
Brody, E., 168
Brody, E. M., 212
Brody, J. A., 21
Bronte, L., 120
Brown, A. S., 89
Brubaker, T., 180
Bunting, S. M., 168
Burack-Weiss, A., 211, 214, 221
Burghardt, S., 66
Byerts, T., 240

Cafferata, G., 168
Callahan, D., 6
Callahan, J. I., 237
Charpentier, M. O., 192
Chimento, T., 67
Circirelli, V. G., 171
Clark, M., 26
Cloward, R. A., 153
Cobb, J., 20
Coe, R. M., 200
Cohen, E. S., 210
Cohen, J. B., 21
Cohen, S., 208
Compton, B., 41, 42, 48
Congdon, J., 249
Conley, R. W., 237
Conway, M., 20
Coons, D. H., 23, 210
Cox, E. O., 39, 75, 99, 133, 140, 169, 170, 171, 172, 178, 191
Cox, F. M., 64
Crystal, S., 7
Curley, M., 77
Cutler, L., 170, 176
Cwikel, J., 209

# SUBJECT INDEX

Income (*continued*)
   supplemental, 157–158
   values and attitudes about,
      149–152
Independence, 26
Individuals, empowerment-oriented
   practice with, 110–115
Institute for Retired Professionals,
   124
Intergenerational Equity Movement,
   7
International Executive Service
   Corps of Retired Executives,
   8
Interpersonal intervention
   in empowerment-oriented prac-
      tice, 51, 54–55, 56
   in family caregiving, 179–180
   in nursing homes, 215–220
   for problems with housing,
      248–249
Intervention strategies. *See also* Personal intervention; Interpersonal intervention; Environmental intervention;
   Political intervention
   dimensions of, 50–55
   for empowerment-oriented prac-
      tice, 48–50
   for family caregiving, 174–185
   for housing problems, 248–254
   for income and health care needs,
      148–149, 151–152
   neighborhood, 253–254
   in nursing homes, 215–228
   relationship among, 55–57
   sanction for, 41–42
   for working with individuals,
      111–112

Knowledge. *See also* Education;
   Learning, phases of
   as component of empowerment
      process, 37–38
   development of, 93, 94
   for influencing social policy,
      76–78
   transfer of, 46
Knowledge gap, 201–202

Late life education. *See* Education;
   Survival skills
Learning, phases of, 122–123
Leisure activities, 8
Life review process, 195–196
Living In For the Elderly (LIFE), 222
Lobbyists, 72
Long-term care, 161. *See also* In-
   home care; Nursing homes
Losses, 20–21, 198

Massachusetts Association of Older
   Americans, 77
Mediation of family disputes,
   178–179
Medicaid, 147, 173, 234
Medical model. *See* Biomedical
   model
Medicare, 147, 173, 234
Memory, 23
Mental health, 22–23
Metropolitan Organizational People,
   78
Middle-old, 4
Minorities, demographic trends and,
   4

National Association of Retired
   Federal Employees (NARFE),
   31
National Association of Social
   Workers (NASW), 11, 40, 212
National Center for Policy Alter-
   natives, 78
National Citizens' Coalition for Nurs-
   ing Home Reform (NCCNHR),
   223
National Coalition of Nursing Home
   Reform (NCNHR), 212
National Council on Aging, 139
National Institute of Mental Health,
   126
National Low-Income Housing Coali-
   tion, 78
National Stroke Association, 54
Neighborhood interventions,
   253–254
New School for Social Research,
   124

TO THE OWNER OF THIS BOOK:

We hope that you have found *Empowerment-Oriented Social Work Practice with the Elderly* useful. So that this book can be improved in a future edition, would you take the time to complete this sheet and return it? Thank you.

School and address: _____

Department: _____

Instructor's name: _____

1. What I like most about this book is: _____

_____

2. What I like least about this book is: _____

_____

3. My general reaction to this book is: _____

_____

4. The name of the course in which I used this book is: _____

_____

5. Were all of the chapters of the book assigned for you to read? _____

   If not, which ones weren't? _____

_____

6. In the space below, or on a separate sheet of paper, please write specific suggestions for improving this book and anything else you'd care to share about your experience in using the book.

_____

_____

_____

_____

_____

Optional:

Your name: _____ Date: _____

May Brooks/Cole quote you either in promotion for *Empowerment-Oriented Social Work Practice with the Elderly* or in future publishing ventures?

Yes: _____ No: _____

Sincerely,

*Enid O. Cox*
*Ruth J. Parsons*

- - - - - - - - - - - - - - - - - - - - - - - - - - - - - - - - - - - - - - - - - - - - -
FOLD HERE

- - - - - - - - - - - - - - - - - - - - - - - - - - - - - - - - - - - - - - - - - - - - -
FOLD HERE